Dinner: A Love Story

Dinner:
A Love Story

It all begins

at the

family table

Jenny Rosenstrach

Photographs by Jennifer Causey

An Imprint of HarperCollinsPublishers

Recipe for Mexican Chocolate Icebox Cookies from *Maida Heatter's Book of Great Chocolate Desserts,* published by Andrews McMeel Publishing. Reprinted by permission of Andrews McMeel Publishing.

Jim Lahey pizza crust recipe from *My Bread: The Revolutionary No-Work, No-Knead Method* by Jim Lahey. Copyright © 2009 by Jim Lahey. Used by permission of W. W. Norton & Company, Inc.

Braised Beef Short Ribs recipe and Swedish Meatball recipe: Jenny Rosentrach, *Bon Appétit* © 2011.

HarperCollins books may be purchased for educational, business, or sales promotional use. For information please write: Special Markets Department, HarperCollins Publishers, 10 East 53rd Street, New York, NY 10022.

FIRST EDITION

Book design by Leah Carlson-Stanisic
Illustrations by Ava Savitsky and Chelsea Cardinal
Photographs on title page, page 84, and page 186 by Jennifer Livingston

Library of Congress Cataloging-in-Publication Data has been applied for.

ISBN-978-0-06-208090-5

12 13 14 15 16 OV/QGT 10 9 8 7 6 5 4 3 2 1

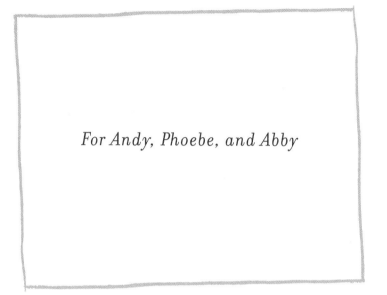

For Andy, Phoebe, and Abby

Contents

A Note from Jenny

elcome to *Dinner: A Love Story*, the book that's all about family meals, however you might define "family" and however you might define "meals." Before I get down to the business of explaining what you will find in the next three hundred pages, I'd like to tell you a bit about what you *won't* find.

✳ You will not find dire warnings that your children are going to become meth addicts if you're not eating with them five nights a week.

✳ You will not find lyrical musings on the Japanese eggplant or tender odes to the fleeting beauty of beet greens, kabocha squash, or garlic scapes.

✳ You will not be told that family dinner is a problem that can be figured out in *three easy steps*!!!

✳ You will not hear me describe family dinner as a problem. A problem is a flood in the basement or a bedbug on your pillow or a letter from the IRS saying you owe them $120,000. A problem is something that, once solved, gets you right back to where you started, but poorer or angrier. Preparing your mother's crispy vinegary pork chops and sharing them with people you love, potentially making your life richer and happier, is, in my opinion, the opposite of a problem.

✳ (Disclaimer: You may, however, catch me referring to certain family dinner scenarios, such as having two working parents and two kids under two, as not merely problematic but also "soul crushing" and "harrowing.")

✳ You will not read the insidious phrase: "So delicious your kid will love it, too!" Therefore, you will not have the urge to throw this book across the room when your kid tries the kale and decidedly doesn't *love it, too.*

✳ You will not hear me suggest, even for one second, that you should do what I have done and document in a dedicated diary every dinner you've cooked and eaten for the past fourteen years. (This strategy should be employed only under special circumstances and only after being officially approved by your institution's chief warden.)

✳ Olives. I'm sorry. I know it's a major culinary weakness, but I really don't like olives, so you won't find them anywhere in these pages.

✳ You will not hear me claim that family dinner is the magic bullet, the answer to your prayers, the only way to raise happy children. But I will say that it has done more to foster togetherness and impart meaning and joy into my family life on a daily basis than just about anything else I can think of.

Dinner: A Love Story

The Confession: How It All Began

Two years ago, I went to lunch with my friend Lori at Sam's, a Jewish deli in New York City's Garment District. At the time, I was her editor at a parenting magazine, and the goal of the lunch was to come up with story ideas for the next few issues. Lori is that friend you want to follow around with a notebook and pencil. She's always reading an advance copy of some novel that everyone else is going to be reading in book clubs six months later. She's the friend who sees the Oscar-winning film before it wins the Oscar and who is constantly sending me links to things she thinks I'll find interesting—Michael Ruhlman food rants, Gwyneth Paltrow juice diets, George Saunders essays. I'm usually the one jotting down notes and interrupting her to ask things like, "Wait, this Jack White person—you say there is no relation whatsoever to Jack *Black*?"

When she sat down on this particular afternoon, though, she looked distracted, a little upset. After some small talk, she leaned over and whispered something to me.

"Can I confess something to you?"

"Of *course*," I told her, preparing myself for an admission of a passionate affair . . . or drinking while breast-feeding . . . or spanking . . . or, I don't know, she looked kinda freaked . . . maybe she was in trouble with the law? "You can tell me anything."

She went on. "Do you want to know the one thing I feel most guilty about as a mother?" She was staring into her matzoh brei, too ashamed to look at me.

Okay, now I was a little frightened. She had two kids, ages five and two. What could be so bad?

"I've never once cooked a meal for my children," she said. She looked up at me with shiny eyes.

I'm not proud to admit it, but my first thought was: *So that's how she manages to read the* New York Times *every freaking day from cover to cover! Even the Metro section!*

My second thought was: *How did we get to the point where mothers break down in tears because they don't know how to cook dinner?*

What would Betty Friedan say?

"Lori!" I practically screamed at her. If it weren't for the gentle-looking Wallace Shawn doppelganger sitting at the table next to us, I would have grabbed her across the sour pickles and yelled "Get a grip!" But all I said was, "*That* is your confession? That's *all*?" She was too upset to answer.

Lori's shame was probably in high relief that day because she knew she was sitting across from someone who regularly, some might say pathologically, cooked dinner for her family. She knew me well enough to know that since 1998, I've written down what I've cooked or eaten every night in a "dinner diary" (more on this in a minute). In addition to editing features at *Cookie*, the parenting magazine, I oversaw the food department and was in the midst of cowriting a family meal cookbook with two colleagues who were equally enthusiastic about cooking for their children. Lori had once told me that her three months in the *Cookie* office, filling in for someone on maternity leave, were pure torture—everywhere she looked, she said, she was reminded of her culinary shortcomings.

"It's not like I feel bad about it *sometimes*," she said. "I feel bad about it at every meal, three times a day, seven days a week."

"Yeah, but it's not like you're feeding your kids *antifreeze*," I told her. She was mostly giving them turkey dogs or things from the prepared section at Whole Foods. "And what about Larry?" I said. Larry was her husband, who loved to cook but didn't get home in time for dinner during the week. "Do you think he is in a coffee shop right now crying into soup with one of his friends? Somehow I doubt it—and I think you should follow his lead."

"I know," she said. "It's pathetic."

"No, it's not pathetic. But you say this like you're the first parent in history to feel handicapped by guilt. No one has it all together." I thought of my friend Terry, who the week before had pulled her SUV to the curb to say hi while I was walking the dog but before long switched gears to park so she could really get into how awful she felt about missing her daughter's soccer trophy presentation the weekend before. She wasn't just talking it through—she was wailing, clearly dealing with some existential parent angst. "And I was just dropping off Max across town," she said, like Marlon Brando in the last scene of *On the Waterfront*. "I could've *been there*."

"I *know* I'm not the only one," Lori continued. "But I feel like if I could just get my act together to make dinner for my kids, then everything else would fall into place. The problem is I know the kids won't eat whatever I attempt to make . . . so I end up saying, Well, why even bother trying? Only to wake up hating myself even more, thinking, *If I can't make my kids dinner, what can I do exactly? What kind of mother doesn't cook for her children?*"

I cut her off. "Okay, stop. You're a good mother! Just look at how *guilty* you feel! I think that means you care *too* much."

She laughed. "I wish I could carry you around with me so I could get a pep talk anytime I need it."

I thought about that. It wasn't such a bad idea.

We hatched a plan right there at the table. I would become Lori's "Dinner Doula." I'd give her onion-chopping tutorials, interview her children about what they would and wouldn't eat, plan some menus, deconstruct her family's weekly schedule, write up shopping lists for her on the weekends, and do lots of good old-fashioned, roll-up-your-sleeves *strategizing*. But more important, I would hold her hand and give her emotional support. You know how a traditional doula takes care of the mom so mom can take care of the baby? That's what I wanted to do for her.

The first thing I told her was not to put so much pressure on herself. Lori is like a lot of parents I know. She had it in her head that she was supposed to "cook" in a certain way—insert visions of Donna Reed here—and to do it that way every single night, a scenario more commonly known as Setting Yourself Up for Failure. On top of that, she had read every Center for Addiction and Substance Abuse study and every article about every CASA study, and she was haunted by their message: that kids who eat with their parents do better in school, are less likely to do drugs, etc., etc., etc. I wanted to help Lori (a) stop obsessing over these alarmist studies and (b) learn a few things, take some baby steps in the kitchen.

But a funny thing happened. Over the next few weeks, as I became Lori's Dinner Doula, she became my muse. In the process of "coaching" her, I realized how many more layers there were to the age-old "what's for dinner" problem, which had been my beat in lifestyle magazines for more than a decade. Sure, there were all the usual stumbling blocks (not enough time, not enough energy, not enough ideas), but for a lot of parents dinner was no longer the part of the day to unwind and share the family news. In fact, it was often the opposite—it was a major source of psychological stress. Every time mom makes a meal that her kid doesn't eat or that ends up being devoured hyena-like in thirty seconds flat (without a single word uttered in between bites, let alone a thank you) or eaten while siblings are screaming at each other across the untouched spinach, or if dinner is, God forbid, a frozen pizza that is eaten with the babysitter or with only one parent, she sees it as a referendum on her own self-worth. It's not much dinner she's looking at; it's a giant report card. And Lori wasn't the only one in the world feeling like she was getting Fs every night.

Lori and I wrote a magazine story about our six-week regimen of basic chicken roasting and picky-eater strategizing, but her breakdown stayed with me long after the story was finished. I couldn't shake the feeling that there was a void out there for parents who believed in the importance of family dinner, who, like me, believed dinner went a long way toward helping us connect more with our kids, but who, like Lori and her husband, didn't have any idea how to make it happen on a regular basis. Maybe I could help them. And, who knows, maybe I could even help people who weren't parents yet or people whose definition of family might never include children. All I knew was that I had been keeping that dinner diary for twelve years—four years before I even had kids—and I knew I had something to say, maybe even something to *teach*, about the importance of a shared meal with people you love.

So in March 2010, I launched Dinner: A Love Story, a website devoted to family dinner. The goal was to take what I'd learned as a food editor and a mother and try to be everyone's doula, providing recipes and strategies, pep talks and encouragement, whenever parents felt like they needed it. What I attempted to do with the website, and what I hope to continue to do with this book, is to change the conversation about dinner and all the dread that came along with it. I had no interest in shaming or scaring anyone into eating with their kids. I wanted the website to feel inviting and homemade, to give real-life-based instruction,

to be different. I want it to be like the family dinner table we all aspire to have—a judgment-free zone; a happy, instructive place where you always feel welcome; a place where strategies and parenting philosophies are passed around right along with the Zucchini Fries (page 212).

Now, back to that diary . . . I would understand if this is where I lose you. Seriously. What kind of person, you'd like to know, writes down every dinner she cooks for fourteen years straight? My response to that is (a) Please don't give up on me before you get to the Pork Shoulder Ragù (page 179) and (b) please know that while keeping a diary in the early days of cooking was instrumental in getting the ball rolling on family dinner, I'd like to make it very clear that there are plenty of less troublesome ways to achieve the same result. This is the way I did it because I am one of those sad, deluded people who still believe that the mere act of writing something down will give me some sense of control over it. I will go into more detail about the diary system in a few pages, but you should know that there are several dozen other strategies in this book that will help you get into a rhythm with family dinner, and not a single one of them will make you question your obsessive tendencies.

How Do You Use This Book?

*T**hose of you already** familiar with my blog know that, for the most part, my focus is on family dinner with my husband, Andy, and my two elementary-school-aged daughters, Abby and Phoebe, who are capable of sitting upright in a chair, using a fork semicorrectly, not spilling their milk all over the chicken I just spent a half hour making, and occasionally even participating in a conversation. Also, most of the time they are eating a meal that resembles (or is at least related to) the meal on their parents' plates. This description may sound like an idyllic little picture of a foreign land you hope to visit someday, but in fact each milestone listed above—as well as many not listed, such as "Not Pinching Nose at the Mention of the Word *Egg*," which we are still working on—was hard-earned and generally helped along by the simple phenomenon of children *growing up*. It took years to get to the point where we could execute a regular old weeknight meal in a way that was relaxing for everyone. Years! In fact, knowing what I know now, I don't even recommend attempting a sit-down meal with your kids until your youngest is at least three (more on that in Part 3). Before my youngest turned three, we were in survival mode at dinner hour. And before that—I can't remember . . . What exactly did I do before I had kids?

I think of our dinner narrative as being divided into three distinct phases, which also happens to be how this book is organized:

✯ Phase 1: Just Married, or the years Andy and I were establishing a dinner routine, building a repertoire and a relationship in the kitchen.

✯ Phase 2: New Parenthood, or the years it felt like a bomb exploded any semblance of routine and normalcy in the kitchen.

✯ Phase 3: Family Dinner, or the years the angels began to sing.

This book will cover all three of these phases of family dinner—the charming parts, the messy parts, the really annoying parts, the crazy-fun parts. Every meal that you read about in the next three hundred or so pages is a real meal. And I don't mean "real" in the way the real food movement folks mean "real" (i.e., wholesome and unprocessed, though they are that, too). I mean that these meals really happened. These are the meals and menus we have served up for family dinners, romantic dinners, dinners for bosses, dinners for friends, dinners for one, dinners for two, dinners for food snobs, dinners for seven five-year-olds, and five seven-year-olds, ski house vacation dinners, beach house vacation dinners, quick Tuesday night dinners, long, luxurious Sunday night dinners, engagement dinners, birthday dinners, outdoor dinners, dinners after the soccer game, dinners before trick-or-treating, picnic dinners, patio dinners, snow-day dinners, potluck dinners, date-night dinners, and dinners for just about any occasion that can happen in the span of saying "I do" (or "I do want to sign that lease with you") to sending your two kids off to UNC with a full scholarship to play soccer (she says hopefully). Though there weren't enough pages in this book to flesh out all four thousand dinners I've recorded in my diary, you'll be getting a "greatest hits" in chronological order beginning in 1998 and ending in 2011. Nothing has been engineered, nothing has been reimagined and refined by a test kitchen staffed with culinary school graduates. On a few occasions, I've enlisted some help wrangling an unwritten family favorite into conventional format or tweaked some recipes that were in desperate need of updating. (Trust me, the gloppy baked pasta I made for dinner guests in 1998 wouldn't fly in 2012.) But other than that, every meal you see here has been cooked and eaten at least a half dozen times by someone in my house. And in my house, we eat well.

My hope is that this collection of recipes and stories might offer a game plan, or at least a little inspiration, for any home cook at any level. It is as much for the novice who doesn't know where to start as it is for the gourmand who doesn't know how to start *over* when she suddenly finds herself feeding an intractable toddler stuck in a white-food-only phase. This book is for the person who never thought too hard about home-cooked meals until the moment he or she became a parent. It's for mothers and fathers—working, staying home, single, divorced, any kind—who crave more quality time with their children and have a sneaking suspicion that the answer may lie in the ritual of family dinner, in the ritual of sitting down together at the end of the day to slow down and listen to each other. This book is, in fact, for *anyone* interested in learning how to execute a meal to be shared with someone they love and discovering how so many good, happy things can trickle down from doing so.

In other words, I'm thinking this book might just be for everyone.

A Note About the Recipes

All *the recipes in* this book, unless otherwise noted, serve four, even the ones in Part 1, when the idea of living with kids, let alone feeding them, was about as realistic a proposition as flying to the moon. This is because almost every meal I've included is one that has made the evolutionary leap from our table for two to our table for four—and yes, often with a dollop of ketchup on the side.

You'll see that some of the recipes are written in conventional style, with the ingredients itemized at the top, and some are written more casually, as though I'm standing next to you and we're having a conversation (e.g., "Add a few glugs of olive oil and a handful of chopped fresh mint"). This inconsistency is not an oversight. I've thought a lot about recipe structure in my career as a food editor (and once even had a spirited debate about it on my blog) and I've come to this conclusion: Cooking from conventional recipes is how you start, but cooking from casual recipes is how you grow. If you cook regularly enough, there will come a day when you won't need to measure out the quarter teaspoon of cayenne or set the timer when a recipe says cook for "3 minutes per side." Just like parenting, you will have to accept there will be snags, but eventually you'll learn to trust your instincts.

Rituals, Relationships, Repertoires

{ *or, how we taught ourselves to cook* }

My mother went back to school when I was in fourth grade. She had been a full-time mom for almost ten years, and once my twin brother, Phil, my older sister, Lynn, and I were occupied all day with play rehearsals, calligraphy club, tennis lessons, and ballet and tap classes (and people say overscheduling is a new phenomenon?) she decided it was time for her to get back in the game. I remember the day she told us. We were all in the car and she was about to start chauffeuring us around the county to our various activities. But before she shifted into drive, she said she had some news.

"I'm going to law school," she said. "I'm going to be a lawyer." There was a stack of pamphlets and applications on the passenger seat and she held them up as if to offer proof.

This was thirty years ago, so the exact details of what she said are hazy, but I have a clear memory of how she looked from the backseat of our tan Oldsmobile Cutlass: proud. Until that moment, I don't think it had ever occurred to me that my mom had her own dreams or that she could spend time doing something that didn't involve her children. But I was proud of her, too. And telling my friends I had a mom in law school was going to be fun. I just had a few questions. Like: *If you're in law school all day, who is going to drive me to soccer practice?* And: *Who is going to pick me up from play rehearsal?* And: *On Thursdays I have Hebrew school until five thirty and then Pointe at six, so how am I supposed to get from one place to another?*

"Don't worry, Jenny," she said. "My classes are at night, so your life will proceed just as it always has."

Whew.

And then, the whammy: "But for three nights a week, Dad's going to be in charge of dinner."

Um . . . *what?*

My dad didn't cook. His contribution to the dinner table was a loaf of bread picked up at Grand Central Station before his twenty-five-minute commute home to our house in southern Westchester. (On most nights it was a baguette; on special nights it was a challah with white raisins.) But one thing you could say about Dad—no matter what was going on at the midtown marketing firm where he worked, he walked in the door every night between six thirty and seven o'clock. He never missed dinner. I didn't realize this in 1981, but his spotless attendance record at the table was obviously a much bigger contribution to dinner hour than the raisin challah, delicious as it was. The moment he walked in was the moment we all started gravitating to the kitchen to peek inside pots and tear off pieces of the fresh bread he set on a cutting board on the table. His arrival, announced by the creaky swing, then slam, of the back screen door, was the signal that dinner was about to be served. I'm not sure my brain even had a part in this decision. All it knew was that my body was being summoned to its seven o'clock magnetic north: the family dinner table.

And yet my dad's presence at dinner, as important as it was, was different from *cooking* that dinner. Until this point, on the rare nights that he had been in charge of feeding us, it usually meant we hit the McDonald's drive-thru. Even my ten-year-old optimistic self knew we weren't going to be dining on Happy Meals three times a week for four years.

"What are we going to eat?" I asked my mother.

"We'll figure it out," she said.

They figured it out all right. They figured it out in the form of Breaded Chicken Cutlets. Later, when I had kids and was forced to compete with the chickenless chicken nugget, I'd call this dinner "crispy chicken" or "Grandma Jody's Chicken" (named after my mom), but in 1981 we just called it Chicken Cutlets Again? It must have been the only thing my mom taught my dad how to make, because other than the occasional bowl of spaghetti with "butter sauce," that's what we ate three nights a week for eight night-school semesters. Sometimes my mom would set up the dredging station with three plates—one for the flour, one for the beaten egg, one for the bread crumbs—while she waited for my dad to come home from work. He started taking an earlier train to accommodate her new schedule, and as soon as he walked in they'd exchange a few pleasantries while he took off his coat and she put hers on, then kiss each other hello and good-bye. With Tom Brokaw wrapping up the *Nightly News* on the tiny black-and-white kitchen TV, Dad would finish what my mom had started, standing at the mustard-colored Formica counters moving the cutlets from plate to plate, then finally into the hot skillet. By seven o'clock there would be a homemade meal on the table for my brother, my sister, and me. A decade later, when Mom was partner in her own firm and Dad would be the first one home, he would often prep the chicken dredging station for her.

From a ten-year-old's perspective, my parents' thrice-weekly do-si-do routine was seamless, and their acts of sacrifice for the family expected. But now as the mother of two girls (one who is almost ten herself), I know better than to assume it was as easy as it looked. I'm sure I was too busy memorizing the lyrics to "Food Glorious Food" to notice all the backstage coordinating that had to happen in order for our complicated little lives to continue running smoothly—and in order for us to sit down to a home-cooked dinner with at least one parent every night while my mom was able to go off and learn about torts and civil procedure and pursue a career.

What did I learn from this besides the desire never to see another breaded chicken cutlet for as long as I lived? Well, for starters, I had a front-row seat to an equality-minded marriage. A marriage where parental roles were flexible, where the pendulum of responsibility swung from spouse to spouse depending on the circumstances, and a marriage where, at the end of the day, the kids came first (unless there is only one beautiful plump apricot left in the bowl, in which case, the mom *always* comes first). I also learned about the importance of sharing a meal with people who loved me enough to tag-team dredge my chicken.

So a decade and a half later, when I got married and settled in Brooklyn Heights, I had a very clear sense of what family dinner looked like. And so did my new husband, Andy, who also grew up in a house where both parents worked and where dinner was a command performance for every member of the family. We had other things in common, too: We went to the same college (where we met), we had the same career path (publishing), we had both highlighted large sections in chapter 1 of *The Autobiography of Benjamin Franklin*, and thanks to our parents, we both had highly cultivated guilt complexes, specifically as they related to dinner.

Even before we had kids, before I was adding up the hours at home and at work and trying to make the numbers come out even, I felt guilty about staying late at work and missing dinner. And so did Andy. If either of us made after-work plans that precluded eating together, the abandoner always asked the abandoned if it was okay. As in, "Is it okay if I go out on Thursday with Brian who is flying in from Chicago for one night to see me?" or "Is it okay if my college roommate's dad wants to take me and his daughter to that new Jean-Georges restaurant Vong?" It is somewhat astounding for me to think about this so many years later, especially now that we have children and the whole idea of guilt has been ratcheted up to levels I couldn't have grasped back in those days—because of course the answer was always yes. Of course! What kind of marriage required spousal permission for a gin and tonic with a college friend who had flown in from one thousand miles away? It was more than permission, though. It was respect. Respect for each other, respect for the ritual, respect for the meatballs.

Because, it turns out, those meatballs don't just appear on the table by themselves. And it also turns out that just because you have a clear idea of what dinner is supposed to look like, it doesn't necessarily mean it's an easy thing to execute—especially if your cooking skills are not as highly developed as your guilt complexes. Neither of us really knew how to get a meal on the table when we first got married, which is to say, we didn't really know how to *cook*. It's not that I was afraid of cooking or hadn't spent time in the kitchen as a kid. I spent a *lot* of time there. But my strength was baking, specifically baking from scratch, which I defined as "anything not purchased from the Entenmann's section of the Grand Union." That meant Betty Crocker brownies from the box counted as "from scratch" as did Jiffy corn muffins. I'm pretty sure no week went by in the 1980s when I didn't bake a batch of "homemade" Duncan Hines chocolate chip cookies for my sister and brother. (Remember? The box mix that came with the "butter flavor" squeeze packet?)

I don't want to sell myself too short here, though. I did have one or two house specialties, like chocolate croissants, which I concocted by slicing open a frozen Sara Lee crescent roll, stuffing it with half a Hershey bar, then nuking it for exactly 35 seconds. And I had a few meals I could put together in a pinch: Kraft macaroni and cheese topped with browned ground beef (I still make this from time to time: it's childhood in a bowl); buttered and salted skinny egg noodles; and Steak-umm sandwiches, which I think I had for every weekday lunch in the summer of 1984. I didn't think too hard about the difference between fresh foods and packaged or processed ones. Until my mother handed me a garlic clove in 1989, I distinctly remember thinking that the only form of garlic was powdered and jarred, with a McCormick label slapped across the front of it.

So for a while, there would be more microwaved veggie burgers than osso buco at our just-married Brooklyn dinner table. Not only because our culinary skills weren't quite where they needed to be, but because we had yet to figure out how crucial shopping and planning were in the dinner equation. I had yet to figure out the dinner diary system.

The dinner diary . . . What drives a person to write down what she cooks or eats for dinner every night in a blank book? And to do this every night for fourteen years and counting? I've been thinking about this question for a long time, and I have a few theories, none of which, amazingly, involve an obsessive-compulsive diagnosis. The rationale I like the best is this: It always bothered me that Andy and I spend so many of our waking hours planning for dinner only for all traces of that meal to disappear forever in fifteen minutes. When we were first married, I can remember on more than one occasion opening my eyes in bed on a Sunday morning and seeing my new husband staring right back at me, wide awake. As soon as he felt it was safe to engage his sleep-greedy wife in conversation, the first thing he'd say was not "Good morning" or "How did you sleep?" but "What should we do for dinner tonight?" Then the rest of the day seemed to be headed in one direction: the meal. Writing down what that meal was made the effort and the event itself seem less fleeting and more meaningful. Or maybe that's just what I tell myself.

But on Sunday, February 22, 1998, the very first date on the very first page of my dinner diary, I didn't care about theories. I had one thing on my mind when I opened up the blank green book that Andy bought me for the previous Christmas: How do I make dinner happen? How can I ensure that I will never again have to endure the agonizing back-and-forth weeknight email exchange that began around five o'clock and usually went something like this:

AW: What should we do for dinner?
JR: I don't know. What do you think?
AW: I don't know, what are you in the mood for?
JR: Something healthy? Salad?
AW: Just had a big salad for lunch. Pasta?
JR: Nah, Jennifer Aniston lost thirty pounds by not eating pasta.
AW: Well what, then?
JR: I don't know.
AW: Sweet.

When, by some miracle, we did decide on a meal, we'd usually have to cram in an express shop at the supermarket on our way home. And since we were in our mid-twenties and therefore never leaving work before our bosses left, that meant we weren't home until after eight o'clock, by which point we'd be starving and opt for ten-minute spaghetti with Ragú Robusto instead of thirty-minute ditalini with amatriciana sauce, or whatever recipe sounded good when we were flipping through *Food & Wine* at the beach a few days earlier. What added to the stress was that I had no confidence in the kitchen, no confidence in my improvisational abilities. I had not yet trained myself to look at a lone onion and envision spaghetti with caramelized onions. I had not yet learned that I wasn't going to be arrested if a recipe called for smoked paprika and I only had the regular kind. I was a recipe girl. I liked to follow them *by the letter*. I was not an improviser. Not an off-roader. If given a choice between those two diverging roads in the yellow wood, I'd have chosen the more traveled one *every time*.

So on that February Sunday, in an attempt to preempt all this dinner angst, I wrote down a lineup of everything I wanted to cook that week on the first page of my blank book. This is what it looked like:

My Dinner Diary: Week one, year one.

Then we drew up a shopping list based on that lineup and hit the supermarket. It wasn't sexy and it wasn't necessarily original, but our advance planning system worked. The day we started doing this was the day cooking and eating together started resembling the meals I grew up with, dinners that were relaxing and satisfying. So what if I had to put up with friend after friend picking up my diary from the kitchen counter, then, after realizing what it was, asking, "Jenny? Is everything okay?"

Things could not have been more okay—on the food front and beyond. I was starting to shape a theory about dinner. I found that if I was eating well, there was a good chance that I was living well, too. I found that when I prioritized dinner, a lot of other things seemed to fall into place: We worked more efficiently to get out of our magazine offices on time (Andy was at *Esquire* and I was at *Biography*, a small publication from A&E), we had a dedicated time and place to unload whatever was annoying us about work and everything else, and we spent less money by cooking our own food, which meant we never felt guilty about treating ourselves to dinner out on the weekend. And perhaps most important, the simple act of carving out the ritual—a delicious homemade ritual—gave every day purpose and meaning, no matter what else was going on in our lives. A decade later, when a *New York Times* reporter wrote a story about my diary habit, all kinds of people got in touch to tell me they did the same thing or to offer their own theories about why someone might be compelled to record the fact that she ate a spinach frittata on September 19, 1999. The letter that meant the most to me and that helped make sense of my dinner compulsion more than any other was from a man named Rudy. He told me that his wife started her dinner diary habit fifty years ago after experiencing a tremendous (unspecified) loss. He wrote: "She never told me this, but I think she started [writing down what she made for dinner] when she was depressed, and it was a mechanism to cope with her depression, showing that she is taking care of herself."

Taking care of ourselves—and to some degree our marriage—officially began on that Sunday, February 22, 1998, with chicken cacciatore, which we made for Andy's brother, Tony, and his wife, Trish. That meal has fallen out of the rotation, but two of the five listed that week are still going strong: chicken pot pie (which you'll read about later) and Curried Chicken with Apples (page 14), which not only introduced me to the basic technique of making a quick skillet meal but also later proved to be the perfect starter curry for my kids. In fact, I think of that recipe and my dad's chicken cutlets as two of the most meaningful dinners in this whole book.

Breaded Chicken Cutlets (aka Grandma Jody's Chicken)

In spite of my desire to never eat breaded chicken cutlets again, this was the first meal I ever made for Andy (at twenty-two, my meal repertoire was about as varied as my dad's) and in the years since, the chicken has proven to be a real lifesaver in the slap-it-together weeknight meal department. Plus, if you have this in your repertoire, you can make "chicken pizza" (page 148), chicken Milanese (just top with an arugula and tomato salad that has been tossed with oil and vinegar), and real chicken fingers.
Total time: 25 minutes

> Few generous glugs of olive oil (5 to 6 tablespoons), more as necessary (you are not deep-frying here, but pretty close)
>
> 2 eggs, lightly beaten
>
> ¾ cup all-purpose flour
>
> 1½ cups plain bread crumbs or Kellogg's Corn Flake Crumbs that have been salted and peppered (see note on next page)
>
> 4 boneless chicken breasts (about 1¼ pounds), rinsed and patted dry and pounded like crazy (see sidebar, page 12)

Add the oil to a large skillet set over medium-high heat.

Set up your dredging stations: one rimmed plate for the eggs, one plate for the flour, and one plate for the bread crumbs. Using a fork, coat your chicken pieces first in the flour (shaking off any excess), then in the egg, then in the crumbs, pressing the chicken into the crumbs to thoroughly coat.

Fry each breast in the oil for 3 to 4 minutes on each side. (I usually do two at a time, but I've been known to cram all of them in at once and then spend the entire meal wishing I had just sucked it up and waited the 6 extra minutes.) The cutlets are cooked when chicken is firm to the touch but not rock hard.

Remove and drain the chicken onto a paper-towel-lined dinner plate tented with foil if you have more pieces to fry. Add more oil to the pan and fry the remaining breasts.

★ *Note:* Feel free to add any of the following to the bread crumbs: a pinch of cayenne, a teaspoon dry mustard, fresh thyme or oregano leaves, some ground flax, sesame seeds, or freshly grated Parmesan.

WHAT'S UP WITH POUNDING CHICKEN?

Flattening out a chicken breast with a meat pounder will leave you with chicken that cooks more evenly and tastes more tender.

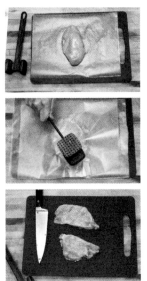

☑ To pound, place your chicken cutlets one at a time in between two sheets of wax paper set over a cutting board.

☑ Then whack the poor thing in the center while simultaneously pushing out toward the edges until the breast is about 1/3 inch thick. (The important thing is that it's all the same thickness.)

☑ The chicken will likely increase in surface area so if it gets too large and unwieldy to handle, you can cut the pounded breast in two pieces before dredging.

How much better does this look than nuggets? Grandma Jody's Chicken (page 11), topped with arugula and summer tomatoes.

Starter Curry: Curried Chicken with Apples

The original recipe we clipped from the *New York Times* had us concocting our own curry with turmeric, cumin, coriander, and cayenne, but more often than not, I fall back on my decent-enough store-bought madras curry blend. This is a constantly evolving dish and we never make it the same way twice. For instance, only in the past year did we start adding coconut milk to the broth—it's just enough to make the dish feel slightly decadent. Total time: 30 minutes

 2 tablespoons canola oil, plus more as needed

 ½ large onion, chopped

 1 garlic clove, minced

 ½ large stalk celery, chopped

 1 large apple, such as Granny Smith, peeled, cored, and
  cut into bite-size pieces

 1 teaspoon grated peeled fresh ginger

 2 tablespoons madras curry powder

 3 medium-size boneless chicken breasts (about 1½ pounds),
  rinsed and patted dry, cut into bite-size cubes, salted and peppered

 ½ cup chicken broth

 ¼ cup light coconut milk

 Handful of frozen peas (optional)

 Few dollops of plain yogurt

 Suggested garnishes: chopped cilantro or mint,
  sliced or chopped almonds

Heat the oil in a deep, large skillet over medium-high heat. Add the onion and sauté until it begins to soften, about 2 minutes.

Add the garlic, celery, apple, and ginger. Cook for 2 to 3 minutes and then add the curry powder, stirring to combine.

Push the ingredients to one side of the pan, add a little more oil, and brown the chicken on all sides. (If your pan is too stuffed, you can do it in two batches.) Stir all of the ingredients together then add the broth and coconut milk. Bring to a boil and then reduce to a simmer. Add the peas (if using) then cover and cook 10 more minutes, until chicken is cooked through.

Serve with basmati rice or flatbread and top with a dollop of yogurt and desired garnishes.

March 1998

. . . .

A Recipe Starter Kit

*A*t least once a month, maybe twice, for the fourteen years that I've been married to Andy, we've received a fat envelope in the mail from his mother, Emily. Nine times out of ten it's an article she clipped from the *Washington Post* (even today, she remains dubious of an emailed link), and most likely the *Post* clipping features either the latest buffoonery on display by a politician or a travel piece highlighting a particular city in the Middle East, where she and Andy's dad, Steve, spent seven years in the Foreign Service in the late 1960s and early '70s. Every now and then she sends a food-related clipping, like one from *Cooking Light* (her favorite food magazine) or the newsletter from the Center for Science in the Public Interest. (She was definitely the first to alert me to the saturated-fat horror show of movie-theater popcorn.)

But the holy grail of mailers arrived in 1998, about six months after I married

Best wedding present ever, courtesy of my
mother-in-law: Andy's favorite childhood recipes
handwritten on genuine index cards.

Great Grandma Turano's Meat Balls & Sauce
(Via Grandma T. & mom)

Sauce
Brown in olive oil w~~~~ or sauce pan.
- 1 clove minced gar~~~
- ¼ C. chopped oni~~~
- C ½ c. sliced mushro~~~

add: 1 t. salt, & pep~~~
1 C. Tomato ~~~
1 T. sugar ~~~
Can~~~
1 15 oz. swee~~~

Meat Loaf
- 1 lb. or more chopped (lean) beef,
  turkey, or combo)
- 1 C. Italian bread crumbs
- 2 eggs (one's O.K.)
- 1 C. Tomato juice or small can
  tomato sauce w. water.
- 1 onion, chopped
- 1-2 stalks celery, chopped
- 1 green pepper, chopped
- 1-2 T. chopped parsley
- 1 tsp. Worcestershire sauce
- 1 tsp. salt
- Herbs: thyme,~~~

Mix t~~~

Port ~~~
- 1 ~~~ tenderloin (approx 3 lb~~~
- 1 cup dried cranberries
- 1 cup cranberry juice co~~~
- 1 cup tawny port (~~~
- 3 Tablespoons brown ~~~
- 2 Tablespoons soy sau~~~
- 1 t. ground pepper
- ¼ t. salt
- 2-3 cloves garlic ~~~
Cooking spray, ~~~

Chicken alla Cacciatora
- 2 whole chicken breasts (4 boneless
  chicken breasts, or chicken breast halves or breast w.
  bones).
- Sprinkle w. salt, pepper, & flour.
- Brown lightly in 2-4 T. olive oil.
  Take chicken out of pan. Add to
  pan:
  1 large onion, chopped fine
  1-2 stalk diced celery
  1 clove diced garlic
  ~~~fore

- 2 eggs
- a little ch~~~
Form into sm~~~
balls in frying~~~
to sauce abou~~~
serving.

Serve over pasta. Yum-Yum!
☺

Andy. It came addressed to both of us: a little stack of white index cards on which were scribbled a half dozen of the recipes that Andy grew up eating at his kitchen table. The recipes were so basic—breaded pork chops! meatloaf! porcupine meatballs—so simple, and for him, so infused with nostalgia. I imagined they had been copied from recipe cards given to her by her mother-in-law or grandparents or from really old cookbooks that showed softly lit aspic buffets on yellowed pages. Whatever their provenance, though (I never asked—what would be more romance dashing than finding out they came from *Cooking Light*?), it doesn't really matter. Within a few months, we had made each one of the recipes enough times to commit to memory, and twelve years later we both still think of the little index card cache as our family dinner starter kit.

Porcupine Meatballs

I would like to go on record and say that this recipe might best represent our whole philosophy of cooking: It's fast, easy, nostalgic, delicious, and only went up in value once we had kids. One note: Unless you are under four feet tall, you will probably need something acidic (a green salad with vinegary dressing) to cut the sweetness of the braising liquid. **Total time: 45 minutes**

1 pound ground beef or dark turkey

½ cup uncooked rice

1 tablespoon finely chopped onion

2 tablespoons diced green bell pepper

1 teaspoon salt

1 garlic clove, minced

2 cups tomato juice

4 whole cloves

½ teaspoon cinnamon

2 tablespoons sugar

1 tablespoon Worcestershire sauce

Combine the meat, rice, onion, bell pepper, salt, and garlic in a large bowl. Shape the mixture into small balls, about 1 inch wide.

In a deep skillet, whisk together the tomato juice, cloves, cinnamon, sugar, and Worcestershire sauce and bring to a simmer.

Drop in the meatballs and cover the skillet. Simmer for 30 minutes, or until rice is cooked and spiky, gently flipping over and spooning braising liquid over exposed meatballs from time to time.

Don't forget to remove the cloves before serving. (But if you do forget, don't worry—it will give you something to laugh about every single time you make it from that day forward.)

Breaded Vinegary Pork Chops

This version has been adapted slightly. The original called for Progresso Italian bread crumbs, but we've upgraded to panko (available in better supermarkets and all Asian markets) kicked up with lemon zest, to add extra crunch. Total time: 1 hour 25 minutes (includes 1 hour marinating time)

4 bone-in pork chops (about 2 pounds), pounded to ½ inch thickness
    (see sidebar, page 12, for a quick pounding tutorial)

1 cup red wine vinegar

1½ cups panko

Zest from ½ lemon

1 tablespoon chopped fresh thyme

1 tablespoon chopped fresh oregano

Salt and pepper to taste

½ cup all-purpose flour

2 eggs, beaten

Olive oil

Arrange the pork in a single layer in a large baking dish and cover with the vinegar. Let sit for 1 hour at room temperature.

In a small bowl, combine the panko, zest, thyme, oregano, and salt and pepper. Set up your dredging stations: one rimmed dish for the flour, one for the eggs, and one for the panko mixture.

Heat a large cast-iron or heavy nonstick skillet over medium heat and add a few glugs of olive oil. Using a fork, dredge each chop first in the flour, then in the egg, then in the panko; make sure you coat the sides as well as the tops and bottoms, as every inch of crust is crucial. Drop the chops into the hot oil. Working in two batches, cook the pork chops until crispy and cooked through (about 4 minutes on each side), wiping out skillet with a paper towel after first batch and adding more oil as necessary.

Emily's Meat Loaf

For her holiday party one year, my friend Elizabeth served a row of meat loaves that were presented on her finest China platters and had been stuffed with spinach and cheese. I loved that, and occasionally follow her lead for just a regular Tuesday night meal. To stuff, place half the meatloaf mixture in the loaf pan. Using a spoon, make a well down the length of the middle, then add thawed frozen spinach and mozzarella cheese into the well. Cover with remaining mixture and proceed as directed. Total time: 1 hour 15 minutes

    1½ pounds ground lean beef, turkey, veal, pork,
        or combination

    1 cup Italian bread crumbs

    2 eggs, whisked

    1 cup tomato juice or 1 8-ounce can tomato sauce
        whisked with water to make 1 cup

    1 small onion, chopped

    1 stalk celery, chopped

    3 to 4 tablespoons cored, seeded, and chopped
        bell pepper (any color)

    2 tablespoons chopped fresh parsley

    1 tablespoon fresh thyme leaves

    1 tablespoon Worcestershire sauce

    1 teaspoon salt

    1 tablespoon ketchup

    2 strips smoky bacon

Preheat the oven to 350°F.

In a large bowl, use your hands to thoroughly mix together the meat, bread crumbs, eggs, tomato juice, onion, celery, bell pepper, parsley, thyme, Worcestershire sauce, and salt. Add the meat mixture to a loaf pan, spreading ketchup on top. Lay bacon strips on top of ketchup and bake for 1 hour. The loaf is done when a knife inserted into the middle feels hot to the touch or when internal temperature reads 160°F.

We call this our recipe door—four of our favorite family recipes, painted inside our cabinet by the stove. See page 194 for Great-Grandma Turano's Meatballs.

A LETTER TO MY YOUNGER, NEWLY BETROTHED SELF

Dear Younger Self,

Congratulations on your engagement! Having been married to your soon-to-be husband for nearly a decade and a half, I can say with conviction that you've done an excellent job choosing a life partner. I know you are worried about Andy's inability to remember when the recycling bins need to be dragged out to the curb, and that it's really annoying when he leaves dresser drawers and kitchen cabinets open, but trust me, these are shortcomings that will be easily overlooked as soon as you taste his meltingly tender braised pork ragù. Also: the flee-to-the-suburbs vs. stay-in-the-city decision? I don't want to give away the ending, but please work on repeating this mantra as you fight and freak out together: *It's a nice problem.*

Okay, enough about the next fourteen years of marriage! What about the next ten months of wedding planning? I'll bet you are getting a ton of advice from parents and friends and bloggers and you have a million decisions to make! Empire waist or A-line? Rabbi or justice of the peace? Where to have the ceremony? The reception? And perhaps most exciting: What to register for? I know I'm an old lady now, but I remember *exactly* how psyched I was . . . you are . . . to hit Crate & Barrel with a clipboard and pencil to start noting SKU numbers for wineglasses and chip-and-dip platters and all those other sophisticated accoutrements of adult living. Someone else is footing the bill so you can finally afford to buy that pasta pot with the built-in strainer! Hooray!

Except I'm here from the future to tell you that you will not use that pasta pot with the built-in strainer more than once, maybe twice, and it is currently enjoying its second life as a very expensive leak-catching bucket in the basement. The problem was that the pot—with its aluminum base but stainless-steel sides (stainless: poor conductor of heat; avoid)—took about 45 minutes to bring water to a boil. The strainer? I can tell you now that both you and Andy tend to favor the freestanding colander that you can use for all occasions, not just one that fits into this particular rotten pot. It will take a few more years and a few more purchases before you discover a hard-earned truth: When confronted with anything claiming to be two in one, you should *run the other way*. (The one exception here is the Spoonula—a silicone spatula and spoon combo that I find to be life-changing in the scrambled eggs department.)

You should also know this: The chip-and-dip platter? Dork move.

The point of this visit from your future, however, is not to make fun of you. That, as we both know, is Andy's job. (And my! He does it so well!) The purpose of my letter is to *help* you. So on the next page, I'm going to tell you the six most important kitchen items to register for, the ones which fifteen years from now you are still going to be using and *loving* on a daily basis.

Much love,

Your Future Self, 10/4/11

Jenny

Dear Future Self,

Thank you for your very helpful advice. I just have one question: What's a blogger?

Love,

Younger Self, 12/16/96

Jenny

SIX REGISTRY ITEMS YOU'LL NEVER REGRET

(continued from previous page)

3-Quart Sauté Pan with Lid. (All-Clad stainless) You are probably thinking, *Wait, you just told me to* avoid *stainless.* Wrong: I told you to avoid it on its own. All-Clad has a line of cookware with an aluminum core (a metal with excellent heat retention prop-erties) and a stainless exterior. (Stainless wears well, looks cool, and is easy to clean.) As soon as you discover the genius of a skillet dinner (like Andy's Thai-spiced Salmon, which, I'm sorry to say, you'll have to wait another decade for), this pan becomes an absolute workhouse. There will be a point in your life when you decide to just leave it on the stovetop and never put it away.

5½-Quart Round Dutch Oven. (Le Creuset) There have been a few times when I wished I had the 7¼-quart one, but only a few, and the point is this: You need this pot more than any other on the list. A home without a Dutch oven filled with soup simmer-ing on the stovetop or a piece of meat braising in the oven is no home at all! And it will take you only a few years to develop the patina that makes your mother's fifty-year-old 3½-quart Le Creuset look so awesome. (Also, good thing you inherited that 3½-quart one from mom, or I'd have to tell you to register for that, too, since you use it every time you make Marcella Hazan's milk-braised pork loin. Which is to say, you will use it often.)

4-Quart Casserole with Lid. (All-Clad Stainless) You registered for this pot because back then it was called the "Soup for Two." You are such a hopeless romantic! (And FYI: still are.) But I'm glad you picked this one because it will make many meals for you and your beloved, not just soup, and if you hadn't lost it before your move from Brooklyn to . . . I'm not telling you where . . . you would still be using it thrice-weekly for rice and pastas for your family of four. (No, not four *kids*. What are you *insane*?) You will eventually replace it with a Dansk enamel pot found on eBay for next to nothing, but it remains to be seen if this one will last as long as the rest of the All-Clad line has. Buy this workhorse and this time, try to *hold on to it*.

Three Knives. (Wüsthof) You'll want either the 5-inch or 7-inch chef's knife (or both, so you can cook together and not fight over who gets the good one), which will be used for chopping about eight million future onions and shallots and . . . Are you serious? How old are you again? A shallot is a small, delicately flavored onion, with purplish skin that, when minced finely, makes it an excellent addition for salad dressings! You'll also want a 7-inch serrated bread knife, which will come in handy for making Andy's beloved tomato sandwiches—there will be a *lot* of these once he discovers them in the summer of 2001—and a 3-inch paring knife, essential for mincing garlic or peeling the skin off an apple in one smooth, coiling motion.

P.S.: That reminds me: Buy stock in Apple! *As much as you can afford.*

April 1998

. . . .

The Happy Birthday Scallops

kay, so I might have been lying just a tiny bit when I said that we are
completely self-taught when it comes to churning out a steady stream
of edible dinners. Because there was that one birthday—my twenty-
fourth, in 1995—when I opened a card from Andy to find three or four cooking
class descriptions that had been ripped from the New School of Culinary Arts
catalog. I could choose "The Food and Wine of Italy" or "A Middle Eastern Feast"
or even a class taught by David Bouley, owner of Restaurant Bouley in New York
and the closest thing 1995 had to a celebrity chef. Since that one was already filled
to capacity, I chose a French cooking class that promised I would learn "classic
culinary principles" and the basics of "balance and texture." And so a few Saturday nights later, I showed up to a West Village brownstone and joined eight other
apron-clad students around the kitchen's island facing our professor, a restaurant chef who was taking time off to teach. As far as I could tell, I got my money's
worth about ten minutes into the class, the moment he taught us the trick for re-
moving the stench of garlic from your fingers. (Rub them against stainless steel.)
But since other students probably weren't so easily satisfied, he went on to walk
us through a basic recipe for scallops. Really basic. Like six-ingredients-and-
10-minutes'-cooking-time basic. To the point where I wondered if I even needed
a professional's help with it. But I soon learned that packed into this unassuming
little recipe were a few core culinary principles that would see me through hundreds of future meals. Including:

✳ Deep flavor comes from browning and searing. To optimize browning
and searing, make sure whatever meat or fish you are cooking is patted dry and is as close to room temperature as possible. (Also: poking

and prodding every few seconds to see if the crust has formed is the surest way to *prevent* a crust from forming.)

✳ The crumbly brown bits left in the pan after the meat or fish have cooked are the building blocks of sauce. Just deglaze by adding wine or broth and bringing to a boil while scraping the bits off the bottom of the pan. (But be warned: Deglazing can also mean "disappearing" if you're not watching your sauce closely. Once it has thickened, remove from the heat *immediately.*)

✳ You cannot go wrong when you start and finish with butter. And also: Butter is much less likely to burn if you heat it in a pan with olive oil.

✳ Adding acid (a drizzle of vinegar, a spoonful of tangy buttermilk, or in the case of these scallops, a simple squeeze of lemon) will always add brightness to an otherwise boring and flat dish. I'll never forget an interview I read with Mario Batali that reconfirmed this. He said the easiest way to pretend you know what you're doing in the kitchen is to talk about the "acidity" level of a dish.

✳ The best recipes are usually the simplest. Look for recipes that call for a few high-quality fresh ingredients instead of a long list of sauces, spices, and pantry staples. They'll taste fresher and you'll be more likely to cook them.

You might call this a birthday gift that kept on giving. I came home from the class and taught Andy everything I learned. And a dozen years later the scallop recipe remains a keeper.

Pan-Seared Sea Scallops

If I had been the one assigning names to shellfish, bay scallops would be the big scallops since they start with *B* and sea scallops would be the small ones since they start with *S*. But someone else decidedly less logical than me was given the task, so I have been forced to remember the difference by reminding myself that it's the opposite of what it should be. Trust me, you will never forget this ridiculous, ass-backward trick now that you know it. Bay scallops = small ones; sea scallops = big ones. This recipe calls for the big ones. **Total time: 15 minutes**

> 3 tablespoons unsalted butter
>
> 1 tablespoon olive oil
>
> 20–24 sea scallops, rinsed and patted dry, tough whitish muscle on the side peeled off with fingers, and salted and peppered
>
> 2 garlic cloves, minced
>
> ½ cup dry white wine
>
> Juice from ½ lemon (about 1 tablespoon)
>
> Corn-Bacon Hash (optional; next page)

In a large skillet set over medium-high heat, add 1 tablespoon of the butter and the oil.

When the pan is hot but not smoking, add as many scallops as you can without crowding the pan and cook for 1½ to 2 minutes per side. (When you flip them be sure to get your spatula or tongs all the way under the scallop so you don't lose the brown crust. If using tongs, push scallops firmly from underneath before grabbing and flipping.) Remove from the pan and cook any remaining scallops.

Once you have seared all the scallops, lower the heat to medium, melt the remaining 2 tablespoons butter, add the garlic, and cook for 30 seconds. (Do not let the garlic burn.)

Add wine and lemon juice and crank the heat to high, scraping the fish bits as the liquid boils down. Watch the sauce vigilantly as it boils (you don't want it to reduce to nothing). When it looks slightly syrupy, remove the pan from the heat and drizzle the sauce over the cooked scallops, reserving some if you are serving this with Corn-Bacon Hash (below). Which I definitely recommend, along with a fresh grape tomato salad that's been tossed with olive oil, basil, salt, and pepper.

Corn-Bacon Hash

Total time: 10 minutes

In a large skillet set over medium heat, cook **1 strip of bacon** until crisp, about 2 minutes. Remove the bacon from the pan, blot with a paper towel, chop into pieces, and place in a large bowl. Add **1 minced small shallot** to the bacon fat in the pan and stir until soft, about 1 minute. Add the kernels that have been cut from **4 ears of corn** and cook for 2 minutes. Remove to the bowl. Add **5 or 6 chopped basil leaves, salt** and **pepper** to taste, and, if you have it, whatever pan sauce is left from the scallops. Toss and serve.

January 1999

· ·

Loserati Special: Chicken Pot Pie

I first reunited with my childhood friend Laurie at a midtown Così on a snowy day in 1999. We had lost touch after high school—she went to college in the Midwest, then traveled to Israel and Japan (where, among other things, she took a job in a strip bar), while I was struggling to figure out a career in New York City, twenty miles from where I grew up. Laurie was voted "Most Likely to Be a Starving Writer" in the superlative section of our high-school yearbook. As early as fourth grade her papier-mâché fruits in art class looked like they belonged next to Brancusis rather than gold spray-painted macaroni art. We sat with each other in Hebrew school, where Laurie would sketch cartoons of friends and enemies, and then I had to guess who they were by writing it in the blank line she'd draw under each caricature. She called this game "Famous Faces," and we got in big trouble, to my goody two-shoed horror, when our teacher confiscated the sheet on which the teacher herself was depicted covered in warts and wearing a witch's hat. There was my handwriting right below the cartoon: *Ms. Batia.*

We were always different, but our relationship was the kind that could be picked up right where we left off, even after a six-year hiatus. And that's what we did on that snowy day at Così, eating smoked turkey and honey mustard sandwiches. We both wanted to be writers and confessed that we'd give just about anything to write a book that would land on *Oprah* or, at the very least, in the *Westchester Gazette*. We got so caught up in our dreaming and scheming that we didn't realize we had been there for nearly three hours. We made a date to continue the conversation on a Friday after work and pretty soon we were official writing partners with a standing date that I looked forward to all week long.

We kept this up for almost three years, meeting every Friday at a coffee shop on the corner of Seventeenth Street and Irving Place. The goal was to think of story ideas we could pitch to magazine and book editors, even though we didn't know any editors besides Andy, who was still at *Esquire*, and Laurie's friend Ariel, who had an entry-level job at a new celebrity magazine called *InStyle*. Of course we hardly ever talked about ideas during our Idea Meetings. We talked about her dates—*What kind of doctor was he?* I asked. *"Jewish!"* she replied; about what we would say if Ben Stiller were sitting next to us (we were both in love with him); about her father, who she was only now learning was a con artist with multiple identities; about how I thought I might have a shot at being a better, darker writer if I had a father who was a con artist with multiple identities; about how badly we wanted to be respected novelists like Ellen Gilchrist, the author of our favorite book *Net of Jewels*; about how one day, "years from now," when we both had Pulitzers and *Vanity Fair* contracts, we'd return to this cafe and admire the plaque above "our" table that read LAURIE'S AND JENNY'S WORLD DOMINATION STARTED HERE.

Turns out that our world domination began with two short assignments for *InStyle*. (Ariel came through for us!) I was assigned a 250-word luxury hotel roundup, and for the same issue, Laurie had to report a trend piece on some breath tablets, which were apparently turning up in all the Birkin bags of the Hollywood ingenues. Since our literary debuts would be in the same issue, we decided it called for not just a party, but a *proper reading*, like the kind we'd seen in Page Six of the *New York Post* items that usually contained the word *literati*. ("All the literati showed up at Half King last night for Candace Bushnell's latest book party.") Our reading, though, was to be attended by the self-proclaimed *loserati*—the two of us, of course, plus Andy and the Jewish Doctor—and I would bake us all a chicken pot pie. Judging by Laurie's reaction to this menu suggestion, you might have thought I had invented the dish myself.

"That is *genius*, Jenny!" she said. "How do you *think* of these things?"

So on the night of the reading, we crowded into her tiny East Village apartment. I simmered some vegetables in broth and chopped up some chicken while Laurie set up a few folding chairs and fashioned a lectern out of an IKEA stool, on top of which she placed a glass of water. When it was time for the reading, Andy introduced us as the world's "next Matt Damon and Ben Affleck."

I went first. "As many of the new breed of fashion-turned hotel designers well know, whether it's a suite or a suit, the materials make all the difference . . ."

Laurie closed with her story titled something like "What's Hot Right *Now*."

And then we ate our chicken pot pie. It was so good that Laurie demanded I teach her how to do it, then proceeded to serve the dish to every dinner guest she hosted for the next decade. "Chicken pot pie is perfect for every occasion," she emailed me years later, after her first book came out—a graphic memoir about her father. "The reason I love it so much," she continued, "is because it can have as much or as little irony as it needs to have, depending on who I'm serving it to." And she was right. When comfort food became all the rage, we made it almost every weekend for friends who were up on these kinds of rages. And a decade later, when our kids were old enough to hold forks, I added little pastry-monograms to their own personal pies (see page 174) and they loved the dinner simply and unironically. And, of course, no matter when Laurie comes over for dinner (even these days, miles away from our downtown cafe, which is now a lame-o singles bar), pot pie is the first recipe I think of making, before realizing that maybe someone who has now *actually* been in Page Six and on the *Today Show* and so much more might be ready to move on to something bigger.

Chicken Pot Pie with Sweet Potatoes

This recipe taught me a trick that I use all the time in other recipes: If you whisk flour into milk, it prevents the milk from curdling when you add it to hot liquids. This comes in handy any time you want to replace cream in a recipe with skim or 1% milk. Also, feel free to replace the sweet potatoes with red or Yukon Gold potatoes. Total time: 60 minutes

1 cup chicken broth

1 small sweet potato or yam, peeled and diced (or red or Yukon Gold potato)

1 medium carrot, peeled and chopped

1/2 medium onion, chopped

Leaves from 2 sprigs fresh thyme

Salt and pepper to taste

1/2 cup milk (any kind)

2 tablespoons all-purpose flour

2 cups cooked chicken, shredded with two forks
    (store-bought rotisserie-style is ideal)

1/3 cup frozen peas

1 store-bought 9-inch pie crust

1 egg, lightly beaten

Preheat the oven to 425°F.

In a medium saucepan, bring the broth to a boil. Add the sweet potato, carrot, onion, thyme, and salt and pepper. Simmer for 15 minutes, or until the vegetables are soft.

While the vegetables are simmering, in a measuring cup or small bowl, whisk together the milk and flour.

Once veggies are soft, slowly add the flour–milk mixture, stirring until the filling has thickened. (That's the flour working.) Remove the pan from the heat and stir in the chicken and peas.

Add the pot pie filling to a 9-inch pie plate. Cover with the pie crust and cut a few slits on the top to allow the steam to escape while baking. Using a pastry brush, paint with the egg wash, which will result in a nice golden sheen.

Bake the pie for 25 to 30 minutes, until filling looks bubbly inside.

April 1999
Entertaining, Part 1

aurie was impressed with nearly everything I cooked, but the reality is, I had very little sense of what I was doing when it came to cooking for other people—a concept most grown-ups know as "entertaining"—even though I supposedly "entertained" all the time. I knew that I *wanted* to cook for other people and that I *liked* to cook for other people but found out pretty quickly that execution was trickier than my Martha Stewart books had led me to believe. (From *where* exactly does one procure silver candelabras and silky, bow-tied blouses with shoulder pads that seemed to be the required uniform of the Westport, Connecticut, hostess?)

The good news, though, was that cooking for people came with no pressure at this stage in our lives—mostly because we seemed to be the only ones in our social circle who could actually dream up something other than pasta or, more to the point, recognize if there was enough Parmesan in the risotto or salt in the marinade. I was not yet plagued by the anxieties that would come later as I started

Holiday Party Notes 1999

What We Bought (Made/)	What was Brought	What is left
2 lbs thin chicken (satay)		none (big hit!)
3 (total) containers hummus/babag.		1 container
2 huge bags pita		1 bag
2 small containers olives		none
3 bags edamame		½ bag
2 dozen cookies		none
3 dozen Xmas sugar cookies		2 dozen
2 dozen brownies		8
1½ foot thick kielbasa		none
2½ feet of thin spicy kielbasa		none
2 inch stack of salami		none
4 hunks of cheese (½ lb. of each)		¼ of each is left
150 lbs of knishes (100) "big hit!!" *		90% !!
100 homemade Crackers (waste of time)		30
1 thin bottle VODKA (Phil)		¼
1 huge bottle GIN (Lynn)		all of it
cranberry juice — one bottle		¾
3 bottles tonic		2 left
1 bottle ~~tonic~~ ginger ale		none
30 bottles beer	24 bottles (30?)	12 left
1 huge bottle white 1 little bottle white		all
3 bottles red	5 bottles	3

* Evan brought them

befriending food writers and editors. (*Is the beef grass fed? Is asparagus in season? Is Humboldt Fog cliché? Is risotto—how could you not know this Jenny?—too 1997? See Part 3.*) Most of our guests were not yet discerning types—they were hungry types. They were just grateful to eat a meal that was free and didn't arrive by messenger bike.

I had so much to learn when it came to entertaining—but thankfully, I didn't know that then. For starters, no one had told me the rule that I would subsequently read and edit seventeen thousand times in the course of my food editing career: *Never make something for company that you haven't made before.* I should back up and say that labeling our regular crew of guests "company" makes me laugh. There was Evan who lived around the corner from us and whom we nicknamed Kramer because he liked to buzz himself in to see what was up—invariably on a Sunday night while a stew simmered on the stovetop. There were the college roommates who seemed much more concerned about the supply of beer than how badly we overcooked the pork loin. And there was, of course, Laurie, who would stand there in disbelief at any meal before her, even if it was as quotidian as spaghetti and meatballs, impressed by the fact that I had somehow strategically mixed together a few ingredients procured at Key Food to form something edible.

"How did you *do* this?" she'd ask.

"It's called cooking," I'd say.

But the point is, we would often wing it when we had friends for dinner—giving not nearly enough thought to the timing of a meal, the quantity of food as it related to number of guests, the degree of difficulty, how much hands-on time it required. I remember once leaving my midtown office at six o'clock even though guests were coming at seven and I hadn't yet done the shopping for my menu: A Barbara Kafka roasted pork loin with apples with Emeril's three-potato "lasagna," which looked good in the book but which I would soon discover required a mandoline, a do-or-die demand to use whole nutmeg, *not* ground, plus, I think, that nearly extinct bird that François Mitterand requested for a last meal as he lay dying. To make matters worse, I was chained to the kitchen all night long instead of hanging in the living room with my guests as they shoveled cubes of yellow cheese into their mouths with toothpicks. All of which brings me to Rule #2: *Always read a recipe through before you make it.* You will avoid the above described agita and, God willing, never experience the unfortunate moment when you come across the directive "Refrigerate for 4 hours" in a recipe as you pour a second glass of Pinot Gris for your friend who expects to be sitting down at the (unset) table within the hour. Just saying.

I did manage to do a few things right. For instance, I tried to (Rule #3) *select menus and dishes that required no doneness assessment.* That is, I never wanted to break out a meat thermometer or compare the "give" on a slab of beef to the palm of my hand to determine its medium rareness—not in public at least. Simple one-pound fillets of fish terrified me. A rib eye? Forget it. The pressure of overcooking or undercooking them was just too much for me to bear. So I mostly stuck with recipes that required minimal culinary instinct, or to be slightly more generous, dishes that had some built-in forgiveness in the technique. Like stews, braises, baked pastas, soups—in general, recipes with ingredients that get mixed together, dumped together, cooked down together. So that if there was a mistake—the wrong amount, the wrong chop, the wrong ingredient—it was much easier to keep it hidden. I found that these dishes were almost impossible to undercook or overcook. Plus, once they were in the oven, they allowed me to sit and eat yellow cheese cubes with my guests instead of slaving over a stove. I can't recommend this strategy highly enough to fledgling entertainers (minus the cheese cubes).

✳ Three Make-Ahead Meals for Entertaining

Pomegranate Pork Loin with Cabbage

Pork loin is a lean cut of meat, so make sure you drizzle lots of pan sauce on the slices when you serve. And don't skimp on the cabbage either. Total time: 2 hours 30 minutes

3 tablespoons olive oil

1 boneless pork loin (2½ to 3 pounds),
    patted dry and salted and peppered

1 large onion, chopped

1 garlic clove, minced

1 teaspoon Chinese Five Spice (optional)

Salt and pepper

Dash or two of soy sauce

About 3 cups of any combination of red wine,
    pomegranate juice, and chicken broth
    (I usually do a third/a third/a third)

½ head red cabbage, shredded

In a large Dutch oven set over medium-high heat, add the oil. Brown the pork loin on all sides so you get a nice golden crust, about 5 minutes per side. Remove to a plate. Add the onion, garlic, Chinese Five Spice (if using), and salt and pepper and cook until soft, about 5 minutes.

Return the pork to the pot. Add the soy sauce and your combination of red wine, pomegranate juice, and broth to allow the liquid to come a third of the way up the loin. Bring to a boil and then cover and simmer for 2 to 3 hours, flipping once halfway through. (Monitor the liquid level to make sure a third of loin is always submerged—add more juice or wine if not.) The longer it simmers, the better.

About 10 minutes before you serve, add the red cabbage to the pot. Remove the pork and slice. Bring the braising liquid to a boil and cook until it is slightly thickened, 2 to 3 minutes. (It won't get syrupy because there is not enough fat in the meat.) Serve the pork with the braising liquid and cabbage spooned on top.

We are total suckers for pork, and so are the kids. This pomegranate braised loin is not as hard as it looks—and yet, even tastier than it looks.

Braised Beef Short Ribs

This dish—a simplified version of a Balthazar recipe—is a real showstopper in the winter, and the longer it sits in the oven, the meltier and tastier it becomes. A few years later, when we had kids, we'd give them a serving of these at seven o'clock, and two hours later, when they were in bed, we'd serve the rest to our guests. **Total time: 3 hours 30 minutes (includes 3 hours hands-off braising time)**

 5 pounds beef short ribs, cut crosswise into 2-inch pieces

 Salt and pepper

 3 tablespoons olive oil

 3 medium carrots, peeled and chopped

 2 stalks celery, chopped

 3 onions, chopped

 1 tablespoon tomato paste

 3 tablespoons all-purpose flour

 1 bottle dry red wine

 Herbs: 2 sprigs fresh rosemary, 8 sprigs fresh parsley, and 6 sprigs fresh thyme tied with kitchen string

 1 head garlic, halved crosswise

 4 cups beef broth

Preheat the oven to 350°F.

Season the short ribs with salt and pepper. Heat the oil in a large Dutch oven over medium-high heat, and in batches, brown the short ribs 4 to 6 minutes each side. Remove the short ribs and add the carrots, celery, and onions. Cook until the onions are soft and golden, 5 to 10 minutes. Add the tomato paste and flour and cook 2 to 3 minutes.

Whisk in the wine and then return short ribs to the pot. Bring to a boil and cook until the wine is reduced by about half. Add the herbs, garlic, and broth to the pot. Bring to a boil and cover. Transfer the pot to the oven and cook until the meat is falling apart, about 3 hours. (You might want to stir them around every hour or so.)

When you are ready to eat, transfer the short ribs to a serving platter with a slotted spoon. Using a colander, strain the sauce into a medium saucepan. Cook the sauce over medium heat until it thickens, about 5 minutes. Adjust the seasoning to taste, spoon the sauce over the short ribs, and serve.

Baked Ziti with Sausage and Vegetables

You can prepare this in advance (and refrigerate) up until the final step, when you bake for 30 minutes. Just be sure to bring the dish to room temperature before you throw it in the oven. Total time: 1 hour

½ pound ziti

1½ cups crushed tomatoes

½ cup shredded Italian fontina cheese

½ cup shredded ricotta salata

1 cup baby spinach

8 shakes oregano

2 tablespoons butter

2 garlic cloves, minced

Shake of red pepper flakes

3 cups mushrooms, sliced

2 links sweet Italian sausage, casings removed

Pinch of salt and pepper

1 tablespoon all-purpose flour

2 tablespoons tomato paste

2 cups whole milk

¼ teaspoon nutmeg

½ cup plain bread crumbs

1 tablespoon olive oil

Preheat the oven to 400°F.

In a large saucepan, bring 3 quarts of salted water to a boil, add the pasta, and cook for about 8 minutes. (The pasta will finish cooking during baking.) Drain the pasta well and rinse with cold water.

In a deep baking dish, combine the pasta, tomatoes, cheeses, spinach, and oregano.

In a large saucepan, melt the butter over low heat and add the garlic and pepper flakes; cook, stirring, for about 2 minutes. Add the mushrooms and sausage (breaking up the links with a fork) and the salt and pepper. Cook until the mushrooms are tender, about 5 minutes.

Add the flour to the mushroom–sausage mixture and cook, stirring continually for 1 minute. Add the tomato paste, milk, and nutmeg. Bring to a boil, whisking, and simmer for 30 seconds. Pour the sauce over the pasta in the baking dish. In a separate bowl, combine the bread crumbs and oil. Sprinkle over the pasta and bake for 30 minutes.

kay, back to the rules. Even before I started keeping a dinner diary, I was recording comments next to recipes in cookbooks. Sometimes my scribbles were straight-up reviews about what I cooked for people ("Yum! Will make this again!") or edits ("less salt than called for here"), but quite frequently they related to specific ingredients. The price of those ingredients was often an issue. ("Raspberries too expensive!" I wrote on a *Silver Palate* pie recipe.) My friend Kate keeps a mental list of ingredients she calls "page turners," so when she sees things like cider vinegar or cream of tartar or cornstarch listed in a recipe, she immediately turns the page. She's the first one to admit how irrational her fears are, but when I wrote about the topic on my blog, it turns out almost everyone has his or her own comprehensive list of page turners: puff pastry, marjoram, tarragon, fish sauce, fennel, caraway seeds. One reader even commented, "Mayo is my page turner. It freaks me out."

My advice is to break down your fears and force yourself to expand your horizons so that you may expand your pantry. The more I bit the bullet and just bought the expensive or scary-sounding ingredient, the more prepared I was when I was designing a menu for guests. I had things in my kitchen that were downright exotic by my 1998 standards: tarragon vinegar, Sriracha sauce, fleur de sel. And a few that should probably not have registered as exotic but did anyway: Worcestershire sauce, whole nutmeg, bay leaves. I found that as I built my pantry, it made entertaining easier, less overwhelming. If I had a stocked pantry, I wasn't starting from zero every time, and this opened up doors to other exciting places. So, in summation, Rule #4: *Don't let unfamiliar ingredients scare you off.* You will be amazed how much more frequently you will see that ingredient called for in recipes once it is in your pantry waiting to be used. (It's like the SAT vocabulary list in eleventh grade: Remember how much more often you saw the word *plethora* after you learned what it meant?)

Now for Rule #5, which has been laid down many times before (most notably by Julia Child) but, based on my experience as a host and a guest at many dinner parties, somehow still hasn't sunk in: *Don't apologize if something goes wrong.* Because nine times out of ten, that "something" has not gone wrong at all in anyone's mind but the cook's. I can't tell you how many times I've listened to my dinner host say something like "I'm sorry that the pasta is too mushy" or "This sauce was much lighter the last time I made it for Ted and Jane" or "Ach! This kale is too bland—I should've added more horseradish." What ends up happening is that instead of thinking about how grateful I am that someone has cooked dinner for me, and instead of focusing on the very pleasant conversation around the table, I start analyzing the pasta and the kale in ways I never would have had she not mentioned them. *Yeah, she's right, it would taste better with more horseradish.* There are exceptions, of course. Like when I was still honing my whole chicken roasting technique and ended up carving up a salmonella special to my sister and her fiancé. There were many sorrys dished up that night alongside the Middle Eastern food we ended up ordering for delivery.

Now these rules are all fine and good when you're making dinner for a few friends and neighbors, but what happens when it's time for a bonafide party, the kind of event where you consider peeling the price tag off the bottom of your wedding registry stemware (but in our case, just consider)? We only had these kinds of affairs once a year—our annual holiday party—but, other than the plastic wine glasses, we got seriously into them, buying festive invitations at Kate's Paperie and star garlands at Crate and Barrel; unearthing our Frank Sinatra and Phil Spector holiday albums; dog-earring dozens of Martha Stewart's hors d'oeuvres recipes, and using the diary to record everything along the way. And when I say everything, I mean everything. Not just what I was going to buy and what I was going to make but also who showed up, who didn't, what was left over, what went fast, what was a huge hit, what was a complete doozy. In addition to providing some very helpful hints—"Less food, more beer" or "People like sausage" or "Never again offer one hundred knishes"—each postmortem gives me a snapshot of the year we were completing. The increase in size of our social network from new jobs didn't necessarily correlate to an increase in real-estate square footage, so it was an annual struggle to make sure the guest list stayed manageable. Every year, on the day of the holiday party, Andy and I would look at the way-too-long list of names and the way-too-long to-do and to-cook lists and swear to each other that this was the last year we were going to do this party. Which brings me to my last rule, Rule #6: *In spite of the pain, remember it's worth it.* Because then, every year, on the day after the holiday party—or the day after the dinner party or the bridal shower or the birthday celebration or whatever production we were going to the ends of the earth to coordinate—we would wake up, recount all the fun we had, then start planning the next one.

September 1999

Starter Cookbooks

My *mother-in-law's handwritten recipes* were special for obvious reasons, but there was also something special about the new recipes we were discovering on our own. This effort involved regular scouring of *Gourmet*, the *New York Times* Living section, and the cookbooks that were starting to populate our shelves. By 1998, we had amassed a nice little library in our kitchen—surely owing, in part, to my cookbook-of-the-month membership. (To join, This Exciting Offer: ten cookbooks for only $1!) We had my mom's copy of *Mastering the Art of French Cooking*, a newly revised and updated *Joy of Cooking*, a bunch of Emeril books, and of course, *The Silver Palate Cookbook*. Almost anything I make from this last book, even today, qualifies as special.

I'll never forget the day I got it. It was 1992. I was wrapping up my summer job teaching tennis before heading off to my senior year in college, when one of my "students" (a mom of three young kids) handed me a paperback copy as an end-of-summer thank-you gift. In my memory of this moment, there's organ music, and a beam of sunlight lasers like a spotlight on the cover. The inscription on the first page was *Good luck with your cooking endeavors! Love, Dyane.*

Dyane told me that *The Silver Palate* cookbook had changed her life and that if I was going to learn anything about cooking (I guess I had expressed some vague interest in between overhead drills), I needed to study this book for the aspiring gourmet. Different from *Julia*, different from *Joy*, this one was revolutionary, with recipes calling for fancy ingredients like arugula and gorgonzola.

I filed the book away and didn't reach for it again until the following summer after I had graduated and spent a few weeks in Florence visiting my new boyfriend, Andy, who was "studying art." Like every other person who visits Italy for the first time, I returned to New York determined to teach myself how to cook, especially since I was now going to be on my own. I was planning to move out when summer was over. No more dining hall. No more Mom.

The Silver Palate was already a raging success—it had been published more than a decade earlier and had sold millions of copies—but the typical owner of it was more like Dyane (someone who could make use of, say, the "Bridge and Poker Sandwiches" sidebar) than like me (someone who didn't realize that chicken stock and chicken broth were the same thing).

So I spent the summer stumbling through a few of the recipes that seemed unintimidating (or, at bare minimum, recognizable) to a girl who ordered sweetbreads once, thinking they were glazed pastries. When Andy came back from Italy, I made him Tortellini with Gorgonzola Cream Sauce to celebrate our reunion. The recipe called for the sauce—a mix of vermouth, cream, and stock—to be "reduced" by a third, which I took to mean "pour a third of the sauce down the drain." For Thanksgiving that year, I baked the Cracklin' Corn Bread (with bacon, oh man) but somehow forgot the butter, prompting my mom to remind me for the fifteen subsequent Thanksgiving corn breads, "Did you remember the butter?"

But as I cooked and dined out and got married to the guy who liked (or pretended to like?) my tortellini, more of the fancy-sounding recipes (escabeche, taramasalata, chicken dijonnaise) seemed less like dishes served at garden parties I'd never be invited to and more like things I could try out on a few friends. I started using the book less as a cookbook and more as a culinary literacy test, flipping through the pages every few months to quiz myself on recipes. Had I heard of all the ingredients? Could I figure out how to make it just using the ingredient list and not the instructions? Even now, two decades later, I still go back to my *Silver Palate* all the time—for the gazpacho, the zucchini bread, the butternut squash and apple soup—and more often than not, I manage to get it right.

What's Held Up from My Kitchen Library, ca. 1998

The Silver Palate Cookbook, by Julee Rosso and Sheila Lukins. See previous page.

Mastering the Art of French Cooking, by Julia Child, Louise Bertholle, and Simone Beck. Even if you only ever end up making her beef bourguignon and coq au vin, it will be worth it.

Martha Stewart's Hors d'Oeuvres Handbook, by Martha Stewart. During this period of our lives we had lots of time to make homemade crackers and experiment with savory bread pudding bites. Later, it was all about the no-cook spread of dried sausages, which Martha suggests one serves with "a bounty of mustards."

The Barefoot Contessa Cookbook, by Ina Garten. I now own all her books, but this first one in the series is the one I still use most. I would guess her turkey meat loaf shows up in my dinner diary at least a dozen times in 1999, the year this book came out.

The Classic Italian Cookbook, by Marcella Hazan. After visiting Andy in Italy, I stopped by my local bookstore on the way home from the airport and asked my friend Matt who was working there if he could recommend a good Italian cookbook that might offer even just a hint of what I had just experienced across the Atlantic. As far as I know, Matt never cooked a thing in his life, but he will forever hold a special place in my heart because he handed me this book and, with the understatement of the year, told me, "People seem to really like her."

What I've Added to My Kitchen Library, ca. 2011

How to Cook Everything, by Mark Bittman. In my mind, a kitchen library without this all-purpose book is like having a wardrobe without a pair of jeans. Basic, useful, beloved, I hardly go a week without opening it up for inspiration and information.

How to Cook Everything Vegetarian, by Mark Bittman. This was his answer to the conscious-cooking movement a decade later. It offers the same comprehensive repertoire of basic dishes but all of them plant-based.

The Fine Art of Italian Cooking, by Giuliano Bugialli. This book is filled with authentic Italian dishes from a master, but I now mostly use it for one: the minestrone. My friend Pilar first pointed it out to me, and it's one of those recipes that freezes guests midslurp. "What *is* this?" they all ask. It's that good.

The Gourmet Cookbook, by Ruth Reichl. If I use Bittman for everyday cooking, I use this classic for casual entertaining. The recipes manage to be just exotic enough without being intimidating.

Great Food Fast, by the editors of *Everyday Food*. I think Martha Stewart deserves some kind of medal for inventing the magazine *Everyday Food*. With this book, a compilation of the best of the magazine, she was the first one to tell me *elegant* and *easy* were not mutually exclusive terms when it came to dinner. So far, there are three books in the series, and all are must-haves for a starter library.

....

The Silver Spoon, by the editors at Phaidon Press. I don't use this massive compilation of Italian recipes as frequently as the rest of my food-loving friends do. But I try to channel it every time I write a recipe on my website. It does a great job of making recipes sound conversational—as though you are just taking instructions from a friend—instead of the somewhat scientific way we are used to seeing them in most cookbooks.

....

My Bread, by Jim Lahey. I was petrified of making my own bread before Jim Lahey came to town. His famous no-knead bread recipe is in here, as are dozens of others that will upgrade the most basic corners of your culinary life. The homemade pizza crust is worth the price of admission (much more on this book beginning on page 268).

....

Time for Dinner, by me, Pilar Guzman, and Alanna Stang. It goes without saying I use the recipes from this book all the time. I cowrote it with Alanna and Pilar when I was an editor at *Cookie*. We directed it at parents who were cooking for young kids, but at the end of the day, the recipes are for everyone. That was the point. You don't have to completely change the way you cook when you have kids. You just have to change your mind-set. And your expectations. And maybe your medications.

....

May 2000

. . . .

You Make It, You Own It

As we amassed a small collection of go-to recipes, Andy and I began settling into a regular weeknight cooking routine. But even though we always ate together, we didn't necessarily always cook together. We favored the one-night-on, one-night-off schedule, though it wasn't necessarily a policy that was set in stone. Often I would see a recipe in *Gourmet* and be so eager to get started on it that I couldn't wait for him to come home from work to pitch in. Likewise, he'd scour our growing cookbook collection and select meals that I had no interest in making with him—meals, actually, that I wouldn't have ever selected in the first place. A lot of keepers came out of this trial-and-error period, but more important, a dinner rule that is still in effect twelve years later took root: When one of us discovers a new recipe, cooks it for dinner, and it's a success, it is the cook's responsibility to prepare that dinner from that point forward. Forever. Ad infinitum. We have probably eaten chicken with soy-lime sauce from Mark Bittman's *How to Cook Everything* three dozen times since 1998, and Andy, who was the first to recognize its potential, has prepared it every single one of those times. Likewise, Andy has never made "my" minestrone or my fish cakes or the chicken, sausage, and corn stew I found in *Gourmet* and proceeded to make every Saturday night for two months. It has nothing to do with skills or technique. A meal breaks down along party lines purely by provenance . . . which can come in handy. Quite often I will respond, "How 'bout those black bean burritos" to Andy's inquiry via email, "What should we have for dinner?" as much out of laziness as out of a craving for an easy vegetarian dinner. Because the recipe for "those black bean burritos" belongs to him.

Andy-owned Dinners

As a general rule, the dinners that belong to Andy are healthy, highly flavorful, and allow for the use of heat. Also, between January 1997 and October 1999, I don't think he ever passed up a recipe that called for cilantro.

Arroz con Pollo

Every time this recipe appears in my diary, it's on a weekend (usually Sunday dinner). That's probably because it's not throw-it-together quick and involves a significant amount of hands-on time. Andy's hands, that is. **Total time: 1 hour**

1 tablespoon dried oregano

1½ teaspoons ground cumin

1½ teaspoons chili powder

Salt and pepper

4 to 5 boneless chicken thighs or breasts,
    rinsed and patted dry

Vegetable oil

½ onion, chopped

1 garlic clove, minced

1 small jalapeño pepper, minced and
    seeded if you don't want the extra heat

1½ cups uncooked rice

1 15-ounce can tomato puree

1 cup chicken broth

Handful of frozen peas

Handful of chopped grape tomatoes

Chopped cilantro, for garnish

Preheat the oven to 375°F.

Combine the oregano, cumin, chili powder, and salt and pepper and rub the mixture all over the chicken, pressing it so it sticks on all sides of the chicken. (Use *all* of the spice mixture.) In a large pot (a Dutch oven works), cook the chicken in a few glugs of vegetable oil over medium-high heat until browned on both sides. Transfer the chicken to a bowl.

To the pot, add the onion, garlic, and jalapeño pepper and cook about 1 minute over medium-low heat, making sure garlic doesn't burn. Add the rice to the pot, turn up the heat to medium-high, and cook about 2 minutes.

Add the tomato puree, broth, peas, grape tomatoes, and chicken. Bring to a simmer, cover, and transfer to the oven. Bake 30 minutes, or until the chicken has been cooked through and the rice is tender. Garnish with cilantro.

Black Bean Burritos

These didn't actually start making regular appearances until about a decade later. But even ten years later, with kids, a dog, and a mortgage, the law remains unchanged. He made it the first night as well as the next two dozen times it appeared on our family table. It's always our first choice for Meatless Mondays and based on a recipe that originally appeared in the *Gourmet Today* cookbook. Total time: 35 minutes

    3 tablespoons red wine vinegar

    2 tablespoons sugar

    1 teaspoon salt

    ½ small red onion, thinly sliced

    3 tablespoons vegetable oil, plus more for frying

    1 garlic clove, minced

    3 scallions (white and light green parts), chopped

    1 teaspoon ground cumin

½ jalapeño pepper, minced

Salt and pepper to taste

2 15-ounce cans black beans, rinsed and drained

Kernels from 1 ear fresh corn or ½ cup frozen

6 8-inch whole wheat tortillas

2 large handfuls grated cheddar cheese

Handful finely chopped cilantro

Toppings: sour cream, salsa, lime wedges

Quick-pickle your onions: Bring vinegar, sugar, 2 cups of water, and salt to a boil in a small saucepan. Add the onion and simmer, uncovered, about 3 minutes. Drain.

Heat the oil in a skillet over medium heat until hot but not smoking. Add the garlic, scallions, cumin, jalapeño pepper, and salt and pepper and cook, stirring, about 1 minute. Stir in the beans, mashing them with a fork. Add another ⅓ cup water and cook, stirring until most of the liquid is absorbed, about 5 minutes. Toss in corn and remove from the heat.

Spread the bean filling across the middle of each tortilla, leaving some space at both ends.

Sprinkle each tortilla with cheese, your now quick-pickled onions, and a little cilantro. Fold the ends of the tortillas over the filling as shown at right, enclosing filling tightly. Heat more oil in a skillet over medium-high heat. Add 2 burritos at a time, seam side down, and fry until lightly browned on the underside, about 2 minutes. Turn over and fry until golden, another 2 minutes. Repeat with remaining burritos and serve with desired toppings.

HOW TO FOLD A BURRITO

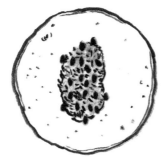

1. Spread filling in center

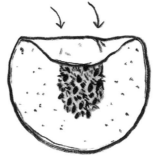

2. Fold over top flap

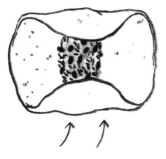

3. Fold bottom flap

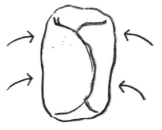

4. Fold in side flaps

Spaghetti with Clams (and Extras)

This is best eaten outside with an ocean view. If you can't swing that, then at least try to secure the freshest clams possible. We often forego the pasta and just have the clams, soaking up the briny broth with crusty bread. Total time: 25 minutes

> 1 pound spaghetti
>
> 1 small shallot, chopped
>
> 1 garlic clove, minced
>
> Few shakes of red pepper flakes
>
> Freshly ground black pepper
>
> 2 tablespoons olive oil
>
> 24 to 36 fresh clams (we usually use littlenecks), rinsed
>
> 1/2 cup dry white wine
>
> Handful of chopped fresh herbs, such as basil, parsley, and chives
>
> Handful of chopped fresh tomatoes (any kind)
>
> Handful of corn off the cob (optional)

Make the spaghetti according to the package directions. In a separate large stockpot or Dutch oven set over medium heat, sauté the shallot, garlic, pepper flakes, and black pepper in the oil. (It's not necessary to salt—the clams are naturally briny.)

Add the clams, wine, and herbs. When the clams steam open (10 to 15 minutes), add the tomatoes and corn (if using) and cook another 2 to 3 minutes. Discard any clams that haven't opened and then toss the whole thing with pasta, making sure to scoop lots of the broth into the bowl. Serve with crusty bread for sopping.

Jenny-owned Dinners

Though I never realized it until right now as I looked at the meals I cooked again and again during this era, a Jenny recipe can be described as "traditional with a twist." Most of the dinners I made veered toward simple, basic comfort foods.

Fish Cakes

You will often read that fish cakes are a good solution for leftover fish. My answer to that is: If you make fish cakes on the first night instead of the second, there is no chance of having any leftovers in the first place. This recipe makes about 10 small cakes. Total time: 40 minutes

For the Dipping Sauce

½ cup sour cream

2 tablespoons fresh lime juice

½ teaspoon sugar

1 tablespoon chopped fresh cilantro

For the Fish

3 firm flaky whitefish fillets, such as cod or orange roughy
    (about 1¼ pounds total)

½ teaspoon chili powder

½ teaspoon dried oregano

Salt and pepper

⅓ cup mayonnaise

1 egg, lightly whisked

1 tablespoon fresh lime juice

1 large baking potato, baked and flaked (bake it in the microwave for
    10 minutes so it's quick)

Handful of cilantro, finely chopped

2 cups bread crumbs (panko or regular)

A decade after first discovering fish cakes, I'm still the only cook in the house who has ever made them for the kids.

3 tablespoons vegetable oil

Lime wedges, for serving

Preheat the oven to 450°F.

To make the dipping sauce: In a small bowl, whisk together the sour cream, lime juice, sugar, and cilantro and set aside.

To make the fish cakes: Sprinkle fish fillets with the chili powder, oregano, and salt and pepper and roast 5 to 7 minutes, until cooked through. Let cool, then using a fork, flake into pieces.

In a mixing bowl, whisk together the mayonnaise, egg, and lime juice. Add the fish to the bowl along with the potato, cilantro, and more salt. Toss and, if you have time, refrigerate for 30 minutes. (This will make it easier to pack the mixture into patties, but it's not a do-or-die move.)

Pack the fish mixture into patties and coat each in bread crumbs that have been spread on a dinner plate. (If you haven't had time to chill the mixture, the patties will be delicate, so do this carefully. Also: I find wetting your hands prevents sticking.)

Heat the oil in a large skillet over medium heat. Fry the patties in batches of four and cook until the crusts are golden brown, about 5 minutes per side. Serve with the lime wedges and dipping sauce.

Roast Vegetables with Polenta

This is an excellent meal to keep in mind when you are staring at an end-of-the-week crisper containing the last scraps of vegetables. And the polenta alone (separate from the vegetables) made many appearances alongside hunks of braised meat. **Total time: 1 hour 30 minutes (includes hands-off chill time)**

1 cup polenta (not quick cooking)

2 tablespoons unsalted butter,
    plus more for greasing pie plate

¼ cup Parmesan cheese, grated,
    plus more for serving

1 10-ounce package white mushrooms
    (wiped with a paper towel and destemmed; see note)

1 small onion, chopped

1 small container grape tomatoes (about 2 cups)

Olive oil

Salt and pepper

Leaves from 2 sprigs fresh thyme

Bring 4 cups salted water to a boil. Add the polenta gradually, whisking constantly. Reduce the heat to low and cook, stirring constantly, until the polenta is thick and pulls away from sides, 12 to 14 minutes. Remove from heat and stir in the butter. Spoon the polenta into a buttered pie dish or square shallow baking dish. Sprinkle with the Parmesan and refrigerate for 1 hour.

Preheat the oven to 400°F.

Meanwhile, in a large bowl, toss together the mushrooms, onions, and tomatoes with the oil, salt and pepper, and thyme leaves. Add to a baking dish lined with foil and roast, along with the polenta (in its own dish, after the polenta has been chilled), for 25 to 30 minutes, until the tomatoes are shrively. Remove the vegetables and broil the polenta for the last few minutes so it gets golden on top. Spoon polenta into pasta bowls and top with the vegetables and more grated Parmesan.

★ *Note:* To clean mushrooms, wipe their tops with a damp paper towel. You don't want to submerge them in water or else they'll be waterlogged and won't cook correctly.

Salmon Salad

I love this recipe because you can boil everything in shifts in the same pot of water. There are endless variations to it, too. In the summer we grill the salmon and replace the Yukon Golds with blue potatoes. And if the corn is summer sweet, it will be love at first bite. **Total time: 35 minutes**

For the Vinaigrette

¼ cup red wine vinegar

2 teaspoons mustard

1 teaspoon sugar

Squeeze of fresh lemon or lime

½ cup olive oil

For the Salmon

1 salmon fillet (about 1 pound)

Salt and pepper

4 potatoes (Yukon Gold, red, or blue if you can find them), peeled and quartered

2 ears corn

Handful of thin green beans, trimmed and chopped into 1-inch pieces

1 cup cherry or grape tomatoes, halved

1 cucumber, peeled, seeded, and chopped

5 to 6 scallions (white and light green parts), chopped

2 tablespoons chopped fresh cilantro

Preheat the oven to 400°F.

To make the vinaigrette: In a small bowl, whisk together the vinegar, mustard, sugar, lemon juice, and oil and set aside.

Make the salmon: Sprinkle the salmon with salt and pepper. Roast in a foil-lined baking dish for 15 minutes. (If you prefer to grill the fish, brush with a mixture of olive oil, salt, pepper, and a dash of honey and cook over medium-hot coals, 4 to 5 minutes on each side.)

Meanwhile, bring a medium pot of water to a boil. Add the potatoes and cook until a knife slices through them with no resistance, about 12 minutes. Using a slotted spoon, remove the potatoes to a large serving bowl. Add the corn to the same pot of water. Boil for 4 minutes. Remove to a cutting board, allow to cool, slice off the kernels, and add to the serving bowl. Add beans to the same pot of water and cook for 3 minutes. Remove with a slotted spoon and add to the serving bowl. Add the tomatoes, cucumber, scallions, and cilantro to the bowl. Toss with the vinaigrette and serve.

A first-ballot Hall-of-Famer, for sure: Salmon Salad (page 62),
which we've probably eaten once a month for the last fifteen
years. Good all year, but best in the summer.

THE BLAME GAME
(OR, WHY MY WEAKNESS IS ALL YOUR FAULT)

Dear Andy,

You know how grateful I am for all you bring to this marriage. How grateful I am for your mastery of the grill, for your I'm-in-your-corner-no-matter-what reaction to whatever story I bring home from work. For your unfailingly impeccable musical taste. (I fully recognize that if it weren't for you, I would likely still be on a steady listening diet of Billy Joel and Edie Brickell.) But. But. But. But. Have you taken a look at our bar lately? Gin and vermouth and three kinds of bourbon and the Costco-size bottle of Grey Goose, and twenty-one-year-old rum . . . and . . . and . . . I hardly recognize myself! You know how much I believe in equality in this marriage, but I feel it's necessary to place the blame for this disturbing sight along with my now nonnegotiable 6:00 p.m. cocktail squarely on you and your long line of alcohol enthusiasts. As you know, I come from a long line of Westchester Jews, from a house where there was always an Entenmann's cake in the snack drawer and a lone, unopened bottle of crème de menthe in the liquor cabinet. And yet, since we've met, since I've been working on various demanding jobs and assignments, I now find myself looking at the clock every two minutes from 5:30 leading up to 6:00, or as your father would say, leading up to that blessed moment when "the sun goes over the yardarm." I used to be such a nice Jewish girl and now I find myself keeping a mental tally of our wine supply as though it's as basic a staple as milk or peanut butter. I find myself getting the Bombay Sapphire out at 5:56, the highball glass out at 5:57, the ice cubes stacked up at 5:58, the lime sliced at 5:59, and then waiting, waiting, waiting that interminable sixty seconds until I can mix in my fizzy tonic and start to sip. So anyway, thanks a lot. And thank your Syrah-drinking Mom, your vodka-tonic drinking Dad, and your Old Fashioned–drinking Grandma (may she rest in peace) for me, too.

Love,

Jenny

Dear Jenny,

You're scaring me. Looking at the clock every two minutes? As basic as milk? You can blame me for leading you to water, but come on: You can't blame me for your thirst. Anyway, thank you for the kind words, and while my mastery of the grill is highly debatable, I'll return the compliments a million-fold: Were it not for you, I would, in addition to being a much less fulfilled and happy person, probably still be eating penne with Ragú Robusto every night in front of the Yankees game.

I would also probably not be addicted to dessert.

When I was growing up, the son of an Italian mom, dessert was something you had on special occasions. On somebody's birthday, we'd have a Duncan Hines cake. In the summer, when the peaches were running wild, we'd have a cobbler on Saturday night. During the holidays, we'd make a huge batch of Christmas cookies, and we'd frost them as a family. But most nights, we'd have nothing. Or maybe some fruit. You know, like normal people. And then I met you. For you—and for the Rosenstrach clan at large (no offense, beloved in-laws)—dessert is just a given, a natural extension of dinner. And lunch. And snacks, too. You eat something nonsweet, you follow it with a dessert. I'm not talking here about an Oreo or two or an occasional bowl of ice cream. I'm talking about the heavy artillery. Chocolate truffle cakes. Chocolate mousse cakes. Chocolate candy bars. Dove ice-cream bars. The truly insidious thing about all this stuff, for a non-dessert guy like me, is that it tastes really, really good. God, does it taste good. So, over the years, as you wore me down, I started to indulge a little, then a little more, and next thing I knew, I started needing—not craving but *needing*—a dessert after every meal. When I finish dinner these days, I head straight for the pantry for my fix, and do you realize what I see when I open it up? Seriously, have you looked lately? A bar of 72% dark chocolate. And a *one-pound* bar of dark chocolate with almonds from Trader Joe's. And a box of chocolate mints. And some chewy oatmeal raisin cookies. And do you know what the worst part is? I bought all of it! The only person I can blame is myself, which is always a terrible place to be. Do you see what you've done to me?

Love,

Andy

P.S. It's not crème de menthe in your dad's "liquor cabinet," by the way. It's Tia Maria, which tastes like coffee, and if you carbon-dated that bottle, I think you'd find it's older than Mexico itself.

June 2000

. . . .

Crushing on the Cook

I remember what I was wearing the day I met Michelle and Bill for dinner at a restaurant in Chelsea. Actually, I should rephrase that. I remember what I *wasn't* wearing the day I met Michelle and Bill on a warm spring night at a restaurant in Chelsea: something attractive. I remember this because of how starkly I contrasted with Michelle, who was the wife of Andy's co-worker and who was dressed in a tailored crisp-white blouse and a delicate gold chain that came together in a small loop at the nape of her beautiful tan-but-not-too-tan neck. Her hair was short and stylish and her light brown eyes were so pretty and sparkly that I think I might have blushed when we were introduced.

"How come you didn't tell me how *beautiful* she is?" I whispered to Andy when she excused herself to the bathroom. He looked at me like I was crazy.

"I never met her before! And anyway, what does it matter?" he asked.

"Well, for starters, I wouldn't have worn this dumpy ribbed turtleneck that I bought my senior year of high school." My hair was unbrushed and there wasn't a whole lot of thought directed toward accessories that morning before I rushed off to work nine hours earlier. There might have been a jumper involved, too. I don't know, it was the decade of the Donna Karan bodysuit—not that that is much of an excuse—but I've tried to block this part out. The general recollection thirteen years later, though, is that I somehow missed an opportunity to put my best, coolest foot forward with this woman whom I wanted to be my friend in a way that probably wasn't so appropriate for a person technically categorized as a "grown-up."

Michelle was too nice to hold my outfit against me. Too nice, in fact, to have even noticed how decidedly unfashionable I was. It turned out we had so much in common. She was from a nice Jewish family and was raised "like fine China" (as Bill once said), just like me. She played tennis just like me. And, best of all, she not only loved to cook, but she was a talented cook with amazing taste and an even better aesthetic. (She seemed to be serving everything on simple, sculptural white plates way before Donna Hay and *Real Simple* were.) Andy and Bill got along well, too, and so we all seized on the rare couple friendship where everyone liked each other. I had such a crush on Michelle. To the point where Laurie had to take me aside one afternoon during the honeymoon phase of my new friendship and ask, "Do you think you could stop talking about Michelle all the time when you are spending the day with me?"

In my dinner diary, Michelle and Bill are penned in almost every weekend between May 2000 and August 2003, including once when they drove to meet us on vacation in South Carolina carrying a 1993 Château d'Yquem. ("We brought you something extraordinary," she announced when she entered the house.) If I made something delicious for Andy, then we'd both say at the same time, "We have to make this for Michelle and Bill!" I remember eating a chilled pea soup *amuse-bouche* at Bouley Bakery and thinking how much Michelle and Bill would appreciate an *amuse-bouche* at our house! I agonized over menus when they'd come over, mixing up lichee martinis and experimenting with weird Syrian spice mixtures from Brooklyn's Atlantic Avenue. They cared about fresh, good food in a way I had never seen before, and more important they were fabulous guests and friends.

But I liked going to their house more. The perfect tennis opponent for me was always someone who could crush me—and Michelle was the equivalent in the kitchen. She could cook her ass off and was an endless source of inspiring recipes, which I would steal and pass off as my own to other friends. I can't think of one time I've been to her house and haven't learned something about cooking or tasted something that I wanted to replicate in my own house for other twice-removed guests who could never trace the provenance of the dish. For a while there, I wondered if my crush on her was affecting the way I tasted my food. (You know? Kind of like that *New Yorker* phenomenon where you assume the writing is good and smart just by virtue of the fact that it is in the *New Yorker*?) But then I'd cook her meal and receive the same ooohs and ahhs that I'd dish out when she cooked it for me. So yes, it was the food in its own right that was special—not just that it was cooked for me by this special person with sparkly eyes who to this day is still a great friend. But actually, I'm not sure why it even matters.

Greek-Style Shrimp with Feta

The key to this dish is to buy prepeeled shrimp—which significantly cuts back on your hands-on time—and to remember a rule that actually applies to any recipe: You are rarely going to regret using more cheese than called for. Total time: 30 minutes

2 garlic cloves, minced

3 tablespoons olive oil

1 28-ounce can tomatoes, drained (*very* important)

1 pound shrimp, peeled

4 to 6 ounces crumbled feta (a little less than 1 cup)

2 sprigs fresh parsley, chopped

Juice from ½ lemon (about 2 tablespoons)

Salt and pepper to taste

Preheat the oven to 425°F.

Sauté the garlic in the oil in an ovenproof skillet set over medium heat for 1 minute. (Do not let the garlic burn.) Add the tomatoes, lower the heat slightly, and stir, breaking up the tomatoes with a wooden spoon or kitchen scissors if you have them. Cook for 5 minutes. Nestle in the shrimp, toss around a little, turn heat back to medium, and cook until the shrimp starts to turn pink all over, about 2 minutes. Sprinkle the feta on top and place the skillet in the oven. Bake for 5 minutes, or until cheese is melty. Remove from the oven and add the parsley, lemon juice, and salt and pepper. Serve with white rice or crusty bread.

Bourbon-Marinated Grilled Pork Tenderloin

In the summer, we serve this with grilled peaches (recipe follows). During colder months, it's delicious pan-roasted with a few firm apple slices that have been sautéed and browned in butter. Total time: 2 hours 25 minutes (includes 2 hours hands-off marinating time)

¼ cup bourbon

¼ cup soy sauce

2 tablespoons brown sugar

3 tablespoons olive oil

2-inch piece fresh ginger, peeled and roughly chopped

1 pork tenderloin (about 1 pound)

In a large zipper-lock bag, combine the bourbon, soy sauce, sugar, oil, and ginger. Add the pork and marinate for at least 2 hours and up to 4. When you are ready to grill, remove the tenderloin from the bag, reserving the marinade, and grill it over medium-hot coals for 15 to 20 minutes, turning every 5 minutes, until the middle is firm but not hard to the touch. (A meat thermometer should read 140°F.) Add the marinade to a small saucepan and bring to a boil; boil until it becomes slightly thickened, about 2 minutes. Slice the pork on a cutting board and transfer to a platter, spooning the sauce over the top.

Alternatively, you could pan-roast the pork. Marinate as directed, but instead of preparing the grill, preheat your oven to 425°F. Set an ovenproof pan fitted with a lid (like a small Dutch oven) over medium-high heat. Add a few tablespoons of oil to the pan. Remove the pork from the bag (allowing excess marinade to drip off), reserve the marinade, and brown the loin on all sides, about 8 minutes total. Cover and transfer the pot to the oven and roast for another 12 to 15 minutes, until the thickest part of the loin registers 140°F on a meat thermometer. Remove the loin from the pot, slice, and transfer to a platter. In the same pot, add the reserved marinade and bring it to a boil; boil until it becomes slightly thickened, about 2 minutes. Spoon the sauce over the top of the pork slices.

Grilled Peaches

Total time: 5 to 10 minutes

Halve **3 to 4 juicy unpeeled peaches.** On the flesh side brush on either **melted butter** or **canola oil** and a sprinkling of **brown sugar**. Grill the peaches for 5 minutes, turning frequently so they don't burn.

Alternatively, you can broil the peaches. Prepare as directed above and then place the peach halves on a cookie sheet flesh side up; broil for 10 minutes, or until they are golden and shrively. Cut the peaches into wedges, if desired, and serve.

Mexican Chocolate Icebox Cookies

These cookies are adapted from a Maida Heatter recipe. I love watching people eat them for the first time because it takes a second or two for the heat to kick in, and when it does, the eater is totally delighted—if slightly confused. Michelle used to serve them warm with cinnamon ice cream. Insane. Makes about 4 dozen cookies
Total time: 2 hours 35 minutes (includes 2-hour chill time)

1½ cups all-purpose flour

¾ cup cocoa powder

¾ teaspoon cinnamon

¼ teaspoon cayenne

¼ teaspoon salt

¼ teaspoon freshly ground black pepper

12 tablespoons unsalted butter, room temperature

1 cup sugar

1½ teaspoons vanilla extract

1 egg

Sift together the flour, cocoa powder, cinnamon, cayenne, salt, and pepper in a medium bowl.

In a large bowl, cream together the butter and sugar. Beat in the vanilla and egg.

Using your mixer, gradually add the dry mixture to the butter mixture until dough is uniform in color and no unmixed flour remains. Using lightly floured hands, divide the dough into two pieces and shape each half into a log (about 8 inches long). Wrap tightly in wax paper or plastic wrap and freeze inside two tall drinking glasses on their sides (so cookie dough doesn't flatten on one side) for a minimum of 2 hours and up to 6 weeks.

When ready to use, preheat the oven to 375°F. Slice the frozen dough in rounds (about ¼ inch thick), place in baking sheets, and bake for 8 to 10 minutes. The cookies are ready when they feel a bit firm at the edges. Monitor them closely because the cookie's dark color makes it hard to detect when they're burning. Store in an airtight container when cool.

December 2000

Back-Pocket Recipes

*W*hen *I was little,* I had a ballet teacher who forbade me to take jazz until a certain age. All I wanted in the world was to buy a pair of those cool Capezio shoes and leg warmers (and maybe even wear them to school with my belted neon yellow sweatshirt), but she was adamant: You cannot learn how to riff off classic movement until you have a solid grasp of what the fundamentals of classic movement are in the first place. I think about this all the time when I write on my blog about "Back Pocket" dinners—basic dishes you can pull out of your back pocket without consulting a recipe—the kinds of meals I was discovering in these early days, which could teach me not just a recipe but a foundational technique. For me, this means risottos, stir-fries, omelets, rice and beans, marinara,

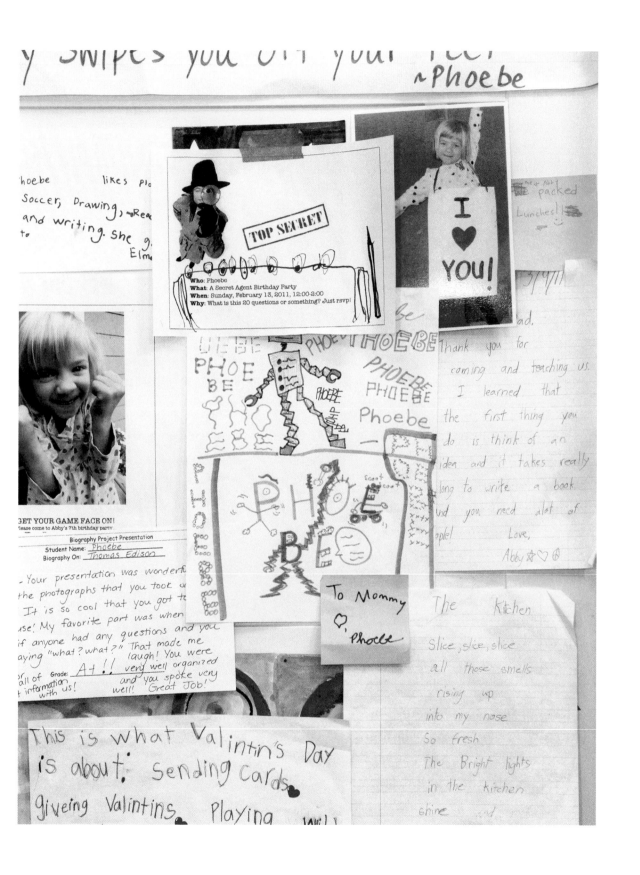

y swipes you off your feet
~Phoebe

TOP SECRET

Who: Phoebe
What: A Secret Agent Birthday Party
When: Sunday, February 13, 2011, 12:00-2:00
Why: What is this 20 questions or something? Just rsvp!

hoebe   likes pla
Soccer, Drawing, Rea
and writing. she g
to
Elm

I ♥ YOU!

...ad.

Thank you for
coming and teaching us.
I learned that
the first thing you
do is think of an
idea and it takes really
long to write a book
and you need alot of
...ople!   Love,
Abby ☆ ♡ ☺

PHOEBE
PHOE BE
PHOEBE
PHOEBE
Phoebe
—

GET YOUR GAME FACE ON!
Please come to Abby's 7th birthday party.

Biography Project Presentation
Student Name: _Phoebe_
Biography On: _Thomas Edison_

-Your presentation was wonderf
the photographs that you took a
It is so cool that you got t
...se! My favorite part was when
if anyone had any questions and you
...aying "what? what?" That made me
laugh! You were
...r all of Grade: _A+!!_ very well organized
...t information and you spoke very
with us!   well! Great Job!

To Mommy
♡ Phoebe

The Kitchen

Slice, slice, slice
all those smells
rising up
into my nose
So fresh
The Bright lights
in the kitchen
shine

This is what Valintin's Day
is about: Sending cards,
giveing Valintins, Playing

simple pasta dishes with cheese and vegetables. They are not the kinds of dishes you will find in a David Chang cookbook because that is not the point. The point is that they are building blocks. Once you learn the fundamental rules of browning meat or stirring risotto, you will be in the position of knowing how to break those rules, having fun, and making something your own.

Back-Pocket Risotto

Total time: 40 minutes

Add **3 tablespoons olive oil** and **1 tablespoon butter** to a medium saucepan set over medium heat. Add **½ small chopped onion**, season with **salt** and **pepper**, and cook until the onion is softened, about 2 minutes.

Add **1½ cups Arborio rice** to pan and stir until each grain is covered with oil. In a second smaller saucepan or a microwave, heat **2½ cups milk** (any kind—whole, skim, low-fat) with **2½ cups chicken broth** until warm but not boiling.

Add ⅓ cup of your hot liquid to the rice, stir, and simmer until all liquid is absorbed, about 3 minutes. Keep repeating until all the liquid has been absorbed and the rice is cooked through but still firm, about 30 minutes. (You don't have to stir constantly, but I find it's helpful to never be too far away from the stove when you are making risotto.)

Remove from the heat and stir in **½ cup grated Parmesan cheese** and another tablespoon of butter.

Riff

Add **½ pound cooked Italian sausage** or **cooked bacon crumbles** and a handful of **frozen peas** to the pot once the risotto has cooked through.

Back-Pocket Tacos

Total time: 50 minutes

In a small Dutch oven or a medium, straight-sided pot, heat **2 tablespoons olive oil** over medium-high heat. Add **1¼ pounds boneless chicken breasts** (which have been salted and peppered) and brown all over (about 3 minutes a side; the chicken does not have to cook through). Remove from pot.

To the same pot, add **½ chopped onion, 1 minced garlic clove**, a dash of **red pepper flakes, salt**, and **pepper**. Cook until the onion is soft, about 3 minutes. Add one **15-ounce can diced tomatoes, 1 tablespoon chili powder, 1 dried red chili, 1 bay leaf**, and a few hefty shakes of **dried oregano.** Stir to combine and add the chicken back to the pot, nestling the breasts in the liquid. Bring to a boil and then lower the heat, cover the pot, and simmer for 25 minutes.

While the chicken simmers, prepare small bowls of toppings: **avocado chunks, shredded cheddar cheese, corn off the cob, cilantro, lime wedges, sour cream.** Warm **4 to 6 8-inch whole wheat tortillas** (wrapped in foil) in a 350°F oven.

Once the chicken has cooked, remove it from the pot, and using two forks, shred it into pieces on a cutting board. (There is no art to this; in fact, the less artfully done, the better.) Add the shreds back to the sauce, stir everything together, then stuff into the tortillas. Add the desired toppings.

Riff

Replace the chicken with a pork tenderloin that has been cut into three or four pieces.

Back-Pocket Pasta with Herbs and Bread Crumbs

Total time: 35 minutes

Cook **1 pound pasta** in water that has been sprinkled with a generous amount of salt. While the pasta is cooking, add **3 tablespoons olive oil** to a large skillet set over medium heat. Cook **2 minced garlic cloves** and **½ large chopped onion** until soft. Drain the pasta, reserving 1 cup of the pasta water scooped out with a coffee mug or heatproof measuring cup.

Add about **¼ cup of the pasta water** to the skillet and swirl with the onions and oil until it has emulsified and looks silky.

Add the pasta to the skillet and toss it until every piece is shiny with oil. Dump into a large pasta bowl and stir in **¾ cup finely grated Parmesan cheese**. (You may need to add more pasta water if it still appears too stiff.)

To the hot skillet, add **½ cup bread crumbs** and fry until brown and toasty, about 1 minute. Add to the pasta along with a handful of **chopped herbs**, such as **fresh parsley, oregano,** and **thyme**.

Riff

Toss in any of the following roasted vegetables with the bread crumbs: **cauliflower, butternut squash, brussels sprouts,** or **broccoli.** Or, omit the bread crumbs and just toss in **4 to 5 chopped fresh summer tomatoes.** Extra Parm and few zests of **lemon** won't hurt either.

April 2001

Undercover

Quite often during this period of our lives, if you didn't find me at my dinner table by seven o'clock, you might have found me hiding in a bathroom stall of a restaurant, scribbling notes about the overcooked duck breast I had just been served. I wasn't doing this for my diary's sake—by some miracle, I knew someone who knew someone who knew someone named Jim, who ran a restaurant consulting business. Jim sent Andy and me undercover to eat for *free* in various restaurants around New York (which, as my contract stipulated, shall go unnamed), and all I had to do in return was deliver a QAR (quality assurance report) that deconstructed everything from whether the host smiled at me when I walked in the door, to whether the bartender upsold me on the gin in my gin and tonic, to whether the three-course meal plus wine (jackpot!) was something I'd come back for another time. This last part was hard for me, as I'd pretty much come back for *any* meal if (a) someone else was making it for me, (b) someone else was doing dishes, and (c) it was *free!*

For these dinners we were undercover in more ways than one. Most of the places we reviewed you might call high end (at least when you compared them to the places we could afford) and located in the kinds of neighborhoods in New York where you can't help but ask yourself, "Who *lives* here?" (Only answers we could come up with: an Icahn or a Radziwell?) We often felt like impostors, as though we were playing grown-up in a pretend world filled with grown-up things like white linen, fifty-dollar bottles of Rioja (I remember pronouncing it with the *j* sound in my head the first time I drank a glass), and a palate-cleanser course that was almost always a cold melon soup. I might have been imagining this, but it felt like everywhere we went, the waitstaff and even some of the patrons would cock their heads to the side when they saw us as if to say, *Awwww, look at the kids having their engagement dinner.* Because why else would we be in a place like that if we weren't celebrating something big? What twenty-six-year-old goes to a three- or four-star restaurant on a Tuesday night just for the hell of it? None that I knew anyway.

The thing is, Andy and I have always excelled at celebrating. Particularly celebrating in a restaurant. It was a quality I admired in him right from the beginning. I'll never forget when we were first dating in college and he took me out for a birthday dinner at the nicest restaurant in town even though I would've been 100 percent happy with moo shu pork and dumplings at the Chinese take-out place. (I'll also never forget when he picked me up for that dinner and asked, "Is that what you're going to wear?" while staring at my Levi's with two huge holes ripped in the knees.)

But we didn't just celebrate big moments like birthdays and anniversaries. We made a point to celebrate the small to medium-size moments as well: getting a job offer, getting a raise, completing the GMAT, getting a good magazine assignment, or my favorite reason of all, simply making it through the week. As Andy would say, if you didn't do that every now and then, "What was the point?" (I have also long admired my husband's existential angst.)

These end-of-the-week meals—meals that we were paying for ourselves— were the opposite of the white-linen kind. They took place in restaurants we'd discover by poring over the numbers and rankings in our tattered, well-loved Zagat guide (Tartine in the West Village, Sagapo in Astoria, Elephant in the East Village; any Middle Eastern cafe on Atlantic Avenue); the kind of places where you'd sometimes have to shield your eyes if you found yourself walking by the kitchen, because you just didn't want to know what was going on in there (Hello, Chinatown!); the kind of places that we'd get ridiculously sentimental about ten or twelve years down the road when we had two kids, had more than earned the title Grown-up, and all we wanted to do was pretend we were twenty-six again.

Lamb Kibbeh with Mint-Yogurt Sauce

I think this may have been Andy's first stab at recipe developing. It was inspired by the kibbeh we'd eat on Brooklyn's Atlantic Avenue, an area famous for Middle Eastern food and culture. If you can't find bulgur, you can use quinoa. Total time: 45 minutes

For the Kibbeh

1 pound ground lamb

½ small onion, finely chopped

1 cup cooked bulgur wheat

1 tablespoon Yemeni Spice (recipe follows)

3 tablespoons chopped fresh mint

1 teaspoon salt

For the Mint-Yogurt-Cucumber Sauce

1 6-ounce container plain yogurt

Pinch of salt

2 tablespoons chopped fresh mint

1 tablespoon fresh lemon juice

1 cucumber, peeled, seeded, and chopped

To make the kibbeh: Preheat the outdoor grill.

In a large mixing bowl, use your hands to combine the lamb, onion, bulgur, Yemeni Spice, mint, and salt. Shape the lamb mixture into 8 flattened football shapes.

Grill the lamb for about 5 minutes on each side. Alternatively, you can fry the lamb in a large skillet over medium-high heat for the same amount of time.

While the kibbeh is cooking, in a small bowl, mix together the yogurt, salt, mint, lemon juice, and cucumber.

Serve with the kibbeh.

Yemeni Spice

This was available in virtually every market on Atlantic Avenue—or, at least, the ones run by guys from Yemen. But I realize that's not typical, so here's a quick recipe if you are making your own. Makes approximately $1/3$ cup Total time: 5 minutes

1 tablespoon ground cumin

1 tablespoon ground coriander

$1/4$ teaspoon ground cloves

$1/8$ teaspoon ground cardamom

$1/4$ teaspoon cinnamon

2 tablespoons turmeric

1 tablespoon pepper

In a small bowl, mix together all of the above spices.

New Parenthood

{ *and*
the family
dinner vow }

Slowly, my kitchen—and my life—became overtaken by little people. This is a makeshift dollhouse I made for the girls using magazine photos and masking tape.

*S*tarting *in the summer* of 2000 until spring of the following year, I was preoccupied with two goals.

Goal 1: Finding a New Job. I was working for a start-up magazine and what I really wanted was to work at a bigger magazine—maybe at a women's magazine or a food magazine.

Goal 2: Getting Pregnant. I remember thinking that if I got pregnant before I found a job, then I would put off the hunt for a few months, maybe even put off the career for a while. Wasn't it a little irresponsible to start a job knowing that I was planning to be on leave a few months later?

Both goals had one thing in common: They proved highly elusive. I went on a thousand interviews with intimidating people wearing intimidating shoes and, it seemed, went through as many failed pregnancy tests. Month after month I'd check for the two pink lines across the window, crossing out and circling days on my year-at-a-glance calendars, which were shoved inside my diary. (Not my dinner diary!) I'd read and reread the section "How to Tell if You're Pregnant" in my *Mayo Clinic Guide to Pregnancy* and dream of the day that I could use the other eight zillion pages of the book, which I bought in a bout of supreme hubris the year before, when it was a foregone conclusion that I would be able to get pregnant 1-2-3, and be on my merry way toward growing a family in Brooklyn.

It almost became a race to see which one would happen first: the new job or the new baby. And I felt oddly disconnected from the competition—like I was just leaning back watching, with no idea how dramatically the result of the contest would affect the next decade of my life. Because I didn't have any idea how dramatically it was going to affect the next decade of my life.

The job won. I was hired as a senior editor at *Real Simple* (tag line: "Making Time for What Matters"), which was only in its second year of existence and had just been taken over by a new editor, Carrie. Carrie had two teenage daughters and had started out as a "cub reporter," as she always called it, at *Life* twenty-five years earlier, in the same building, the storied Time-Life Building on Sixth Avenue and Fifty-first Street.

Carrie told me she hired me because I had never worked at a women's magazine. She needed fresh ideas, new people with new ways of thinking who hadn't written and rewritten the same "How to Lose Weight" pieces for six other magazines. She loved that I had been at a start-up like *Biography*, where I got my hands involved in everything—book reviews, lots of profile writing, a little recipe editing. She especially liked this last credential. She needed someone to help out in the food department. We shook hands on my suddenly doubled salary and I started two weeks later. I was thrilled—but also a total wreck, terrified that I was going to screw up or, worse, be discovered as a fraud who was wholly undeserving of this opportunity.

My *Mayo Clinic* told me that a stressful environment is not conducive to getting pregnant. I got pregnant a month after I started the job.

If I hadn't been so stressed out, I would have found this hilarious. Instead, I was consumed by the Conversation I was going to have to have with the boss. The conversation in which I was going to tell Carrie I was pregnant and presumably in which she would respond with outrage over my lack of commitment. (And by that I meant my three months "off" for maternity leave. It never even crossed my mind that I wasn't going to return to work after maternity leave, reporting from nine to five, five days a week as always.) When I finally got in to see Carrie—the night before September 11—she seemed to know my news already. This didn't stop me from blurting out, "I'm pregnant," and then, in the same breath, "butI*fully* planoncomingbackaftera*really*shortmaternityleaveI*promise*!" She laughed a laugh that carried the distinct tone of wisdom, then officially became the first person to say to me: "Don't say that. You have no idea how you'll feel once you have the baby."

I was shocked by this statement.

"No, no, no," I told her. "I love my job here too much to not come back." It was true. By this point, Carrie had put me in charge of managing the food team and had given me free rein to assign first-person essays to my favorite writers—like Ellen Gilchrist, who actually said yes. My direct boss, a guy named Tom, had taught me more in those first five months than I had learned in the ten years leading up to it. I was no longer nervous about my work—just stunned by my good fortune. I couldn't believe that I had a job that seemed designed expressly for me.

Carrie had always been a full-time working mother—she was one of those moms who was on the phone with the office while she was in labor—but did her best to impress upon me how serious and how *personal* the work-vs.-stay-at-home decision was. She also warned me not to be disappointed or shocked if I felt different about my job specifically—or about my career generally—once I became a mother.

I nodded with a very serious expression on my face, but I was thinking something like, *Yeah, whatever. So many women work and have kids. How hard could it be? Isn't that what this magazine is about? Making Time for What Matters? Mastering the Juggle? Figuring Out the Balance?* I went back to editing my Ellen Gilchrist essay and brainstorming eight different dinners you could make with the same eight ingredients. Since the magazine was still pretty young, we had some late nights finishing up the big issues—Carrie was a demanding boss and knew exactly what she wanted, albeit sometimes letting us all know exactly what she wanted on the day before an issue was shipped to the printer. Although it did occur to me that this might become inconvenient with a baby around, it didn't hold me back. I felt like I was hitting my professional stride, culminating one night on my way out when Carrie, coming out of Tom's office held up a story outline I had just proposed, then shouted down the hall, *"Brilliant, Jenny!"*

I would subsequently call up this moment hundreds of times in the next few years—compliments from bosses are few and far between in my experience—but I replayed the scene like crazy on maternity leave. Because when Phoebe was born on a February Sunday in 2002—more details on that in a few pages—I wasn't necessarily shocked by how much love and happiness she brought me. I was shocked by how this little six-pound nine-ounce thing could be the source of so much guilt. I'd be in a rocking chair with Phoebe in her sunny nursery and wonder how on earth I was going to ever leave her for eight straight hours every day with someone I didn't even know. What was I thinking? How could I do this? And then I'd think of the *Brilliant, Jenny!* moment.

Ten years and many not-necessarily-brilliant professional moments later, it seems like such a ridiculous memory—one I'm sure Carrie has no recollection of—but it was my first taste of real professional pride and the first sign that I had not just a *job* to come back to but a *career* to look forward to. I am embarrassed to admit how much that moment made me want to work harder and get more praise and feel more proud. And I was embarrassed that this feeling, this drive to excel, didn't evaporate when I was staring at my newborn daughter.

After a four-month maternity leave, I went back to work. (My first dinner as a working mother on June 17, 2002: Turkey Chili. See opposite page.) The memory of the first few weeks is painful. Not only the leaving Phoebe part, which in eight years never got easy, but also because I became a walking working-mother cliché. These were the golden years of the working-mom manifesto and I read every one of them— quoting my hero Kate Reddy, the scatterbrained but brilliant financial analyst/ mother of two from *I Don't Know How She Does It*, to anyone who would listen. I photocopied Caitlin Flanagan's *Atlantic* article about how working mothers oppress their nannies in the name of their careers and handed it out to all the mothers on staff. I dragged my co-workers to a Peggy Orenstein event to discuss *Flux: Women on Sex, Work, Love, Kids, and Life in a Half-Changed World*. I remember one of them coming by my office to talk about it. (That was the other thing I realized quickly—working mothers loved nothing more than talking about being working mothers.) In the course of the conversation, it came up that she had made a promise to herself when she became a mother: She would always be home in time to say good night to her son. She was one of the hardest-working people on staff—one of the editors I respected the most—and my heart sank a little when she told me this. I wondered, *Am I going to have to stay that late and work that hard and miss that many dinners if I want to keep climbing up the ladder? Do I want to keep climbing up the ladder after all?* Phoebe was probably only about six months

Grilled Pork Tenderloin : Marinate in
bourbon, brown sugar, + soy

6/15 Bouillabasse — OUT
6/16 Larchmont BBQ
6/17 [BACK TO WORK] Turkey Chili [FREEZER]
6/18 Rice Pasta w/ Turkey Sauce [FREEZER]
6/19 Rotisserie Chicken
/20 Scallops with Lentil Rice
/21 Garden of Eden Takeout, Emily + Steve
/22 Larchmont BBQ Lamb+Chicken Shish Kebabs
6/23 Cedar Plank Salmon, spinach, wilted
6/24 Chicken Cacciatore [FREEZER]
25 Pizza w/ Sausage + Peppers + Fresh Tomatoes
26 Pasta w/ Turkey Meat Sauce [FREEZER]
/27 Andy's Chinese
28 Codcakes with Chipotle Lime Sauce
30 29 [Melissa+Brendan's] Grilled Swordfish w/ sugar snap Pea salad
30 Pasta w/ Yogurt + Caramelized Onions
7/1 Turkey Chili [FREEZER]
7/2 Roast Chicken w/ Spinach + Sweet Potatoes
7/3 Grandma Ward's / Mike
7/4 Codcakes w/ Chipotle Lime Sauce

old, and when I went home that night and fed her dinner (breast milk) I made a promise to her and Andy: If I couldn't regularly be home in time for dinner, I wasn't going to stay on that particular career path. I was just going to have to figure out some other way to be Brilliant Jenny.

In order to stick to the plan, I became an obsessive checklister, identifying three realistic tasks to complete every day by 5:50 p.m. At that hour, no matter what I was doing, no matter what I was in the middle of, I was going to stop and walk out the door. If there were certain tasks that had to be completed because other people's days and nights and workloads were depending on my completing them, then I would make sure those tasks had first priority. I figured it would be a lot easier to walk out the door with conviction knowing I wasn't leaving some-one hanging. Of course, this 5:50 "conviction" often manifested itself in poking my head out of my office, checking to make sure the hallway was clear of bosses, sprinting to the elevator bank with my bag and my day's supply of breastmilk clunking behind me, then pressing the Down button a million times as though somehow this would make the elevator come faster, preferably before anyone walked by and saw me leaving before 6:00. Which was still a full hour earlier than most staffers went home for the day.

It would have been helpful if there was a *Mayo Clinic* chapter that addressed the topic of "leaving." Man, I would have read that chapter over and over—leaving your wailing baby in the morning without wanting to slit your wrists; leaving your desk even though you are only a half hour away from completing something that would feel so good to wrap up; leaving the building so no one no-tices that you are actually leaving. I was much more interested in honing that skill than learning how to puree apples and carrots to freeze in ice-cube trays (not that I ever did that either). As long as I was a full-time working mother with a clock to punch or a train to catch—as I would be for eight more years—I never figured out how to leave with grace or with so-called conviction.

But I did it anyway. And as scattered and stressed as I felt doing it, it somehow didn't come across that way to my co-workers. Within the next two years, more than a half-dozen babies would be born to women in my office. Besides the obvi-ous camaraderie this brought to my workdays—more people to talk about Kate Reddy with—it brought a certain degree of drama-squelching perspective, too. I wasn't the first person in the history of the world to have a baby and a job at the same time, and I wasn't going to be the last. It also made me feel better about my decision: In those two baby boom years at the office, a few of the new moms made a point to come up to me and say that they were going to do what I had done—get the hell out of the office at a decent hour no matter what was on their desks. One of the moms, Pilar, who'd become a close friend and whom I'd go on to work with at *Cookie* said, "I was nervous about having a baby until I saw you do it. I didn't think it was possible to still be good at your job after you had a family."

It *goes without saying* that this joined the *Brilliant, Jenny!* moment on my loop of "Nice Things People Said to Me That I Will Draw upon for the Rest of My Life."

Bolting from the office was the hardest part of the equation during these early days of parenting—the phase the next section addresses. Once I was home, it was relatively easy to stick to the dinner vow because we ate in shifts. Phoebe and her sister, Abby, who came along twenty months later and whom you will meet a little further on in this part of the book—were obviously way too little to sit still for a proper dinner with us. So we'd come home, scour the fridge for bits and pieces of chicken and strawberries and broccoli, open a jar of Earth's Best sweet potatoes and dinner would be on the table in ten minutes. Our own dinner, usually something quick, too, but at least involving a fresh herb or two, wouldn't get going until an hour later, when the kids were asleep. We weren't even close to feeling the pressure to all be eating the same thing at the same time—that expectation was years away. But even so, we wanted to sit with them while they ate. As often as possible, we wanted to avoid outsourcing that part of the nightly routine to our full-time babysitter, Devika. And once they were done eating, we wanted to, you know, *spend time* with them, too.

So what ended up happening was this: The girls' bedtimes got pushed later and later to accommodate their selfish working parents. Even though *The Seven O'Clock Bedtime* was a huge best seller at the time, our kids were eating dinner when most of those seven o'clock babies were winding down, and our kids were not going to sleep until about eight thirty. I know parents who say their kids are too hungry to wait that long, too exhausted to stay up that late. I'm sure sleep experts will say this kind of routine would adversely affect their brain development (surely reversed by all those brain-enriching conversations we'd someday have at the table!). But right from the beginning Devika made sure they were eating healthy, hefty snacks later in the afternoon so they wouldn't be starving by the time we got home. In retrospect, this was laying down the groundwork for our nightly ritual. Every now and then, we would attempt an all-parties present family dinner, but that was the exception rather than the norm until Abby turned three ("the norm," of course being very broadly defined, since for a while, especially during the frantic period after Abby was born, no two nights ever looked the same).

This was the way we did it. I do not mean to infer that everyone's schedules should proceed as outlined above. I've heard from a lot of parents—especially those home with their babies all day—that they are less concerned about squeezing in some eleventh-hour family time around the table than they are about wrapping their hands around a cold martini and snagging an hour or two of scream-free chill time before they collapse into the bed they look at with longing *all* day. I also know that after putting in a full day at the office, then coming home and shepherding the baby through her dinner-bath-and-bedtime paces, probably the last thing you may be thinking is, *Hey, honey, now that the baby is asleep, let's take this opportunity to expand our skillet meal repertoire.* What I'd like to come through in the following section is that no matter how different and harried family dinner looked during this new baby phase of our lives, it still served its main purpose: It was our day's deadline. Even when we were in a house in the suburbs with two kids under two and the evening hours between six o'clock and eight thirty felt like we were trapped in a high-speed game of playground dodgeball, even when the girls got a little older and we'd try and fail and try and fail to get them to eat the *same* dinner as us at the *same* time, even though each of us would have our share of late nights at the office, and even though we'd regress to our frozen veggie burger nights more often than I care to admit, the ritual of sitting down together at the end of the day remained our default mode, our time to be together. And a decade later, dinner has happened regularly enough for me to feel I've stayed true to my vow.

February 2002

Nesting and Expecting

My *contractions with Phoebe* started in the middle of a Sunday night, two weeks before her due date. By six in the morning—a brutally cold, slate-gray-winter-sky kind of morning—we were in a Town Car barreling over the Brooklyn Bridge and up the FDR Drive on our way to the hospital. To distract myself from the contractions, I finally decided to read that "How to Breast-feed" section in *What to Expect When You're Expecting*, which I had been putting off all winter. When that stopped working, I dug my fingernails into Andy's arm while he called our parents. His mother said she was so excited she felt like she was going to pass out. Eight hours, one epidural, one spinal, and one emergency C-section later, we were parents. Andy snapped a picture, just after surgery, of all four grandparents leaning over my bed while I held Phoebe. In the photo my mother is weeping.

I was enamored by the living creature in my arms, of course, but what I remember the most was the unconditional, undiscriminating love I felt for everyone else in the room, too. Andy, my parents, and my in-laws. My sister, mom to a newborn herself. My brother. Even the nurse, Carmen, who was first assigned to me. I had an irrepressible urge to tell this woman I loved her, even as she stood over me like a drill sergeant and demanded that I say my good-byes and start thinking about breast-feeding this baby *immediately*. I hadn't retained a single piece of information from *What to Expect*, but it didn't matter. Phoebe was a champion eater right from the start—no book required. Andy slept on a cot all four nights in the hospital—adrenaline was outpacing exhaustion, so we didn't care yet—but on the day after Phoebe was born, he went home to shower and prepare the nest.

About this nesting thing: I'm not sure why I wasn't overwhelmed by the mysterious primal urge during those last few days of pregnancy to cook up batches of

A stash of frozen soup and stews: Money in the bank!

stews and chili for the freezer like all my friends had. In fact, I didn't even know that this phenomenon existed. (Perhaps if I had bothered to read my *What to Expect*, I would have found a description of it in the FAQ section, right there after the question on "Frequency of Urination.") But again, it didn't really matter because when Andy went home—he ran five miles in record time, mopped and Swiffered the apartment, changed the sheets, and cooked up a huge batch of turkey Bolognese for the freezer. U2's "It's a Beautiful Day" was on the stereo, a song he said he didn't even like that much but couldn't resist putting on repeat while he sautéed his onions and browned the meat, before racing back to the hospital to attend a swaddling class. (Holy *Christ* could he swaddle!)

We didn't know what to expect when we brought Phoebe home three days later—we had no idea what we were doing. I remember that first night, putting a sleeping Phoebe in her bassinet next to our bed and asking Andy, "So what do you think? Should we set an alarm for three hours from now so we can wake her up to nurse?" An alarm! Little did I know I wouldn't need to set another alarm clock for eight years. But we knew we could always expect one thing. A kick-ass home-cooked dinner, only about a three-minute thaw away.

Three Nesting Recipes

All good nesting recipes share three main characteristics: They are quick to make, they are easy to double or triple, and they freeze well. We freeze all our sauces, soups, and stews in flattened zipper-lock bags so they are easier to thaw under running water when you need them quickly.

Lazy Bolognese

Though Andy grew up with this recipe, the credit for the name goes to one of my blog readers (identified only as "jillybean"). Before she came along, it was known only as turkey Bolognese. Not to be confused with a real Bolognese, like Marcella Hazan's, which requires lots of time on the stovetop to allow for seemingly gallons of liquid (wine, milk, tomato juice) to be absorbed by the meat. But Lazy Bolognese is just the right speed for New Babydom. Later there will be time for Marcella. **Total time: 35 minutes**

Few glugs of olive oil

1 small onion, chopped

1 garlic clove, minced

½ teaspoon red pepper flakes

Salt and pepper to taste

1 pound ground beef or turkey (if using turkey, dark meat
   is always preferable)

1 heaping tablespoon tomato paste

1 teaspoon fennel seeds

1 teaspoon sugar

¼ cup wine (red or white preferably dry)

1 28-ounce can diced tomatoes, in their juices (or tomato puree)

8 shakes of dried oregano

1 pound tubular pasta (penne, rigatoni, ziti)

Freshly grated Parmesan cheese, for serving

Add the oil to a medium saucepan set over medium-low heat. Add onion, garlic, pepper flakes, and salt and pepper and cook for about 2 minutes, until onion is slightly wilted.

Push everything to one side of the pot, turn up heat slightly, and add the ground meat, breaking it up with a fork as it browns. Once most of the pink is gone, stir it together with onion mixture.

Add the tomato paste, fennel seeds, sugar, and wine and stir everything together. Raise the heat to medium-high and cook until most of the liquid has been absorbed, about 5 minutes. Stir in the tomatoes and oregano. Bring the sauce to a boil and then turn heat to low and simmer uncovered for at least 30 minutes and up to 1 hour.

If you are freezing for later, let the sauce cool at this point and then ladle it into a freezer bag. If you are not freezing for later, while the sauce is simmering (or reheating), prepare the pasta according to package directions. Toss the drained pasta with sauce and serve in bowls topped with freshly grated Parmesan.

Turkey Chili

Serve in bowls with traditional toppings, or add the chili to tortilla chips, melt cheese on top, and eat dinner with your fingers from one plate. Who said I'm not a class act? Total time: 45 minutes

1 large onion, chopped

1 garlic clove, minced

Few glugs of olive oil

1 pound ground turkey (dark meat is always preferable) or beef

Salt and pepper to taste

4 tablespoons chili powder

1 28-ounce can diced tomatoes

1 teaspoon oregano

⅛ teaspoon cayenne

1 bay leaf

¼ teaspoon cinnamon (crucial)

1 14-ounce can black beans, drained

Over medium-low heat, sauté the onion and garlic in the oil about 3 minutes. Turn up the heat to medium-high and brown the meat until it loses its pink color. Add salt, pepper, and the chili powder—get it sizzly so the spices get cooking—and then add the tomatoes and the remaining spices. Turn down the heat, simmer for 10 to 15 minutes, and add the beans. Cook for another 5 minuets, or until the beans are warmed through. Serve with white rice and any combination of the following: avocado chunks, shredded cheddar cheese, chopped fresh cilantro, sour cream.

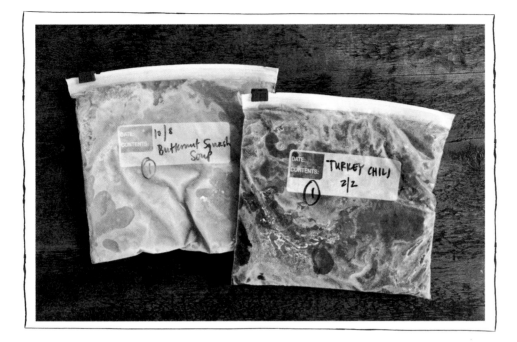

Butternut Squash Soup with Apples

We first found a version of this soup in one of the Barefoot Contessa cookbooks. Ina Garten says she first found it in *The Silver Palate*. Is there any wonder why it's a favorite in our house? Our twist on the recipe is adding all the garnishes at the end. Total time: 60 minutes

1 medium onion, chopped

Few glugs of olive oil

Salt and pepper to taste

Leaves from 1 sprig fresh thyme

1 tablespoon curry powder (optional)

⅛ teaspoon cayenne

1 butternut squash (about 2 pounds), peeled, halved, seeded,
   and cut into 1-inch cubes; if you can find pre-chopped squash,
   by all means, go for it (you want about 4½ cups of squash cubes)

2 apples (Fuji, Macintosh, or Cortland preferred,
   but just about any except Red Delicious will work),
   peeled, cored, and cut into chunks

3½ cups or more chicken broth

Garnishes: Chopped walnuts, chopped chives, sour cream

In a Dutch oven or a large stockpot, brown the onion in oil until wilted, about 3 minutes. Add salt and pepper, thyme, curry powder, and cayenne. Stir in the squash and apples, then add enough broth to cover it all by about a half inch. Bring to a boil and then simmer uncovered for 30 minutes—checking and adding water or broth every 10 minutes to make sure liquid stays at about the same level—until the squash is tender. Turn off the heat and puree with a handheld immersion blender or in batches in the blender (see warning), adding more water or broth until it reaches desired consistency.

Top with walnuts, chives, and sour cream.

Warning: To avoid an explosion, keep the lid on the blender slightly ajar as you whirl. You should do this anytime you are blending hot liquid.

⭐ *Tip:* Three other soups that fit into the nesting category: Chicken Soup with Orzo (page 290); Tomato and White Bean (292), Beluga Lentil with Anchovies (231)

WHO'S GONNA KNOW?

I hated telling people I was pregnant. We were one of those annoy-ing couples who didn't breathe a word to anyone in the first trimester, which made me dread being out to dinner with friends when the waiter would appear to ask us for our drink orders. I never handled it correctly—lying and stammering ("I ran five miles today and feel *so* dehydrated") and almost always giving away the secret without wanting to. My solution was to have people over for dinner instead. When the guests arrived, I would already have poured a glass of wine for myself, which was in fact a cold glass of Welch's white grape juice. (Or, as Andy called it, "my late-harvest Riesling.") When I told my sister the big news the first thing she said was, "But you were drinking *wine* last week!" It's been almost a decade and I think she's still mad at me for the decep-tion. Once I went public, things were a little easier in the drinking department, except for the fact that . . . I couldn't drink. This was not as tragic then as it would have been, say, a few years later when I really needed a glass of wine to buffer the chaos of work from the chaos of home, but I still craved the ritual. When we were on vacation, just at my thirteen-week mark, Andy mixed me the greatest vir-gin cocktail, which we named the 1080 (after the number of the house where we stayed): It was a mixture of apricot nectar, lime juice, club soda, strawberries, and a handful of fresh juicy sliced peaches (measurements pretty much to taste), and it was so good that whenever the peaches are good enough (even when I'm not pregnant) I mix one up and raise a glass with my fourth-grader. (How is it possible that she is in fourth grade?) Then I give her the 1080 and pour myself a real drink.

May 2002

. . . .

Getting a Noncook on Board

he first time the concept of "division of labor" really registered for me was about two weeks into motherhood at 2:00 A.M., when my swaddled little newborn, as warm and delicious as a burrito, decided to finally wake up and make herself heard . . . all night long. Since I was breast-feeding, I was obviously going to have to be the one who had to wake up three, four, five times a night. And what seemed equally obvious to me was that if I was the one breast-feeding around the clock, then Andy should be the one up with her whenever she was awake and *not* hungry. This was so obvious—in both our eyes—that it wasn't even discussed. But there were thornier issues down the road, when we were both back to work and Devika, our babysitter, would call in sick. It was never quite as simple as the alternating tag-you're-it approach. Often it didn't matter whose "turn" it was or who stayed home last time; it came down to whose day was more unmissable. Who had meetings they couldn't skip and, since we were both in publishing, deadlines they couldn't blow. There was no cut-and-dried approach to it, but neither one of us was ever considered the Assumed Stay-at-Homer.

Another big issue was Morning Duty, that is, who would wake up with the baby at five-thirty or six or whatever ungodly hour she decided was the best time to welcome the day. Because this responsibility wasn't something as small and unpredictable as, say, picking up more milk or emptying the diaper genie, we fell into a strict alternating routine: Andy wakes up Monday, Jenny Tuesday, Andy Wednesday, and so on. Though we never actually drafted up our "Morning Duty Constitution," we referred to this document as though it were signed in blood, framed, and hanging on our living room wall. My guess is that we fell out of sequence fewer than ten times in six years. If it was your turn to be on duty, you couldn't get out of it no matter how hard you tried, how tired you were, or how

hung over. I remember one night I came home from a dinner out with friends—a dinner that included a gin-and-tonic and a half bottle of wine. Andy, who was sitting on the couch watching *The Daily Show with Jon Stewart*, turned to me with an evil glint in his eye, and asked, "Psyched for Morning Duty?"

All of these tasks were negotiations to some degree because, with the exception of breast-feeding, both of us were perfectly capable of performing the task at hand no matter how much we dreaded doing so. But what would've happened if this hadn't been the case—if we hadn't both been perfectly capable of executing the task at hand? What happens when one member of the couple dreads the task at hand so much that it is actually causing more resentment than it is alleviating? And what happens when the task at hand is not as petty and expendable as putting your clothes in the hamper (instead of beside the hamper) or swinging by CVS for more wipes? What if we're talking about a duty that sometimes seems much bigger and more relentless than all the other duties combined?

In other words, what happens if you have a spouse who is unwilling, incapable, or shows absolutely zero interest in cooking dinner for the family? And what if you are like that, too, but somehow the responsibility has fallen squarely on your shoulders anyway, every night, all week long, all year long, with no end in sight until your youngest is safely nestled in her first college dorm room?

I am no relationship expert, but I can tell you that there's a higher chance that your *Dinner: A Love Story* will become *Dinner: A Simmering Resentment Story.* I would say that of all the private questions I get from my readers (as opposed to publicly posted on the site for all to read) the one I get the most is this: How do I get my spouse on board to cook when he/she has no interest and/or skills in the kitchen?

I have several pieces of advice for readers in this situation, not one of which requires a legal document to execute. Because if you think about it, there are *so* many things besides the actual *making* of dinner that go into *making dinner happen.* Some of you out there might feel like me—that the braising and the chopping and the simmering is the easy part, dare I say, the *fun* part. It's all the little satellite duties that orbit the meal that fill me with dread. So here are a few duties the Cook should feel free to outsource to the Noncook:

1. Make a decision!

There is nothing I appreciate more than getting an email from Andy at three in the afternoon requesting chicken with Brussels sprouts. Or when Phoebe comes home from school and begs for chicken soup. Just because I have four thousand meal ideas recorded in my diary doesn't necessarily mean I'm brimming with inspiration on any given Tuesday (I've yet to figure out why not). Give someone else the job of thinking up what to cook, so you can relax and just concentrate on the fun part.

Of course, for some people—especially the kinds of people who would never describe cooking as "the fun part"—this is the opposite of good advice. At first blush, the idea of your Noncook requesting spaghetti and clams might sound about as helpful as your boss requesting no sugar next time you go around the block for his double skim latte. But for so many cooks, the decision making, narrowing down, think-work part of dinner can often be the most paralyzing stage of the process, so having a partner in any phase of the planning helps make the meal more of a shared goal than an it's-coming-no-matter-what burden. Even if the Noncook never lifts a finger in the kitchen, it's nice to know he or she was sharing your stress. Which brings me to my next piece of advice.

2. Get home on time.

If you can't get home in time to cook, get home in time to eat. I know this is a tricky one—with demanding work schedules and the kids' early bedtimes, but have the Noncook earmark a night or two during the week when he or she knows for a fact that he or she can get home in time to appreciate your fine effort. It's the least he or she can do.

3. Clean-up duty.

Well, not true. As mentioned above, the Noncook should also be on Clean-up Duty if you got your act together enough to braise a freaking pork loin for the whole family.

4. Praise the pork loin.

Also on the list of duties for the Noncook (and I'm afraid this one is absolutely nonnegotiable), he or she must praise that braised pork loin, as well the braiser of the pork loin, up and down and all around until braiser blushes with pride and appreciation, prompting unappreciative children at the table to ask night after night, "Why do you *always* say that to each other?" Praise is motivating. And no praise is bad for the soul.

5. Take control of the heart sinkers.

By this I mean, take care of all the things in the kitchen that routinely make the Cook's heart sink: discovering the dishes in the dishwasher are clean but unloaded; realizing just as you sit down to dinner that no one has anything to drink or that the soy sauce / ketchup / napkins are not on the table. I think the best birthday present anyone could ever give me would be a little robot that automatically took care of all of these duties, none of which individually take up a lot of time but which collectively can send you spiraling into dark places.

6. Master one meal.

You *don't need to* know how to make fifty different dinners to be a major contributor to family dinner. You just have to know one or maybe even two. (Remember my dad and his chicken cutlets?) Teach your Noncook the easiest recipe in the world, like Baked Sausage with Apples, Potatoes, and Onions and just accept the fact that you'll eat it at least once a week for the next eighteen years. (The Greek-style Shrimp with Feta on page 70 might also fall into this so-easy-a-monkey-could-make-it category, as would any of the nesting freezer meals, pages 98 to 102, especially if they are already cooked and frozen and just in need of a reheat.)

Baked Sausage with Apples, Potatoes, and Onions

Preheat the oven to 425°F. Combine **3 cups whole small potatoes** and **1 onion** (chopped in large chunks) in a large baking dish and toss with **1 tablespoon olive oil**, the leaves from **4 sprigs of fresh thyme**, **salt**, and **pepper**.

Place **4 sweet Italian pork sausages** on top of vegetables. Bake uncovered for 45 minutes, until sausage is brown on top. Using tongs, flip over the sausage and bake for 10 more minutes.

Meanwhile, chop **2 Granny Smith apples** (unpeeled) and toss with a little more **olive oil**, **salt**, and **pepper.** Scatter the apples around the sausage, drizzle **2 tablespoons cider vinegar** over the whole dish, and bake for 5 more minutes. Serve with dollops of **spicy brown or Dijon mustard**.

And *last, one more* duty, this time for the Cook. When you have made dinner for seven straight nights, as well as replenished the toilet paper in both bathrooms, hung up the coats that were left on the bench, dragged the recycling bins to the curb, picked up the kids' wet towels off the bathroom floor, and all those other small tasks that can easily go unnoticed (read: unappreciated), and you feel resentment creeping into your bloodstream, try to remind yourself of the fact that it's never once occurred to you to cut the kids' fingernails or replace the filters in the AC unit or sweep the strewn Cheerios from under the table after breakfast or drain all that weird rusty water out of the boiler in the basement. (What *is* that stuff?) Okay, fine, that's my situation. But you get the idea.

January 2003

It Started with an Egg

When Phoebe was little and just starting out on finger foods, we fed her chicken nuggets as a matter of course. Not those additive-free naked nuggets by the Blue Ribbon guys or the organic kind you can find at Whole Foods and Trader Joe's and just about anywhere else these days, but the kind of nugget shaped like dinosaurs. The kind that listed "chicken" fifth or sixth in the ingredient list, behind things like magnesium oxide and ferrous sulfate. The kind that tasted like sawdust. In 2002, our closest supermarket was Key Food on Montague Street in Brooklyn. And those were the kinds of chicken nuggets that Key Food sold. Nothing natural, nothing organic, nothing real. So that was the chicken we brought back to our house, cut up into microscopic bites, and placed before Phoebe on her high chair tray. I don't know if this makes things better or worse, but we reached for those nuggets with conviction. We grew up with Tyson and Perdue on our dinner tables—why wouldn't we do the same for our kids? It didn't occur to us to question this. Especially since Phoebe had such a varied diet—the notes in her baby book say her favorite foods were Cheerios, strawberries, sweet potatoes, broccoli, turkey, pancakes, pasta shells, any kind of bread, peanut butter, and

American cheese. If I had looked at the label on my packet of American cheese, I might've noticed that there was no cheese listed in the ingredients, but why would I look at the label for any other reason than calorie counting? Why would anyone?

This was four years before Michael Pollan's *The Omnivore's Dilemma* was published, before it became mainstream to question everything on our plates—what was in it and how it got there. *Fast Food Nation,* Eric Schlosser's skewering of the industrialized food industry, had been out since 2001, but I didn't get around to reading it until after Abby was born three years later. Though I hardly had time for pleasure reading, I think the real reason I let the book collect dust on my nightstand was because I wasn't ready to hear the message. (Plus, I rationalized, it was about fast food like McDonald's, not about the food I bought at Key Food, right?) And yes, while it's true that the Real Food movement, the Organic Movement, and the Slow Food movement had all been around for quite some time (not to mention that the year I was born, 1971, marked the opening of a small restaurant in Berkeley called Chez Panisse) I was not a card-carrying member of any of them.

But the food editor at *Real Simple* was. Her name was Jane and I worked with her very closely. She had a sweet set-up—she lived on a farm in Vermont and spent two days a week in our office. She raised organic chickens—long before anyone with a tattoo and a Williamsburg lease was raising organic chickens. In her spare time, she ran a program in her son's school teaching children about where food comes from. "I want them to learn that an apple doesn't grow in the supermarket," she told me. My first thought: *Why, exactly, is that important to know?*

One day she brought me a dozen eggs from her farm. I was delighted and took them home to fry up for a weekend breakfast. Then I cracked one open. The yolk of this egg was yellow, like *really* yellow—orangey gold almost. It was not the customary pale color I was used to finding when I broke open my supermarket eggs. And I have to say—it terrified me. I thought something was wrong. I showed it to Andy.

"Do you think this egg looks okay?" I asked.

"Oh *yeeeaaaeah,* baby! That's what an egg should look like! Fry it up!"

This was 2002. Which means, the first time I tasted what an egg is supposed to *really* taste like—that is a real, fresh, eggy, organic egg—I was thirty-one years old. Thirty-one! And I had *loved* eggs my entire life. But these farm-fresh organic ones seemed to deserve a food category unto themselves—they were rich and flavorful and *gorgeous*, and came in all different colors and sizes. Which made a lot of sense—why hadn't I ever questioned the fact that every single egg from Key Food looked exactly the same?

Those eggs and that question busted open the door of a whole new world for us. Because once we asked that, the next logical question was: What other kitchen basics could be upgraded and change my life the way my organic eggs had? Which led to: What is the difference between all-natural and organic? And soon after: What exactly *were* those nuggets we were feeding Phoebe? Was there any actual yogurt in the Go-gurt? Should I worry that I can't pronounce five of the seven ingredients in our Jif peanut butter? (Related: Was life without Jif peanut butter a life worth living?)

But most important: Once I discovered the answers to all these questions, how was I supposed to apply that information to the family dinner table?

One of the great things about working at *Real Simple* was that whenever I had questions like these, I had an expert at my fingertips to help me figure out the answers. It stood to reason that if Jane was the one to send me out into this new land with its strange new language—cage-free, hormone-free, antibiotic-free, free-range, naturally raised, grass-fed, humanely raised—she was certainly going to be the one to guide me through it, too. Soon after Jane brought me my eggs, we started working on a story together called "Upgrade Your Pantry." We wanted to tell readers about small tweaks they could make to their shopping list that would make almost everything they cooked taste better. Not surprisingly, a lot of products Jane recommended were organic, all-natural, and unprocessed foods. She recommended buying peanut butter that was made with two ingredients: peanuts and salt. She advised replacing iodized table salt with cleaner-tasting kosher or sea salt. She recommended cooking with real organic butter every now and then, instead of cooking with light butter (made with chemicals) all the time. She told me that real Parmesan cheese came from one region of Italy and had "Parmigiano Reggiano" stamped on the rind—anything else, namely the powdery stuff

that came in the green cans, was inferior tasting and not authentic. She also, of course, recommended buying organic eggs. The flavor, she wrote in the story, is "full, rich, and downright eggy."

I edited a lot of stories at *Real Simple*, but that one, more than any other, would have the most lasting effect on the way I cooked and thought about food. I reworked my weekly shopping list (organized by aisle, a classic *Real Simple* move) to reflect what I had learned and I barely noticed that I had officially launched Phase One of our home's own private food revolution.

Come to think of it, we barely noticed Phase Two either: Identify the foods our family ate all the time—chicken, peanut butter, yogurt, milk, strawberries, and bananas—and try to keep those clean. With these products, whenever possible we avoided pesticides, hormones, additives, and anything labeled with unpronounceable ingredients. We had absolutely no problem transitioning away from store-bought chicken nuggets to homemade breaded chicken cutlets (see Grandma Jody's Chicken, page 11), especially when we took pains to make them extra crispy. For peanut butter, we began the transition by mixing Jif with organic, then gradually increasing the amount of natural until Jif was completely out of the equation. And since there was no going back to nonorganic eggs after tasting the real deal, that was an easy switch as well.

Phase Three (shop at the farmers' market as often as possible) and Four (know the provenance of your meat) would come in the next five or six years—a period where the conversation about where our food was coming from was growing too loud to ignore. And it wasn't until fairly recently that we could say our family kitchen was stocked with mostly wholesome, unprocessed ingredients. Unless you count the Mallomars in the fall. And Flav-or-Ices in the summer. And if there is no Gatorade in the refrigerator for Andy after he runs in the morning, I fear he might short-circuit. In other words, we've been mostly good. And so far, that's been good enough.

The egg epiphany was particularly timely because during this phase of parenting—when we'd want to put together a quick healthy meal for two as soon as the baby went to sleep—egg-based dinners were in heavy rotation.

Ricotta and Chard Omelet

Serves 2 Total time: 15 minutes

3 eggs

Dash of water

Salt and pepper

1 tablespoon olive oil

2 tablespoons butter

1 garlic clove, halved

Handful of Swiss chard leaves, washed, stemmed,
    and chopped into small pieces

3 large dollops ricotta

In a small bowl, whisk together the eggs, water, and salt and pepper. Add the oil and 1 tablespoon of the butter to a large cast-iron or nonstick skillet over medium heat. Swirl around the garlic halves and remove them before they brown. (This gives the oil a quick garlic infusion.)

Add a handful of the Swiss chard to the skillet and cook until slightly wilted, about 2 minutes. Remove the Swiss chard from the skillet and set aside.

Melt the remaining tablespoon of butter in the skillet and add the egg mixture to it, tilting the pan to spread evenly. Cook for about 1 minute and then spoon the ricotta and a few cooked chard leaves into the center in a row. (The egg on top should still look a little runny.) Fold one-third of the omelet over the fillings and then fold the other side on top. Cook another 1 to 2 minutes and slide onto a plate. Split in half and serve with any extra chard.

Dinnertime Breakfast Burritos

Serves 2 Total time: 15 minutes

2 8-inch whole wheat tortillas

1 15-ounce can black beans, rinsed and drained

1 bay leaf

1 avocado, chopped

Handful of shredded sharp cheddar cheese

Handful of cilantro, chopped

Sour cream

Salsa

3 eggs

Salt and pepper to taste

4 to 5 dots of cream cheese (optional)

Glug of olive oil

1 tablespoon butter

Hot sauce (optional)

Preheat the oven to 300°F.

Wrap the tortillas in foil and place in the oven.

Heat the black beans in a small saucepan with a bay leaf. Set out the avocado, cheddar, cilantro, sour cream, and salsa.

Whisk together the eggs, a dash of water, and the salt and pepper. Add dots of cream cheese if you have it. (I find this makes them fluffy.)

Add the oil and butter to a large cast-iron or nonstick skillet that has been set over medium-low heat. Add the eggs and scramble until the cream cheese melts into them and they reach desired consistency. (I like mine slightly wet.)

Top each warmed tortilla with eggs, hot sauce (optional), and desired toppings. Wrap and serve.

Spinach Tomato, and Feta Frittata

Total time: 25 minutes

    1 tablespoon olive oil

    2 tablespoons chopped onions or shallots

    Salt and pepper to taste

    Handful of fingerling potatoes,
        thinly sliced into "coins" like thick potato chips
        (about ½ cup)

    8 to 10 grape tomatoes, chopped

    1 garlic clove, minced

    2 cups washed and roughly chopped fresh spinach

    4 eggs

    ⅓ cup crumbled feta, plus more for sprinkling on top

    1 tablespoon chopped fresh herbs, such as parsley or chives

Preheat the broiler. In a cast-iron (or ovenproof) skillet, heat the oil over medium heat. Add onions and salt and pepper and cook about 1 minute.

Push onions to the side of the pan and add the potatoes in a single layer. Cook another 5 minutes, until the potatoes are crispy and mostly cooked through. Add tomatoes and cook, stirring for 1 minute. Add the spinach to the pan and stir until the leaves wilt.

Whisk together the eggs, cheese, and herbs in a small bowl. Pour the egg mixture into the pan and stir lightly to make sure the spinach and potatoes are evenly distributed.

Let cook without stirring for about 2 minutes. When eggs are mostly cooked around the edges, sprinkle more cheese on top and transfer to the oven. Broil for 1 to 2 minutes, until eggs are cooked on top and cheese is slightly golden. Serve cut into pizza-like wedges.

March–August 2003

Sunday Shopping Is the New Date Night

think there are two kinds of people in this world: the kind who would bestow sainthood upon the founder of Fresh Direct and the kind who enjoy shopping for food—whether it's at a summer market in Aix-en-Provence or the Stop & Shop on Main Street. In case you couldn't guess by now, Andy and I fall into the second category. (There's a third category, which comprises at least one member: my friend Jane, a mom of four under four, who hates cooking but loves grocery shopping because she does it alone—*alone* being the operative word—at 10:00 p.m., after all her kids are asleep.)

The truth is, once Phoebe was born, picking up the carton of milk at Key Food practically qualified as date night for us. It was part of our Sunday morning ritual, which also included a menu-planning session with the dinner diary, a strong cup of coffee on Montague Street, a stroll through the Heights with Phoebe in her Snap N' Go, then some Frank Rich reading on the Brooklyn Heights Promenade, with its stunning view of downtown Manhattan. It's highly possible I am over-romanticizing this period in my life, since there were also middle-of-the-night feedings, teething tantrums, crying-it-out sessions that lasted until 5:00 a.m., and weeks on end spent with the song "Victor Vito" in my head.

And for Andy, there was also the schlep home. Our cozy apartment, as romantic as it was with its exposed brick and roof deck, was a fifth-floor walk-up. And carrying a week's worth of groceries ten blocks and then up five flights of stairs gets old even for a category 2 shopping person like him. (I was busy holding our twelve-pound baby.) I think the day we started talking about a house in the suburbs with a driveway where we could park our car was the day Andy came home with our shopping bags, sweating and grumpy, walked straight into the bathroom, stepped on the scale, and determined he was holding 60 pounds of cereal and Goldfish crackers and diapers and jarred baby food. He looked at me and said one word: "Pelham."

There was another large factor that made us think about leaving Brooklyn for the greener pastures of Pelham or Montclair or the "Rivertown" suburbs on the Hudson: finding out I was pregnant with Abby. A week after celebrating Phoebe's first birthday (the cake was decorated with a big yellow duck, honoring her first word), I took a pregnancy test. Even though every fourth person had warned me it's a myth you can't get pregnant while breast-feeding, and even though I have a college degree, which would indicate I'd be smart about heeding this kind of advice, I was both shocked to see the results (I assumed another baby would take a while like it had with Phoebe) and proud. (I hate failing tests.) Andy's reaction was totally different: He was wistful thinking about Phoebe, who would only get nineteen months of our undivided attention.

To clear our heads, we went to Atlantic Avenue, grabbed some spinach and lamb pastries from one of our favorite Middle Eastern markets, then called our real estate broker, Steve. Steve—not my parents, not Andy's parents—was the first person we shared our news with. We needed a three-bedroom apartment ASAP, which, we quickly discovered, we couldn't afford in Brooklyn.

And so just before Abby's arrival, we moved twenty miles up the Hudson River, to the suburbs, to the land of Trader Joe's and Whole Foods and supermarkets with parking lots! To a Dutch Colonial with (seasonal!) views of the Hudson and a drive-in garage that connected to our kitchen via *one* flight of stairs. For Andy, I don't think the novelty of this will ever wear off.

But the one thing that never changed was the Sunday morning shopping ritual. Even though the coffee wasn't quite as strong, even though the drive through the strip malls and big box stores wasn't quite as romantic as a stroll down charming Brooklyn streets, even though our grocery list was beginning to reflect a more unprocessed, sustainable diet, and even though we now had two daughters under two conspiring to prevent us from reading Frank Rich (or anything else) ever again. In spite of all these things, we still had our date night every Sunday morning. And the girls—first in Baby Björns, then in the flip-down cart seat, then with pretend mini shopping carts, then venturing off to the next aisle by themselves to hunt down the salsa, then helping us pack the bags at check-out—tagged right along with us.

Six Items That Are Always on the Shopping List

Before I go shopping, I make sure I have a healthy supply of these six long-lasting pantry friends in the kitchen. I find that even if I have nothing else (except for maybe a few basics like olive oil, soy sauce, and Parmesan cheese), I can almost always churn out a fast healthy meal.

* Whole wheat spaghetti

* Quinoa

* Frozen spinach

* Canned or frozen artichokes

* Eggs

* Onions

Option 1: Spaghetti with Spinach and Artichokes. Cook **1 pound pasta** in a large pot according to package directions. Remove the pasta from the pot and toss it with a little **olive oil** to prevent sticking. In the same pot, add **4 tablespoons**

olive oil and **half a chopped onion** and cook until soft, about 3 minutes. Add a **14-ounce can** (or **1 cup thawed frozen**) **artichoke hearts** (drained and chopped), about ½ **teaspoon lemon zest**, a handful of **frozen spinach** (thawed, squeezed dry), **salt**, and **pepper**, and stir together until heated through. Toss with the pasta and a ton of **grated Parmesan cheese**.

Option 2: Whole Wheat Spaghetti with Caramelized Onions, Spinach, and Parmesan. See page 204 for the recipe.

Option 3: Quinoa with Fried Egg, Spinach, and Soy Sauce. In my house, this has always fallen under the "After-Hours" category, as in: quick enough to make after they go to bed and only ever eaten by Mom and Dad. Subsequently, it only serves 2. (But can be doubled if your kids are more adventurous with quinoa than mine.) Bring **1½ cups water** to a boil in a medium saucepan. Add ¾ **cup quinoa** and simmer, covered, until tender, fluffy, and water is absorbed—about 15 minutes. Let stand, covered, off the heat for 5 minutes, then fluff with a fork and divide into two bowls. While quinoa is cooking, add **2 tablespoons olive oil** and a dash of **sesame oil** to a skillet set over medium-low heat. Swirl a **halved garlic clove** in the oil and remove after 1 minute. Add ½ **medium onion** (sliced) and a dash of **red pepper flakes** to the pan and cook for 8 to 10 minutes, until onions are slightly golden. Add **1 cup frozen chopped spinach**, thawed, or **2 generous handfuls of fresh spinach** and cook until heated through or wilted. Add **2 teaspoons soy sauce**. If you have kitchen scissors, use them to chop the spinach while it cooks (unless you are using frozen). Remove the spinach from the skillet and place it on top of the quinoa. In the same skillet, turn the heat to medium-high, add another drizzle of olive oil, and poach or fry **2 eggs** (over easy). Place each on top of the quinoa and spinach. Drizzle a little more soy sauce on top, and add a sprinkle **of sesame seeds** if you have them and a few drops of **Sriracha** if you want some heat.

Option 4: Spaghetti Omelet. Okay, I'm slightly cheating here, because this one involves leftover pasta. (Do not try it with freshly made pasta. It won't work.) Use **3 eggs** for every 1 cup of **cooked spaghetti**. Fry leftover, unsauced spaghetti in **1 tablespoon olive oil** over medium heat. Add some **salt** and cook for 5 minutes, until crispy on the bottom. Add **1 tablespoon finely chopped onions** or **scallions** and **1 tablespoon chopped parsley**, then flip over like a pancake. Whisk together some **grated Parmesan cheese** and your eggs. Add eggs to the pan and cook until they are done, 2 to 3 minutes. (You can also crack the eggs right into the crisped spaghetti in the pan.) Flip one more time. Serve like a pizza, cut into wedges.

⭐ *Tip:* To thaw frozen spinach quickly, add a block to a colander and then gently run water on top. When it has thawed, press spinach into the colander to squeeze out any excess water. You want to get out as much water as possible.

Dinner: A Love Story

May 2004

Two Under Two

The best way for me to explain how thoroughly our two kids under two decimated family dinner, as well as all semblance of domestic order, is to take a walk through the girls' two baby books. You know, those journals that allow you to chronicle every inch grown, pound gained, hour slept, limb kicked, book read, holiday celebrated, toy chewed?

We took Phoebe's book seriously. To begin with, it's very possible that we spent an entire afternoon searching for the right one—we *definitely* made a special trip from Brooklyn to Manhattan to stroll through my favorite paper store on West Eighteenth Street—a high-ceilinged temple to blank books and notecards and stationery and all things beautiful and right with this world. (Andy called it Jenny's Porn Shop.) It was important to me to find exactly the right book—this was my firstborn we were talking about—and I didn't want to settle for the generic, impersonal Winnie-the-Pooh kind they sold in the shop around the corner. Like many of the tasks on my "Planning for Baby" to-do list, the "Buy baby book" box was checked off a few weeks before Phoebe even entered the world.

The book we settled on was red and blue, with charming little watercolor animals dancing across the cover. It had all the requisite fill-in-the-blank pages: Place baby shower invitation *here*, Place baby announcement *here*, Place envelope with first lock of hair *here*, Place front page of newspaper *here* (headline in the *New York Times* the day Phoebe was born: "Enron Had More Than One Way to Disguise Rapid Rise in Debt"), and as Phoebe grew, I completed each of these tasks with the precision and punctuality of a kindergarten teacher.

Her baby book also contained dozens of blank pages for freestyle recording, and boy, did we ever take to freestyle recording. It seemed there was no detail too

	Sleep Hours	Last nursed	Dinner	Notes
January 20	930 → 545	930	Pasta w/ turkey meat sauce	Full body swaddle
January 21	930 → 200, 205 → 215 → 315, 345 — 645	930	"	half-body swaddle
January 23	1000 → 300, 330 → 630			One ~~night~~ time wake-up not bad
January 24	~~930~~ → 945 — 200, 230 → 315, 330 → 6 30	930		
January 25	10-11, 11-330, 330-430			Serious Regressing
January 26	930 — 1230 up screaming for 1 hour 1:30 — 430 430 → 545			
January 27	Same thing, sucking hands... teething?			
January 29	9:30 — 200, 2:30 — 545 not bad; gave her Tylenol			
January 30	930 — 1245; 100 — 145 → 345. 4:30 → 5:30 Awful!			
Feb 1 — 5	worse, awful, and horrific, then worse			

Pooh tried and tried to stay awake,
but his sleepy eyes had other plans.
© Disney

Feb 6 9:00-4:45; 5:00-7:30 !!! Hallelujah!

Feb 21 8:45-12 15; 12 30 — 1 45; 2 00 — 4 45; 5:00-6:30 nightmare

Mar 13-20 Still feeding twice a night but more predictable: usually first wakeup is betw. 1:00-3:00; 2nd is always at 5:15. Andy's giving her a bottle at first wake-up.

April 14-21 Hallelujah. Five straight nights 8:30 — 6:00 !!!!!!!!!!!

pink puppy to

insignificant to document for eternity. Week 15: *First grabbed her foot and extended it.* Weeks 17–18: *Right now she has her entire fist in her mouth.* Weeks 19–20: *She's playing in her saucersizer but she needs a few more inches before she can really bounce around in it.* There were, of course, significant details, too, like this obvious favorite from weeks 24–25: *We put her in her high chair this week while we ate dinner. She's so much happier sitting up there with the grown-ups than in her bouncy seat on the floor.*

We bought Abby's baby book from a paper store in a strip mall in what was more or less a hit-and-run mission. The trip was early in the morning—timed so we could be home for Phoebe's afternoon nap, which, if the gods were smiling on us, might overlap for at least an hour with an Abby nap. (*But, dear Lord in heaven, I'll even take fifteen minutes, as long as there's just some overlap.*) Abby was already about four weeks old and it wasn't that we forgot about the book. It was that we were lost deep in the land of Two Under Two, also known as the Void, also known as Dante's Tenth Ring of Hell. From what I recall, there was no to-do list lying around reminding me to buy her baby book. The reminder came from Andy, in the form of: "Holy s*%t! I can't believe she's four weeks old already and we have yet to record a single note about her life! Are we terrible parents?"

The only baby book in the strip-mall store that wasn't decorated with fake sepia photos of rattles was . . . a Winnie-the-Pooh baby book. Every page was emblazoned with a chipper little title across the top: "Wonder-filled Days" and "Great Adventures!" and "I Can Do Anything!" And even though the tone was decidedly out of sync with the way I felt on a daily basis, it was going to have to do. We should've probably just gone with a blank book, because with Two Under Two, there weren't many afternoons when I found myself leafing through the themed pages thinking, *I can't wait to write down her first words! Her first plane trip! Her first time crawling.* Most afternoons I was sitting around in a zombie-like state, dead in the eyes, dreaming of sleep.

Abby woke up two or three times a night until she was almost twelve months old, which meant that Andy and I were waking up two or three times a night, which meant that for the rest of the day all we thought about was how to catch up on our sleep. On my morning commute, I gave up on reading the newspaper, choosing instead to snooze the whole thirty-three minutes to New York. (There were many mornings when the conductor announcing "Last stop, Grand Central!" didn't do anything to pull me from my slumber—but Andy's elbow in the ribs would usually do the trick.) I went to bed as soon as we finished dinner, having learned that if I let myself sit on the couch to watch even one minute of *The Bachelor*, there was a 100 percent chance I would crash out, fully clothed, teeth unbrushed, contacts in, the day's mascara caking up my lashes.

Without sleep, everything seemed more dramatic than it actually was. If I couldn't find my office card key, I'd feel like crying. Once, at work, I had to restrain myself from lunging at a coworker who had no kids and who claimed she was "exhausted" from being at a bar so late the night before. "She should be arrested for using that word in that context," said Andy when I relayed the story to him later.

Without sleep, I was a shell of my former self.

It took about eighteen pots of coffee to get me to the point where I could put a sentence together. And once I got to that point, the sentences I put together for Abby's book, instead of being about first checkups and first baths, were mostly about sleep—hers and mine. All the titles and prompts ("My favorite place to walk," "Our first vacation together") were crossed out and replaced with a maniacal stream-of-consciousness monologue that could stand in history as the official document of exhausted motherhood. Where once I might have spent a few pages describing the moment the baby first started kicking in her crib, now, it seemed, the first thing I brought up was how tired we were and how poorly Abby was sleeping. One entry began: *Best night yet!* Followed by one that began: *Never get cocky.*

On the inside of the front cover, I glued an article Andy wrote for *GQ* called "The Waking Wounded," where he talked about the condition as though "we're trapped in the remix version of the Great Human Sleep Deprivation Experiment." He went on to write the phrase that, for me, defined the first five years of parenting: "We no longer *get* tired; we *are* tired." The inside of the back cover attempts to connect what I ate for dinner with how Abby slept every night, thinking maybe the answer to a Glorious Eight Hours lay not in the white noise machine or the perfect swaddle but in the quesadillas with hot jalapeños spiking my breast milk. (Perhaps I should've been looking more closely at those eighteen pots of coffee.)

My favorite page in Abby's baby book is titled "We'll Never Forget!" At the bottom, there is a picture of Piglet snoozing like an angel, while a bee buzzes the quote "Sweet dreams, little one" over his head. The warm-and-fuzzy prompts (like "My cutest gestures . . ." and "Favorite stories about me . . .") are Xed out and replaced with a beleaguered hour-by-hour chronicle of our typical day—from Abby's first squawk at five thirty in the morning, until grown-up bedtime sixteen and a half hours later. I must've at least had the clarity of mind to recognize that someday everything that had to happen in the course of twenty-four hours with two kids under two would be fascinating to read back.

But I know I didn't have the clarity of mind to recognize that these days were going to get easier. If someone had just said to me, You know, Jenny, your days will not *always* look like this. Someday you'll walk in the door after a productive day at work, you will say hello to your children and they will say hello back. You will change into something comfortable, then cook dinner while your girls keep you company and, on good days, say, "That smells good, Mom. What are you making?" You won't have to immediately change a diaper, nurse the baby, change the diaper again, dance to "Old King Cole" on your new *Music Together* CD while attempting to steam broccoli and slice turkey. You won't have to lap the dinner table to soothe a witching-hour baby while your spouse spoon-feeds your toddler. (At least we were all "around" the table.) If someone had just told me that bath time and bedtime wasn't always going to resemble a scene from *Upstairs Downstairs* in double time, with Andy and me darting in and out of the girls' bedrooms, filling water cups and bottles, reading books, searching under the cribs for loveys and pacifiers, nursing, lullabying, changing another diaper, barely even grunting hello as we passed each other in the hallway or headed in opposite directions on the stairway. If someone had told me I wouldn't always have to wait until nine o'clock to eat my own dinner, after which I'd immediately wash the dishes and go right to sleep. If someone had just told me that someday I might even miss all this chaos . . .

. . . then I still, in a million years, wouldn't have believed them. With Two Under Two, we were in the trenches and the only moment of our day that resembled home life as we once knew it was our brief window of adult-only dinner time after the kids were asleep. Needless to say, during this period of dinner-time decimation, there was a special place in my heart for two things:

* The postwork cocktail. I think this is when Andy started referring to his Manhattan and my gin-and-tonic as our "medicine."

* Any recipe with the word *quick* in the title or that promised to limit ingredients and hands-on time.

I let my *Gourmet* subscription lapse but kept renewing *Cooking Light*, mostly because of its Superfast column, which seemed to speak directly to me. At *Real Simple*, it finally clicked why the Fake It, Don't Make It section I edited was so hugely popular. And suddenly, everywhere I looked, there were fifteen-minute dinners, three-ingredient recipes, and quickened versions of classics that seemed to understand that there was no room in my life for a coq au vin recipe that called for hacking up a whole chicken and igniting cognac.

The ones that follow were particularly beloved: They are quick, delicious, and tailor made for parents whose sleep-deprived brains are temporarily incapacitated. In other words, they are mind-numbingly easy.

I know how this is going to sound, but parenting can be hard. Really, really hard. Man, I need a drink.

Spicy Shrimp with Yogurt

This dinner is one of the most popular ones I've run on the blog. It takes about 10 minutes from start to finish—and closer to 5 minutes if you have the spices mixed already. When Phoebe got older, she requested the dish often, so we periodically prepared a stash of the smoky-cinnamony rub to have it ready to go. The spice mixture even gets its own special jar painted with her name. Below are the spice amounts to sprinkle over a shrimp dinner for four. Triple or quadruple if you want to make a stash to have on hand for the next time. Total time: 10 minutes

> ¾ teaspoon salt
>
> ½ teaspoon smoked paprika
>
> ½ teaspoon ground cumin
>
> ½ teaspoon curry powder
>
> ⅛ teaspoon cayenne
>
> ⅛ teaspoon cinnamon
>
> 1¼ pounds shrimp, peeled and deveined
>
> 1 tablespoon butter
>
> Accompaniments: toasted whole wheat naan bread (such as Kontos brand), plain yogurt, cilantro, lime sections

In a small jar, mix together the spices. Sprinkle over the shrimp and toss.

Melt the butter in a large skillet over medium-high heat. Add the shrimp to the pan and sauté 5 minutes, until done, sprinkling on a little more spice as you flip them around to cook.

Serve the shrimp with the accompaniments.

The very definition of a nice problem: A dinner that comes together too quickly, allowing for no time to savor a glass of wine while one prepares it.

Apricot-Mustard Baked Chicken

This chicken takes about 10 minutes to pull together and then about a half hour of hands-off time in the oven. In theory, you could time things so the chicken is ready as soon as the kids go to sleep. But if you can't for the life of you figure out a way to steal the few minutes needed for prep while the kids are awake, then just take care of step 1: Preheat the oven. Total time: 40 minutes

 6 to 8 skin-on chicken pieces (thighs or drumsticks), rinsed and patted dry

 Salt and pepper

 ¾ cup apricot jam

 1 tablespoon grainy mustard

 ¼ cup water

 Leaves from 2 sprigs fresh thyme

Preheat the oven to 400° F.

Place the chicken on a rimmed cookie sheet or baking dish lined with foil or parchment paper, sprinkle with salt and pepper, and bake for 10 minutes.

While the chicken is baking, whisk together the jam, mustard, water, thyme, and a little salt and pepper in a small saucepan over low heat for about 3 minutes. It should be slightly syrupy.

Pull the chicken out of the oven and pour the sauce on top. Continue baking for another 15 minutes. For the last 3 minutes, place the chicken under the broiler on the top rack so it gets golden and crispy looking.

Cacio e Pepe

In addition to being a classic after-the-kids-go-to-bed meal, this dish also holds the honor of being Andy's go-to meal when he's on his own. You can add a touch of cream when you whisk the oil and cheese for a little decadence. We've never gotten the kids on board with this one, so this only serves two. **Total time: 15 minutes**

½ pound spaghetti

¼ cup olive oil

¼ cup freshly grated Parmesan cheese, plus more for serving

12 generous grinds of pepper (hence the "pepe"), plus more for serving

Salt to taste

In a medium pot, prepare the pasta according to package directions. Reserve ¼ cup of the pasta water before draining the spaghetti. While the pasta is cooking, in a large bowl, whisk together the oil, Parmesan, pepper, and salt. Add half of the reserved pasta water gradually, whisking so it becomes emulsified. Toss the spaghetti into a medium bowl, and if cheese isn't distributing evenly, add the remaining pasta water until it does. Top with more cheese and pepper and serve.

Flatbread Pizza with Arugula and Prosciutto

This is also excellent prepared on the stovetop using storebought pizza dough. Use the pan-fried pizza on page 281 as a guide. Total time: 10 minutes

4 pieces flatbread (or naan bread)

1¼ cups shredded Italian fontina cheese
  (or mozzarella or aged provolone)

Few handfuls of arugula

5 to 6 thin slices prosciutto, pulled into pieces

Shaved or shredded Parmesan cheese

Freshly ground black pepper

Olive oil, for drizzling

Broil the flatbread (or toast it in a toaster oven) until golden, about 3 minutes. Remove and flip over. Add the fontina cheese to each untoasted side and return to the toaster oven or broiler until the cheese is bubbly, 2 to 3 more minutes. When the toasts are ready, top with bunches of arugula, a few pieces of prosciutto, Parmesan cheese, pepper, and a drizzle of oil.

★ *Tip:* Other excellent options for the After-Hours dinner: Quinoa with Fried Egg, Spinach, and Soy Sauce (page 121), and anything in the freezer from pages 98–102.

Medicine

Andy's Manhattan

Some recipes will tell you to do **2 parts bourbon** (or rye, which Andy likes, or Canadian whisky, which kind of smells like lighter fluid to me) to **1 part sweet vermouth,** but we find that's a little sweet. So Andy usually does something closer to 3:1. Up to you. Fill a short glass two-thirds full with **ice.** Add **2 dashes of angostura bitters**, sweet vermouth, and whatever bourbon you like. (We like Buffalo Trace and Maker's.) Add a **maraschino cherry** and crush it against the side of the glass with a spoon. Stir.

Jenny's Gin and Tonic

Fill a large glass two-thirds full with **ice.** Add **1 part gin** to **2 parts fresh tonic**. (Nothing will ruin this drink faster than flat tonic.) Squeeze in the juice from a juicy **lime wedge** and then toss the wedge into your drink. Stir.

Martini

As a general rule, a martini is **4 parts gin or vodka** to **1 part dry vermouth**, but even that might be too much vermouth. Either way, we like ours in a short glass over **ice**, stirred, with an **olive** or two or a lemon twist, or—the best—a pickled ramp from the stash our friend Matt delivers every spring.

Dark & Stormy

Get a decent-size highball glass and pack it full of **ice**. Fill the glass halfway with some good **dark rum**. (We use fifteen-year-old El Dorado from Guyana. And there is always Gosling's.) Then—and this part is crucial—top it off with real **ginger beer**. (We used to use Reed's Extra Ginger Brew, but we've recently switched to Regatta, which hails from Bermuda, where they know from cocktails.) Finally, the **lime.** Don't skimp on the lime! Squeeze two wedges into the glass and discard. Take your third wedge, squeeze it, run the fleshy part once around the rim of the glass, and drop it in. Stir.

November 2004

The Wednesday Wife

Around *this time, I* won the lottery. Not a windfall of cash but, to the working mother, something much, *much* better: After a two-year begging and bribing period that involved a batch of Mexican chocolate icebox cookies, my new boss, Kristin, granted me a four-day work week. I was allowed to be home on Wednesdays. Not *work* from home, not check in via *email* from home, but *be* home. Be around. Pick up the dry cleaning. Drop off the overdue library books. Let one-year-old Abby fall asleep on top of me, stomach to stomach, then nap right along with her. Take the girls to Music Together class and hear everyone sing, "Hell*ooooo* to Mommy . . . so glad to see you!" Pick up Phoebe from preschool and actually meet this friend Evie she liked so much. I could even host a playdate where we'd all bake cookies and the girls could wear those little aprons that still had the sales tags on them. If I wanted to—oh happy day!—I could assemble a black bean salad while the sun was still shining and *allow the flavors to mingle* before dinner.

Seven years later, now that I am home all the time—working from home but still physically *home*—none of these activities seem remotely as exciting to me as they did back then. But when I was commuting to work for forty to fifty hours every week, the idea of approaching the day in an active way (as opposed to the putting-out-fires way) was my idea of heaven. Before I struck my four-day deal, I viewed the endless tasks—dry cleaning, bill paying, doctor visits, gift buying for the relentless birthday party circuit—as foreign combatants determined to destabilize my fragile two-working-parent family. But after I was granted my Wednesdays, I embraced my domestic duties in a way that would've made Carol Brady proud. (And Alice too, since she was the one who actually did all the work.) I'd look forward to organizing the toy closet. I'd savor three-hole punching school handouts for my Master Binder. And usually I'd start the morning by asking Andy what I could do that day to make his life a little easier. Andy called this relaxed, helpful impostor his "Wednesday Wife." I loved that so much. But probably only because I knew she'd be gone by Thursday.

Playdate Cookies

My friend Wendy gave me the recipe for these cookies in an email titled "World's Best Chocolate Chip Cookie." I added M&Ms to transform them into these Playdate Cookies. I find giving little kids the task of placing the M&Ms into the cookie dough scoops is all they need to do to feel included (along with the assignment to lick the bowl, of course). Feel free to replace the M&Ms with a mix of chocolate and peanut butter chips, or stir in some chocolate shavings to the batter. Makes 24 cookies Total time: 30 minutes

1½ cups all-purpose flour

½ teaspoon salt

½ teaspoon baking powder

½ teaspoon baking soda

1 stick (8 tablespoons) unsalted butter, room temperature

1 cup light brown sugar, tightly packed

3 tablespoons white sugar

1 egg

2 teaspoons vanilla extract

½ cup good-quality chocolate chips (such as Ghirardelli)

2 1.69-ounce bags M&Ms

Preheat the oven to 375°F.

In a medium bowl, sift together the flour, salt, baking powder, and baking soda. (It was somewhat life-changing when I found out whisking was just as effective as sifting, so that's what I usually do.) In a separate bowl and using a wooden spoon or electric mixer, cream together the butter and sugars. Add the egg and mix until well combined. Add the vanilla and stir. Using a handheld mixer, add the dry mixture to the wet mixture gradually until all the dry mixture has been worked into the batter. Fold in the chocolate chips. Using your hands or two spoons, scoop small rounds of dough onto the cookie sheet about 2 inches apart from each other. Pour the M&Ms into two small bowls (it's important for each helper to have his or her *own* bowl) and ask the kids to stick the candies into the dough rounds until they are all gone. (Sometimes I use my fingers to make the balls round, then I flatten them slightly—it makes for prettier cookies.) Bake for 8 to 10 minutes, until golden. Cool on a rack.

Pork Dumplings

On any normal weeknight a "project" dinner like this, with its individual dumpling stuffing and sealing, would be unthinkable. Which is exactly why Wednesday Wife seized upon it. The recipe takes a little over 1 hour start to finish. As always, if you are enlisting your toddler, you should assume prep time will increase by about 350 percent. Total time: 1 hour 10 minutes

  1 tablespoon vegetable oil, plus more for frying

  Dash of sesame oil

  3 scallions (white and light green parts), chopped

  1 teaspoon grated peeled fresh ginger

  ¾ to 1 pound ground pork

2 teaspoons Chinese Five Spice

2 tablespoons soy sauce

1 8-ounce can water chestnuts, drained and minced

¼ cup minced fresh cilantro

1 12-ounce pack of wonton wrappers

Add the oils to a large skillet over medium heat and cook the scallions and ginger for about 1 minute.

Add the pork, using a spoon to break it up, and increase the heat to medium-high.

Once most of the pink in the pork is gone, add the Chinese Five Spice, soy sauce, water chestnuts, and cilantro. Let the pork cook for another 2 minutes and remove from heat.

Transfer the filling to a bowl. If you are feeling ambitious, pulse the cooled mixture in the bowl of a large food processor. (This is not necessary, but it lends a nice consistency to the filling and prevents it from being too crumbly and messy when you bite into the dumplings.)

Set up your dumpling-assembling station: a bowl of water, the pork filling, and your wontons.

Dip your fingers in the water and dot or "paint" around the edges of a wonton. (This is an excellent task for the kids.) Spoon a small amount of the pork filling into the center and fold one corner over the opposite corner to make a triangle shape. Pinch all sides together and set aside.

Once all the dumplings are assembled, add a tablespoon of vegetable oil to a large skillet set over medium-high heat. Fry in batches, adding more oil as needed, until dumplings are crispy and golden, about 2 minutes on each side.

Serve the dumplings with dipping sauce and snow peas. Dipping sauce note: Instead of making my own (soy sauce, scallions, fresh lime juice and/or rice wine vinegar), I usually use Soyaki sauce.

Fried Flounder with Black Bean and Avocado Salad

Every time we make this dinner it seems like Andy asks, "Why don't we eat this every night?" The key, as always, is to start with the freshest fish you can find. Flounder is a major player in our family kitchen since it's mild enough for the kids and cooks so quickly. You can assemble the salad 10 minutes before you eat dinner and it will taste good, but if you do it a few hours ahead of time and let all the flavors mingle, it will taste better. **Total time: 40 minutes (25 minutes for the fish; 15 minutes for the bean salad)**

For the Black Bean and Avocado Salad

2 14-ounce cans black beans, rinsed and drained

1 cup halved grape tomatoes

4 to 5 scallions (white and light green parts), minced

½ small jalapeño pepper, minced (about 1 tablespoon)

Juice from 1 large lime (about 2 tablespoons)

¼ cup olive oil

Salt and pepper to taste

Few dashes of hot sauce

Handful of chopped cilantro

1 avocado, cut into cubes

In a medium bowl, combine all ingredients. If you are making this way ahead of time, hold off on cutting and adding the avocado until you are ready to serve, as it will brown if its exposed flesh sits around too long.

For the Flounder

½ cup all-purpose flour (salted and peppered)

2 eggs, lightly beaten

1½ cups panko bread crumbs, salted and peppered
   with ¼ teaspoon cayenne mixed in

Olive oil

1¼ pounds flounder fillets,
   cut with kitchen scissors or a sharp knife
   into sandwich-size pieces, which make them easier to flip

Tartar sauce, for serving

Lemon wedges, for serving

Set up your dredging stations: one rimmed plate for the flour, one rimmed plate for the eggs, and one rimmed plate for the panko.

Heat 3 tablespoons olive oil in a large skillet over medium-high heat.

Dredge your fish fillets: first in the flour, then in the egg, then in the panko. Add two fillets at a time to the skillet and fry 2 to 3 minutes on each side, until cooked through. Remove from the skillet, tent with foil to keep warm, and fry the remaining fillets, adding more oil as necessary.

Serve with a dollop of tartar sauce, lemon wedges, and the black bean and avocado salad.

January 2005

Devika's Roti

In one way, it was too bad we were so adamant about being home to make dinner for the kids because we could've had it so easy—Devika, our babysitter, loved to cook. Often she'd show up at our house on Monday mornings and regale us with stories about the meals she and her husband made for her family and friends over the weekend—feasts that seemed to involve about forty-six more people than we were accustomed to cooking for and that would last until early the next day. You could tell it was hard for her to hang back and not make dinner for the girls, and so occasionally our mandate to save the cooking for us went unheeded. She couldn't help herself. We'd come home to find a big dish of macaroni pie (aka homemade mac and cheese) baking away in the oven, or a platter of Chicken Pizza (aka chicken parm) on the counter, ready to be served to two excited children and two tired, grateful parents.

The best kind of night was when we'd walk in the door and see a few of our dinner plates on the counter covered with overturned pasta bowls. (She didn't like to waste foil.) We knew this meant we were going to be eating curry and roti. Hot, spicy curries—chicken, vegetable, duck—were Devika's signatures. She is from Guyana but of Indian descent, and ever since the day she taught Phoebe how to scoop up curry with homemade roti, Phoebe has demanded heat whenever and wherever possible—red pepper flakes on her pizza, hot sauce on her taco, the jalapeño cheese puffs, not the plain ones. When she got older, at playdates she'd break out chips and salsa for a snack and her friends would invariably come running to me, eyes wide open, mouth on fire, begging for a tall glass of ice water. Abby wasn't quite as daring. She'd eat Devika's curry, but she preferred the roti, the freshly made flatbread that Devika would toss in the air like she worked in a pizza parlor, then fry up in a cast-iron skillet. On extra-special nights, the roti would be stuffed with cooked yellow lentils—or dahl—which is the way Abby and I loved them. So much so that Abby would make me save a piece so she could have it for lunch the next day—with peanut butter spread across it.

Devika's Roti

The best thing about this traditional bread is that you don't have to worry about yeast or long rising times. You can find yellow dahl (dried split yellow peas) at better supermarkets or any Indian or Middle Eastern market. **Total time: 1 hour**

½ cup yellow dahl

1 cup water or vegetable broth

½ teaspoon ground cumin

1 garlic clove

2 cups all-purpose flour

2¼ teaspoons baking powder

½ teaspoon salt

3 tablespoons vegetable oil, plus more for frying

¾ cup warm water

Put the dahl in a medium saucepan, add water, bring to a boil, and cook for 15 minutes, until the peas are soft but still holding their shape.

Drain the dahl and set aside to cool. Once cooled, put the dahl in the work bowl of a food processor with the cumin and garlic (those mini food processors come in handy here) and pulse about ten times. You don't want to puree it; you want the dahl to still have some texture. Set aside.

In a large mixing bowl, combine the flour, baking powder, and salt; add oil, then slowly add the water, and using your hands, begin to knead the dough until it's smooth and pillowy, much like pizza dough. Wrap the dough in plastic wrap and set aside for about 10 minutes.

On a lightly floured surface, use a knife or pastry cutter to divide the dough into 8 or 9 pieces. Form into little balls, and flatten each into a disk.

Take the dahl and fold about 1 tablespoon into each disk, pinching the ends together and rolling back into a ball. Let each ball sit for about 2 minutes.

Using a rolling pin, roll out each ball until thin and about 4 to 5 inches in diameter. (This dough is pretty forgiving and can stand up to lots of pulling and rolling.)

Brush the surface of a large cast-iron or nonstick skillet with oil and heat over medium-high heat. Fry each disk for 5 to 10 seconds on each side. As each roti finishes cooking, fold each one in half twice and place on a plate covered with foil to keep them warm.

Serve warm with "starter curry" (page 14) or eat plain with a good-quality peanut butter if you have a kid who won't touch it otherwise.

Devika's Chicken Pizza

Total time: 30 minutes (with store-bought sauce)

8 pan-fried Breaded Chicken Cutlets (page 11)

½ cup store-bought pizza sauce
    (Don Pepino's is my favorite) or
    homemade pizza sauce (page 271)

1 8-ounce ball fresh mozzarella, sliced

½ cup freshly grated Parmesan cheese

Chopped fresh basil, for garnish

Place the fried chicken cutlets in a baking dish as soon as they are finished. Top each cutlet with a thin layer of pizza sauce (to me, there's nothing worse than gloppy tomato sauce under melted cheese, so don't overdo it), a slice or two of mozzarella, and a sprinkle of Parmesan cheese. Broil for 8 to 10 minutes, until the cheese is melted and golden. Garnish with the basil and serve.

April 2005

You Only Get One of Those

Before Abby was born, Andy, Phoebe, and I attended a wedding on the beach in South Carolina. The day could not have been nicer—blue sky, no humidity, about seventy-five—the bride could not have looked cooler (she wore red satin shoes!), and Phoebe could not have behaved any better. She was about nine months old at the time and she sat on my lap during the entire forty-five-minute ceremony and, I could have sworn, squinted as though in deep reflection during the Khalil Gibran reading. After the bride and groom had done their kissing and everyone stood up to follow them to the reception, a friendly older guy who had been seated in front of us did a little cutchy-cutchy-cooing with Phoebe, complimenting her on her stellar behavior. "Such a sweet little girl! Such big cheeks! Such a wonderful disposition!" My heart swelled as usual, until he turned to me and said, "You only get one of these, you know."

These kinds of knowing comments were really starting to bug me—the kinds where people think their own experience with parenting is going to be exactly like everyone else's. I wasn't even pregnant with Abby yet, but I was offended. Just because this guy had one perfect child and one who was thirty, still living at home, drinking hard lemonade and watching *Twin Peaks* marathons all day and night, didn't mean he had to put all that on me. Right?

"And I'm a pediatrician," he added, *ha ha ha ha ha*, "so I know!" He laughed and put his arm around his wife, who of course also found the whole thing terribly amusing, and they went on their way.

I'd be lying if I said I didn't think of this scene when I was pregnant with Abby. Constantly. When she'd bounce and twirl around in my belly like a sparrow trapped in a small attic. (Had Phoebe been this nuts?) Or a year later, when

Abby was four months old, and she decided two days before I was going to return to work that she was no longer going to drink from a bottle—only breast. (Had Phoebe ever refused?) Or a year after that, when she went on a solid-food strike for five weeks. (I'll never forget Andy calling me at work to announce, in triumph, that she had eaten a piece of pear. Only to spit it up later.) For that harrowing stretch, she basically survived on PediaSure while we carted her from doctor to doctor trying to figure out what the problem was.

There was no problem. She was just Abby. And more to the point, she was not Phoebe. I was doing the same thing the oversimplifying pediatrician had done. Comparing the girls' baby books is one thing, but comparing two babies is another thing entirely. Abby was her own person. Abby was the house comedian. Abby was an Olympic-level dollhouse player. And Abby, sweet, charming Abby, was a freaking nightmare when it came to eating what Phoebe (and later, what her parents) ate for dinner. If ever there existed an open-and-shut case exhibiting nature triumphing over nurture, it was mealtime with Phoebe and Abby.

I'm not going to tell you that we solved the problem immediately, but I do want to say that just because she was a different person from her sister, a different person who often demanded a different parenting style (how is it that a mom's raised voice can cause tears from one child and giggles from the other?) didn't mean I was going to capitulate to our tiny terrorist. I can still picture the way Abby would reject food we'd place in front of her: She'd drum her fingers on the high chair tray and slowly turn her head to the side, raising her chin slightly as she did so. It was nearly impossible to keep my cool in these situations, which, as I now know, is exactly why she did it. People ask us all the time how we managed to get through those tough years with her. The short answer is that we did what everyone does and what you have to do: We just kept plowing ahead. But when I look back, there were several other factors that might have helped turn her around. I like to think of these factors as rules for not losing your mind when you are living with and cooking for a picky eater.

How to Triumph over a Tiny Table Terrorist
(or, How Not to Lose Your Mind When
Cooking for a Picky Eater)

1. Hang back. This was a lesson learned the hard way. When Abby was on the Great Food Strike of 2004, this is what we heard from the poor souls who happened to come visit during mealtime. *Don't worry so much. She'll eat when she's hungry! Why are you making yourself so crazy? She'll eventually get too hungry to refuse.* Wow, did these comments make me angry. Even though experts the world over warned against turning feeding time into a power struggle, I dare you to just hang back and relax when your kid eats one bite of pear over the course of an entire month. It was impossible not to worry. It was impossible not to chase her around the house with a pint of Ben & Jerry's. One night we thought we had her right where we wanted her: starving and strapped into her high chair at the kitchen table, a piece of crispy pan-fried white fish flaked into little bites on her little melamine plate. I started feeding her and was astounded when she kept opening up her mouth for more. Andy and I looked at each other, too nervous to say anything for fear of jinxing our good fortune. We should have known better. After about five voracious bites, we realized she was just storing the fish in her cheeks like a squirrel—she somehow knew it would be more dramatic to spit it out all at once than reject the fish in pieces.

Couldn't she see how frustrated we were? Why would she do this to her poor parents who were disintegrating right before her eyes? Because, to a sixteen-month-old, I imagine this sight was probably very entertaining. And also: Because she could. When we finally stopped obsessing over Abby's eating, we did so more out of sheer exhaustion than because of any clear-headed decision-making process. As soon as we let go of our anxiety, she was forced to come up with new ways to torture us—I mean entertain herself—and things gradually become more pleasant at feeding time. To this day, she's not a quantity girl (unless we are talking Japanese food, in which case she eats us all under the table), but she will eat almost anything if it's presented the right way. (See The Marketing Plan, page 166.)

2. Enlist them. You've no doubt heard from many an expert that if you cook with your child, he or she will be more invested in the meal and therefore more likely to eat that meal with gusto. When the girls were older—about five and six—I would discover the wisdom behind these words. But at this stage, when I was dealing with a two- and three-year-old, I couldn't think of anything less appealing than enlisting help from the kids when it came time to measure the oil or stir the batter. (Stirring and pouring are the only tasks toddlers are capable of, and even these require strict supervision while you are busy burning your garlic.) My feeling was that enlisting the kids' help with cooking chicken was ensuring that 100 percent of dinnertime would be frustrating instead of just the usual 50 percent in which you'd be struggling to convince the kid to eat. We preferred lower maintenance methods of personal investment. Like grocery shopping. We found that when they came with us to Trader Joe's and were given the task of picking out their peppers or whole wheat tortillas or Soyaki sauce (we call this "fairy dust" in our house because it will transform any food into an edible one for Abby), that was investment enough. It also helped to show them cookbooks with beautiful photographs. If they had a sense of what a new dish would look like before it was set before them, it took a little of the anxiety out of the equation. It was even better when we let them point to the photo of the meal they wanted to eat for dinner—that way, it made them accountable, that is, they shouldered the blame (or accepted the credit) when it came time to reject it or eat it.

3. Build Their Adventure Muscles. This lesson was the happy byproduct of an essay I wrote for *Cookie* called "30 Days, 30 Dinners." I wrote the story in the middle of a particularly brutal winter when a confluence of factors (too much work, not enough sunshine) resulted in a depressing stretch of uninspired dinners. After noticing how many one-word meal descriptions I was recording in the diary—*Cutlets, Pasta, Pizza*—I decided to break the cycle with a mission called Operation 30 Days. The goal was to try to cook a brand-new dinner every night for a month—brand-new to me and Andy, and brand-new to the girls. If, at the end of thirty days, we only added six keepers to the list, I didn't care. At least we'd be exposing them to new things, and, more important, giving our dinners a shot of much-needed inspiration.

For the kids, we spun the project as a Big Fun Experiment (!!!) with only one rule: They had to try a single bite of something new every night. And if they stopped at one bite? No problem! Every meal was built around one food the girls liked, so we knew we could always extract, de-sauce, or decontaminate individual ingredients to their liking. (See Rule 4: Deconstruct.)

The next month was spent shaking off all the dust that had settled around our dinner ritual: We began texting back and forth about lamb chop preparation during the commute home (a ritual that would get us through many more dinners in the future); we busted out the rolling pin and enlisted the girls' help in shaping homemade tortillas; we broke through Phoebe's soup barrier with a fifteen-minute fish stew; we discovered that kids cannot only defy all expectations and enjoy Brussels sprouts, but that they are also capable of pounding their utensils on the table demanding we serve Brussels sprouts to them every night from that night on . . . *pinky promise Mommy?*

Forming a meal into letters and words also helps the effort!

In the end, out of thirty recipes, only about five of the dishes became part of our regular rotation—but the meals themselves were almost beside the point. For Andy and me, the process of seeking out the best recipe for shrimp curry or rolling out homemade tortillas for fish tacos was crucial for getting *us* excited about cooking dinner again—for putting the love back in the love story. And for the girls, trying new dishes was crucial for flexing what I now call their well-developed adventure muscles. In other words, it was great that the experiment ignited an enduring love for lamb chops, but it was even greater that by the end of the month, they were approaching the table open to the idea of trying something new—*expecting* to try something new. Four years later, as the children of food bloggers ("Operation 365 Days a Year") they do this now without thinking. Though, in the case of quinoa, polenta, and mushrooms, not always without complaining.

Lamb Chops

Total time: 10 minutes

> 3 pounds single-cut lamb chops (or about 3 per kid; 4 per grown-up)
>
> Salt and pepper
>
> Olive oil

Bring the lamb chops to room temperature and sprinkle liberally with salt and pepper. Heat a stovetop grill or a cast-iron pan brushed with a small amount of olive oil over medium-high heat. Cook, turning fairly frequently, for a total of 5 to 6 minutes.

Chicken with Bacon-y Brussels Sprouts

Total time: 35 minutes

2 strips bacon

4 to 6 chicken breasts (about 1¼ pounds),
   pounded to ¼-inch thickness (see sidebar, page 12),
   and seasoned with salt and pepper

2 tablespoons olive oil

½ onion, chopped

Salt and pepper

About ½ pound Brussels sprouts, trimmed and
   roughly chopped (if it's easy to shred them
   in a food processor, this works too)

½ cup chicken broth

In a medium skillet set over medium heat, fry the bacon until crispy. Remove the bacon from the heat and drain a little of the fat from the pan.

Turn up the heat to medium-high and brown the chicken, about 2 minutes on each side. (It does not have to cook through.) Remove from the pan.

Add the oil, onion, and salt and pepper and cook until the onion is soft, about 3 minutes. Add the Brussels sprouts, toss with the onions, and cook about 1 minute. Nestle the chicken breasts in the vegetables, add the broth, and bring to a boil. Once it boils, reduce the heat to a simmer, cover, and cook another 10 minutes, until chicken is cooked through. Crumble the bacon on top.

Orecchiette with Sausage and Crispy Broccoli

Total time: 35 minutes

3½ cups broccoli florets, trimmed

4 tablespoons olive oil, plus more to taste

Kosher salt and pepper to taste

1 pound orecchiette

2 links sweet Italian sausage, casings removed

½ cup grated Parmesan cheese, plus more for serving

1 tablespoon butter

4 heaping tablespoons ricotta (optional)

Preheat the oven to 425°F.

Line a baking dish with foil, add the broccoli, and using a spoon, toss with 3 tablespoons of the oil and salt and pepper. Roast for 15 minutes, or until broccoli looks crispy but not completely brown.

Meanwhile, make the pasta according to the package directions. Strain the orecchiette, reserving ½ cup of the pasta liquid.

Add remaining tablespoon oil to a large skillet set over medium-high heat. Brown the sausage, breaking it up with a fork, until cooked, 5 to 7 minutes. Add half of the reserved pasta water to the skillet and turn heat to high; cook, stirring, until it looks emulsified and saucy. Add the pasta, Parmesan cheese, and butter to the skillet and toss with tongs until everything is evenly distributed, adding more pasta water to loosen as necessary. Divide into four bowls and top with crispy broccoli—if your kids allow it—a little more freshly grated Parmesan cheese, and a dollop of ricotta if you are feeling indulgent.

Salmon salad (page 62), deconstructed.

4. Deconstruct. How many exposures to a new piece of food do those experts say a kid needs before she tries it? Twenty? Twenty-five? Thirty? Whatever the number, we'd regularly exceed it with Abby. She'd turn her nose up at the avocado and shredded cheddar and sour cream when it came time to top her chicken tacos. But there was always something on the table that we knew she'd eat—in this case the chicken and the hard taco shell, separately—no questions asked. Because of Abby, we were forced to develop a style of eating called "Deconstructed Dinner," which I write about all the time on my blog and which saved our asses (or at least our dinners) during Abby's stubborn phase. This is not rocket science, it's exactly what it sounds like: You take a favorite meal like Salmon Salad on page 62 and serve it in its individual components (as shown in photo) so the kids can pick what they like before any green specks or offensive sauces get mixed in. This helped tremendously on the nights when we attempted to sit down together, which we were only attempting on the weekends at this point. Not only did deconstructing allow the rest of us to eat our dinners the way they were "supposed" to be eaten, but it *showed* Abby the way her dinner was supposed to be eaten. Were there times that we just boiled a Hebrew National for her while all of us ate our cobb salads? Of course—a *lot* of times—but we stuck to our guns enough for her to slowly expand her repertoire. Does she inhale duck curry like Phoebe? Does she, like Phoebe, literally cheer "yay" when I announce that we're having black bean burritos? Will she ever eat as enthusiastically and widely as Phoebe? Who knows. Probably not. And anyway, what fun would that be?

Taco Soup

To make this soup for Abby, we would remove the chicken from the soup and put it on a plate with chips, cheese, and avocado even though she rarely touched the avocado. (But we could add a tick in the Exposure column.) To make this even faster, you can use rotisserie chicken. Just decrease simmering time to 10 minutes and add shredded meat during the last 5 minutes. (Then use the chicken carcass to make the homemade stock on page 289!) Total time: 35 minutes

2 chicken boneless breasts (about ¾ pound), rinsed and patted dry

1 tablespoon canola or vegetable oil

½ onion, chopped

1 garlic clove, minced

½ jalapeño pepper, minced

Salt and pepper

4 cups chicken broth

1 dried chile pepper

1 15-ounce can hominy
(found in the international section of your supermarket)

Juice from 1 lime (about 2 tablespoons)

Various toppings: tortilla chips, avocado chunks,
shredded cheddar cheese
(the cheese should not be considered optional)

Brown the chicken in a medium saucepan, about 2 minutes on each side. (It does not have to be cooked through.) To the same pan, add oil and sauté the onion, garlic, jalapeño pepper, and salt and pepper over medium heat for about 3 minutes.

Add the broth, chile pepper, and hominy and bring to a boil. Reduce the heat and simmer for 15 minutes. Remove the chicken from the pot and shred using two forks. Add the shreds back to the pot and simmer for another 5 minutes.

Ladle the soup servings into bowls, then squeeze lime into each bowl add and the toppings.

Grilled Chicken Mediterranean Plate

In the summer, if we're grilling chicken (page 264), we always make twice as much so we can have this quick-to-assemble dinner the next night. It's healthy, flavorful, and, like all great summer meals, does not require an oven, stovetop, or toaster. You can also use a store-bought rotisserie chicken. **Total time: 5 minutes**

4 whole wheat pocketless pita rounds

1 16-ounce container hummus (I like original creamy—none
   of that weird jalapeño or sun-dried tomato action)

1½ cups cooked chicken, shredded or chopped

1 cup crumbled feta

1 Japanese cucumber (the kind that come shrink-wrapped),
   chopped and lightly salted

Fresh herbs, such as thyme or oregano

Olive oil

Freshly ground black pepper

Place the pita rounds on four separate plates. (Or, if you have an Abby, tear the pitas into pieces.) Spread a generous layer of hummus on each pita and top with chicken, feta, cucumber, the herbs, a drizzle of oil, and pepper.

Two-bowl Chopped Salads

This is not so much a recipe as it is a strategy. The idea is that you chop your favorite salad ingredients up into a fine dice, and distribute them among two bowls as you go: "the Definitely Bowl" (to hold everything you know the kids will eat) and "the Maybe Bowl" (to hold anything with deal-breaker potential for the kids). This is a go-to meal for us in the summer when the vegetables are so fresh it kills you to waste a single bite. The key to the chopped salad is, not surprisingly, the fine chop. You want to be able to experience as many different tastes in one bite as possible. Another good rule to keep in mind: You should aim to include something sweet (like fruit), something salty (like feta or bacon), and something crunchy (celery, snap peas, sunflower seeds). Play around with combinations until you find the ones you like.

Set two medium bowls on the counter. Designate one the Maybe Bowl and one the Definitely Bowl. Chop any of the following ingredients and distribute them into the appropriate bowl. Toss with the Basic Vinaigrette (page 163) after everyone has been served.

* Tomatoes

* Corn off the cob

* Kale, destemmed, boiled for 2 minutes, then drained

* Shredded poached chicken

* Cooked bacon

* Sugar snap peas

* Peppers

* Green beans, boiled for 2 minutes

* Bacon

* Hard-boiled eggs

* Asparagus

* Avocados

* Shallots or scallions

* Fruit, such as apples or peaches

* Nuts, such as walnuts, almonds, sunflower seeds

* Fresh herbs, such as chives, thyme, mint, cilantro, basil, parsley

* Cheese, such as feta, blue, Parmesan, Pecorino, cheddar

Basic Vinaigrette

1 tablespoon Dijon mustard

4 tablespoons red or white wine vinegar

Squeeze of honey

Squeeze of fresh lemon

Salt and pepper

Chopped fresh herbs, such as chives, parsley, dill, thyme

½ cup good-quality olive oil

Whisk together all of the ingredients.

Riffs

For Creamy Dressing: Add a tablespoon of **mayonnaise**.

For Balsamic Vinaigrette: Replace red wine vinegar with **balsamic vinegar**.

For Garlic Vinaigrette: Add 1 teaspoon **minced garlic**.

For Citrus Vinaigrette: Replace the wine vinegar with 1 tablespoon each of **fresh lime juice** and **fresh orange juice**, and up the lemon juice to 1 tablespoon.

TO: Postwork Jenny
FROM: Prework Jenny
RE: Family Dinner, Making It Happen
DATE: July 9, 2004

LETTER OF AGREEMENT

I, Prework Jenny, would like to take this opportunity to thank you, Postwork Jenny, for committing to a home-cooked meal tonight. This letter of agreement will provide our terms regarding the event (henceforth referred to as "FAMILY DINNER").

This confirms my commitment to initiate the process of FAMILY DINNER before I leave for a day of doing things I don't feel like doing (henceforth referred to as "WORK"). Said list of processes may include, but are not limited to: deciding what the main dish is, transferring any appropriate product from the freezer to the fridge to allow to thaw (including, but not limited to, raw meat, premade sauces), chopping 2 (two) medium onions, marinating chicken, chopping red potatoes into a medium dice and soaking in water to prevent browning, filling a pot of water and setting it on the stovetop burner, because it's the law that you always end up needing a pot of boiling water for dinner. My commitment will be for the duration 8:00 a.m. to 8:03 a.m.

Your commitment will be for the duration 6:30 p.m. to 7:15 p.m. and will be to (a) walk in the door on time and (b) close the FAMILY DINNER deal.

If FAMILY DINNER is canceled or postponed due to unforeseen events regarding stalled trains and/or chatty officemates at WORK, I reserve the sole discretion to make you feel really, really guilty. Guiltier even than when you missed Music Together last week. If you agree to the terms, please sign and send a duplicate copy of this letter to me before you leave. And don't forget your breast pump.

Sincerely,
Pre-Work Jenny

Jenny

Buttermilk Oven-fried Chicken with Rainbow Salad

....

Total time: 45 minutes

    4 cups buttermilk

    2 tablespoons Dijon mustard

    4 garlic cloves, halved

    6 to 8 chicken drumsticks, skin on

    Cooking spray

    1½ cups plain Kellogg's Corn Flake Crumbs,
       salted and peppered

    1 teaspoon dried oregano

    Leaves from 1 sprig fresh thyme

    ½ teaspoon cayenne

    Salt and black pepper

Before you go to work: In a bowl, whisk together the buttermilk, mustard, and garlic. Add to a large zipper-lock plastic bag with the chicken pieces. Refrigerate for at least 30 minutes and up to 12 hours.

When you walk in the door: Preheat the oven to 400°F. Line a large shallow baking sheet with foil and coat lightly with cooking spray. In a large bowl, combine the corn flake crumbs, herbs, cayenne, and salt and pepper.

Pull the chicken pieces out of the marinade, letting the excess drip off. Dredge each drumstick in the bread crumbs until well coated and then place on baking sheet. Spray the pieces lightly with cooking oil. Bake until golden and cooked through, 35 to 40 minutes. Serve with Rainbow Salad (page 166).

Rainbow Salad

You (and your kids) have probably heard by now that the easiest way to tell if a meal is healthy is by checking to see how many colors are represented—the plate should look like a rainbow. That's how we came up with this salad. Every color on the spectrum is represented: red **(pepper)**, orange **(pepper)**, yellow **(frozen corn)**, green **(peas)**, purple **(cabbage)**. I make it with mostly corn because that is the big draw for the girls. Just finely chop the peppers and cabbage, heat everything in a small saucepan with a little water for about 5 minutes and then add **butter** and **salt**.

September 2005

The Marketing Plan

When *Jessica Seinfeld's book* came out—the one that told us to hide vegetable purees in our kids' food (including dessert) if we were having trouble getting them to eat nutritiously—there was a lot of resistance from parents who felt it was the easy way out and, in the long run, counterproductive to healthy eating. How would a kid learn to choose spinach for himself if he had only ever eaten it pureed into his chocolate fudge brownie? I'd like to take this high-and-mighty stance myself, but the truth is, I find it's almost impossible to feed a kid without employing some sort of trickery or, as I've sometimes heard it referred to in the business pages, marketing.

It is amazing how many marketing principles apply directly to feeding children. (A warning: Success rates are all relative. Do not expect your kid to inhale his broccoli by commanding "Just Do It.") I'm not just talking about using the heart-shaped cookie cutter on the PBJ; I'm talking about strategies for how to roll

out a new food, how to package and rebrand old foods into new ones, how to personalize it so your customer—I mean child—feels special and comes back for more. Here are the main principles we employ on a weekly, sometimes daily basis.

Spinning and Packaging. Like most parents, we figured out pretty quickly that so much of launching a new food in the marketplace, aka the family dinner table, depends on how you spin it. I doubt our kids would have gone within a mile of cauliflower had we not first introduced it to them as "white broccoli." They wouldn't have tasted Brussels sprouts had we not sold them relentlessly as "baby lettuces." Same goes for baked beans ("sweet beans"), yellow and orange bell peppers ("rainbow peppers"), and on and on. I think our most genius move to date has been repackaging fish en papillote as "fish presents." Fish en papillote is a complete meal (protein-veg-starch) that is wrapped up in parchment paper like a gift, then baked, then presented on the plate still in its little package. The kids could hardly believe their luck the first time this showed up on the table. Especially since Andy had built up the suspense as expertly as Steve Jobs might have when releasing Apple's latest change-your-life product.

"Dad, what's for dinner?"

"A present."

"What?"

"A present. I'm giving you a present for dinner."

"But it's not my birthday!"

"Doesn't matter—you deserve it anyway."

"Well, what is it?"

"You're going to have to wait to find out."

When we finally placed the little packages onto their plates and opened them up (we had to do the opening part since the trapped steam inside is *really* hot), we had two girls who were pretty damned excited to eat fish and cabbage. I like to think this is because we took a meal that was unfamiliar (read: scary) and turned it into an adventure, an experience, something a four- and five-year-old might relate to better than a meal whose sole purpose is to provide a vehicle for protein and fiber.

Fish Presents

Total time: 30 to 35 minutes

¼ cup olive oil

Few dashes of red pepper flakes

1½ pounds fish fillets
   (gray sole, flounder, salmon, tilapia, sea bass, snapper)

3 small potatoes (any kind except baking potatoes),
   unpeeled and very thinly sliced

1 lemon, sliced horizontally

½ medium red onion or 1 shallot, sliced

Green vegetables, such as 10 baby bok choy
   (which have been boiled in salted water for 2 minutes),
   10 to 12 asparagus spears, 2 dozen haricots verts,
   or 1 cup stemmed, chopped kale

Chopped fresh herbs, such as chives, parsley, or cilantro

Sesame oil (optional)

Salt and pepper

Preheat the oven to 400°F.

Pour the olive oil into a measuring cup and add the red pepper flakes. Lay down four 15 x 15-inch squares of parchment paper or foil and place 1 fish fillet on top of each sheet. Top each with a few slices of potato, lemon, onion, and desired vegetables and then drizzle with spicy olive oil. (You can use plain olive oil, too, if you want to avoid heat.) Top each packet with fresh herbs, a dash of sesame oil (optional), and salt and pepper.

Next, wrap the presents (see below): Lift the sides of the parchment paper until they meet above the fish. Turn down a few times and fold the ends under the fish—picture the way the deli guy wraps a sandwich—creating a seal so the steam doesn't escape. Slide the presents onto a cookie sheet and bake for 20 minutes. (It's hard to overcook the fish when steaming it like this.) Remove from the oven and serve one present per plate. Be careful when unwrapping, though: Steam is hot.

HOW TO MAKE FISH PRESENTS

1. Place fish and vegetables in center of paper.

2. Pull up sides together, then roll down edges until it lays flat on the fish.

3. Fold overhang underneath bundle.

4. Place fish present on cookie sheet.

Branding. A couple years ago, Andy's brother Tony invited us over for a barbecue. He was serving steak, a food that Phoebe would reliably gobble up as though it were a Hershey bar and that Abby would reliably never deign to touch. Tony marinated a flank steak forever in teriyaki sauce, grilled it, then thinly sliced it. Abby was, of course, skeptical. We begged her and tried to reason with her and explained how steak was exactly like a hamburger, only sliced instead of chopped, blah, blah, blah—can't you see that?—and finally bribed her—I mean *incentivized* her ("You want ice cream tonight, right?")—to have a bite, one bite . . . at which point her stubborn little mind was blown. She had seconds, then thirds, and Tony's Steak was born. When we tried to re-create it at our own house we skipped the teriyaki sauce in favor of a marinade that somehow achieved the perfect balance between sweet and salty, but we still called the finished product Tony's Steak. Without even the tiniest bit of shame. And we will do it forever if we have to. If I'm not mistaken, I think that's called creating brand loyalty. And by the way, *re-branding* is also highly effective strategy. Remember those basic chicken cutlets from chapter 1 (page 11) that I have been eating my whole life? Appropriately, the girls first ate them at my mom's house, so they were rebranded "Grandma Jody's Chicken." No matter what I do to the dish (like add brain-boosting ground flax to the bread crumbs or serve Milanese-style with a vinegary arugula and tomato salad on top), when I call it Grandma Jody's Chicken, it goes down the hatch. In your own kitchen, you might consider slicing the cutlets into thirds and calling them "Chicken Fingers."

Tony's Steak

Total time: 2 to 4 hours (most of which is marinating time)

⅓ cup soy sauce

1 tablespoon brown sugar

1 tablespoon olive oil

1 teaspoon dark sesame oil

½ cup chopped scallions (white and light green parts)

1 garlic clove, chopped

1 teaspoon hot sauce

Juice from 1 lime (about 2 tablespoons)

Salt and pepper

1 flank steak (about 2 pounds)

Add everything to a large zipper-lock plastic bag, seal it, and marinate in the refrigerator for 2 to 4 hours (closer to 4 is better). When it's time to grill, cook the steak 4 to 5 minutes on each side, flipping frequently (or stick under the broiler for 4 to 5 minutes on each side), keeping in mind that flank steak is thin, and it's easy to overcook. Remove and let sit for 10 minutes before cutting. Slice on the bias against the grain, as shown at right.

Customizing. I once heard a marketing guru give a self-helpy speech at a Direct Mail and Database Marketing convention in Des Moines. (In case you are wondering, this convention was every bit as scintillating as it sounds.) This was probably fifteen years ago and while I don't really remember exactly what the theme of the guru's speech was, I do remember how he began it. "What's the sweetest word in the English language?" he asked, stretching the moment out as he sauntered

across the stage in his slightly sheened, well-tailored suit, which I'm pretty sure held a pocket square. A few brave audience members wagered guesses, but none got it right.

"The sweetest word in the English language is your customer's *name!*" He pounded his fist on the podium when he said the word *name*. "If you remember nothing else from this speech, please remember that."

So I can make fun of this guy's liberal use of the phrase "abundance mentality," but I have to admit that I said a silent prayer of thanks to him and his marketing-speak on the day Abby took her first bite of chicken pot pie. It was the same pot pie I had made for Laurie way back when (page 33), the same pot pie I had probably baked three dozen times in the past decade, but for Abby, who had always declined to try one bite, it was something different. That's because this time I had fashioned the letter *A* out of extra crust and stuck it on top of her mini pie. (I had also used ramekins instead of the regular 9-inch plate to maximize the appeal.) The look of delight on her face upon spying her very own, made expressly for her, monogrammed mini chicken pot pie was enough to erase all those years of rejection.

Monogrammed Mini Pot Pies

Total time: 1 hour

Cut **1 store-bought pie crust** (such as Pillsbury or Trader Joe's) into four pieces. Follow the pot pie filling instructions on page 33. Once the filling is ready, spoon it into four ramekins and cover them with the quartered dough, pinching it around the sides to seal. Using a sharp knife, trim the crust on each ramekin, leaving only about a half inch of overhang. This should leave you a few scraps of extra crust. Combine all the scraps into a ball, then roll into a skinny snake. Shape your strand into the appropriate initial, then place on top of your pie. Brush with lightly beaten egg and then bake 15 to 20 minutes in a 425°F oven until crust is golden and filling is bubbly.

A is for Abby: Monogrammed Mini Pot Pies

March 2006

. . . .

The Onion Trick

Over the years, I'm sure my mother has told me a lot of stories about Joan, her best friend from college—whom I've only met a handful of times—but there's only one story that has stuck with me and that I think about almost on a nightly basis. Or at least a weekly basis. It's the onion trick story.

When Joan first got married, she was expected to cook. Which would've been fine except for one problem—she hated to cook. And because this was forty-five years ago, before women actively embraced the role of *not* cooking, she was routinely figuring out ways to pretend she was cooking so her husband wouldn't be disappointed by her complete antipathy toward the kitchen. This is why she started chucking an onion into a 350°F degree oven an hour before he came home from work. Even if she had no use for that onion in the meal she would ultimately make and eat, she felt better knowing her husband was walking into a house permeated by the smell that signaled soups and stews, roasts and braises—meals that require clocking some serious hours in the kitchen. I never did find out what happened at dinnertime, when she'd serve him something that was more likely inspired by Peg Bracken (author of the legendary *I Hate to Cook Cookbook*) or a pouch of Lipton onion soup mix.

I love this story so much and have been known to employ Joan's onion trick at holiday parties that are 100 percent outsourced. (Is there anything more depressing than showing up to a party and not smelling the food?) I'm also proud to say that I've also come up with my very own onion trick over the years, albeit a little more practical. It goes like this:

When I have no idea what I'm going to make for dinner, I start caramelizing an onion and then assume a meal will fall into place from there.

Because when you cook onion slices over low heat for even just 15 minutes, you know you have the start of something special for dinner. The onions, which get all silky and candy sweet, elevate almost any ordinary meal—whether you stuff them into an omelet, sandwich them inside a turkey burger, or heap them on top of pasta pizza or baked potatoes. And most important, your home will smell like you know what you're doing.

How to Caramelize an Onion

In a large skillet set over low heat, add 3 to 4 good glugs of olive oil. Add 2 to 3 onions, sliced, to the pan and cook for at least 15 minutes and up to 45, stirring every few minutes. During the last few minutes, add a small drizzle of balsamic vinegar.

September 2006
Entertaining, Part 2

 e made the mistake of sending out invitations to our Eighth Annual Holiday Party (in 2004) with "Kids Are Welcome!" across the bottom of the card. It was our second holiday party in our new house, but the year before, we kept the guest list manageable (read: we hadn't made any new local friends—either the little or grown-up kind) and Abby was only two months old so it was easy to pass her around like a football to anyone who would take her. The next year, though, we thought it would be "fun" to invite families. It would make it easier for our guests (no need to book a sitter) and also Phoebe and Abby would enjoy themselves more since they could hang out with their friends, too. There was, of course, a small problem with this theory: Abby had just celebrated her first birthday and her idea of hanging out with friends was to hang around my neck and cry if I tried to have a conversation with my friends. Not that this was even a possibility considering that my friends who had brought *their* kids (thanks, Jenny!) looked just as relaxed and festive as I felt.

That was the first time I learned the rule that when entertaining, one kid under five counts for five times as many adults in terms of volume and energy—and I couldn't hack it. It was our Eighth and Final Annual Holiday Party. We consoled ourselves by saying we'd start up the tradition again when the kids were older or at least until they were able to restrain themselves from fighting over the green M&M cookie in the holiday dessert spread or spilling nail polish all over our new rug. In the meantime, we'd just have small dinner parties instead.

And by small, I meant one couple, no kids. That went for our kids, too. During this period, if all went according to plan, the girls were bathed and pajamaed before our dinner guests even rang the doorbell. It wasn't that we worried about them being unruly or unpresentable, or that we feared Phoebe would pillage the crostini plate (okay, maybe we did worry about that). It was more that usually the people we'd have over for dinner were parents of young kids, too. Parents who had already spent the waking part of their day doing what parents do—suffering through another *Teletubbies* marathon, doling out snacks, pretending to lose at Pretty Pretty Princess—and probably didn't feel a real powerful urge to spend valuable babysitting hours doing the same with our kids.

This meant that call time for the guests was on the later side—around eight o'clock—which gave them a chance to say hi to the kids, then move on to the real reason for the party: to have a cocktail and eat something that didn't call for ketchup on the side. So while one of us would shepherd Phoebe and Abby through their bedtime paces—book, backrub, kiss—the other would put the final touches on dinner, which was, for the most part, already done.

That was the other important part of our entertaining strategy (and, actually, still is). We knew that if we were going to ask parents to come at eight, we couldn't start dinner *after* the kids went to bed. We had to start earlier—like four hours earlier with some kind of meat braising in a Dutch oven. If the dinner party occurred anytime between October and the first day of spring, there was about a 90 percent chance that the Dutch oven contained Andy's pork shoulder ragù, which we'd serve on top of pappardelle and which you may have gathered by now might just be my favorite meal in this entire book. It's particularly ideal for a fall or winter night: It's warm and hearty, it makes the house smell insanely good, and it goes well with red wine. Best of all, when everyone is *oohing* and *ahhing* over every bite, we could almost forget—for a few hours, at least—that there were plastic Cinderella shoes strewn about the living room and that we all had to be awake before sunrise the next morning to perform sock puppet shows.

Pork Shoulder Ragù with Pappardelle

Serves 6   Total time: 3½ to 4½ hours (includes 3 to 4 hours braising time)

Because this is pork, it goes well with a salad that has a little sweetness to help cut the porkiness. Greens with apples and shaved fennel? Greens with pistachios and pomegranates? Either would be good. Also, this serves about six normal-size people (or four parents and four kids). If you are cooking for more than that, cook another pound of pasta, up the meat to 3 pounds, and add a few more tomatoes and another ½ cup of red wine. Like all braised meats, it's nearly impossible to get wrong, so don't get too hung up on the exactness of measurements.

> 1 boneless or bone-in pork shoulder roast
>   (about 2 to 2½ pounds)
>
> Salt and pepper

This is our go-to, what we call our dinner party in a pot. Serve over pasta, serve on buns. Also makes the house smell extremely good.

2 tablespoons olive oil, plus more for drizzling

1 tablespoon butter

1 small onion, chopped

1 garlic clove, minced

1 28-ounce can whole or chopped tomatoes,
   with juice

1 cup red wine, plus more as needed

5 sprigs fresh thyme

5 sprigs fresh oregano

Small handful of fennel seeds

1 tablespoon hot sauce, for smokiness (we use Trader Joe's hot chili sauce)

1 pound pappardelle

Freshly grated Parmesean cheese

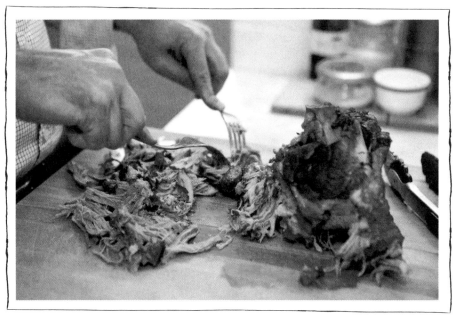

Braise this pork long enough and no cutting is required. Simply get two forks and start pulling.

Preheat the oven to 325°F.

Dry the pork with paper towels and liberally salt and pepper all over. Add the oil and butter to a large Dutch oven and heat over medium-high heat until the butter melts but does not burn. Add the pork roast to the pan and brown it on all sides, 8 to 10 minutes in all.

Add the onion and garlic and sauté for 1 minute. Add the tomatoes, wine, thyme, oregano, fennel, and hot sauce and bring to a boil. Cover and put in the oven. Braise for 3 to 4 hours, turning every hour or so. Add more liquid—water or wine—if needed. (No matter what size pot you are using, the liquid should come to at least one-third of the way up the pork.) The meat is done when it's practically falling apart. Remove the pork to a cutting board, pull it apart with two forks, and then add the pulled meat back to the pot and stir. Remove the herb sprigs.

Cook the pasta according to package directions. When it's ready, put it into individual bowls and top with ragù, lots of Parmesan cheese, and a drizzle of oil.

✳ *Tip:* The Braised Beef Short Ribs (page 40) are great for this kind of entertaining, too.

PULLING OFF A DINNER PARTY
WITH CHILDREN UNDERFOOT

The Schedule

4:00 p.m. One of us starts the pork ragù (page 179) while the other tries to break a record for number of times Dr. Seuss's *Oobleck* can be read in one twelve-hour stretch.

6:30 p.m. Make the kids' dinner. We either give them a few shreds of meat pulled from the pork (it will be edible but not optimal) or, more likely, pull a Trader Joe's pizza out of the freezer.

7:00 p.m. Bathtime begins. One of us gets the kids clean and dressed. If there's any other part of the bedtime routine that can be checked off the list—more *Oobleck* reading, teeth brushing—we check it off the list. While this is going on, the other parent is downstairs assembling the cheese plate, making the salad or side dish, stacking up a pile of plates and utensils, and setting a large pasta pot filled with water on the stovetop. (I am of the belief that there is no task too small to do in advance.)

8:00 p.m. Guests arrive. We introduce them to our beautiful, clean kids! If either daughter has any show-pony trick up her sleeve (hula-hooping, Taylor Swift lip-synching, jump-roping), we do our best to convince them to go for it. We make sure to set out starters and offer our patient guests a strong cocktail during this portion of the program. (Andy is of the belief that this should be a Manhattan; page 137)

8:25 p.m. One of us starts boiling the pasta water.

8:30 p.m. Kids go to bed. One of us heads to the bedroom with the kids and attempts to convince them that the most recent reading of *Oobleck* was their bedtime story. This never ever works. On most nights we read each daughter one book, but on this "very special night," we read one book to both at the same time. (When the girls got older, on nights like this, we also let them sleep over in each other's rooms to minimize the chances of them complaining about bedtime.)

8:40 p.m. Lights out. We trade places: the parent who is with the guests heads upstairs and plants as many bedtime kisses onto foreheads as necessary while the other sets the table. (Note: We do not like to ever leave our guests without at least one host around.) If the stars align, we don't hear from the kids until five thirty or six the next morning.

8:45 p.m. We add the pasta to the boiling water and shred the pork for the ragù.

9:00 p.m. We dish up some pasta with ragù and cheese, place the salad bowl on the table so guests can serve themselves, open up a bottle of Barbera, make a feeble attempt to talk about what's going on in the wider world outside our homes, before all four of us come around to discussing our charming, sleeping children.

Family Dinner

{
or, the

years the

angels began

to sing
}

I spent a lot of time in the first few years of our daughters' lives reading about—sometimes obsessing over—milestones that they hit and missed. How could I not? Every visit to the pediatrician was like report card day: Is she smiling? Is she sleeping through the night? Is she pulling herself up? Is she pointing? ("She *must* be pointing by twelve months," said one clipboard-wielding doctor with a seriousness that scared me.) How many teeth? What percentile? (God, how we hated percentiles.) We stressed about milestones they "missed" and celebrated like crazy over milestones they achieved ahead of the curve. (I'm sure the word *gifted* was thrown around after we saw eight-week-old Phoebe following that spinning mobile with her eyes.) There were milestones I looked forward to—when we could turn their car seats to the forward-facing position. And there were milestones that left me feeling bereft—getting down to the last bag of frozen breast milk a few weeks after I had weaned Abby. I was surprised by how hard it was to say good-bye to that era of lugging ice packs and bottles back and forth to work, where I'd pump behind my closed office door. A Post-it that said *Just a minute, please* switched places from the front of the door to the back of it all day long, and I still have the note stuck on a page in Phoebe's baby book.

As the girls got older, of course, we spent less time focusing on their developmental milestones and more time dreaming about family lifestyle milestones. Going on a transatlantic flight. Going on a family bike ride. *Sleeping until 7:00 a.m.* We were still exhausted. Once, when the kids were one and two and we were very much still in the trenches—hovering, tummy timing, being awake a full four hours before "starting" our workdays in the office—I remember asking my co-worker Tom, a father of two middle-school-aged kids, if I was going to be this tired for the rest of my life. No, he told me. It all turns around at about age six, when they can make their own breakfast. When you don't have to wake up with them to pour the juice and toast their bagels. When they can scroll through the DVR offerings and select *Sponge Bob* for themselves. These were unimaginable milestones to me—*Hold on a sec . . . They eventually learn how to turn on the TV?*

But before we would get to that point, our family hit a more astounding milestone than the one Tom described. It was in 2006, one of my days off from work, and I was playing with the girls (about ages three and four) in Abby's room. The two of them had locked into a pretend game with their new pirate ship and I had a radical thought: What if I left the room, went downstairs, and started making dinner? That is, what if I trusted the girls—trusted some distant inner voice buried underneath all my neuroses—and let them play without me helicoptering over them to make sure no one fell on the corner of the play table or squeezed the finger paints onto Abby's bedspread or licked a 9-volt battery? (Amazing how active my imagination became as soon as I had children.) So I turned on Abby's baby monitor and went downstairs to start making meatballs. With one ear on the monitor I poured a glass of Pinot, whisked my egg, worked the ground meat, shaped and browned the balls, and then placed them one by one in the Dutch oven where Andy's Great-Grandma Turano's tomato sauce was simmering away. At some point I realized I was listening more closely to Lucinda Williams on the iPod than I was to the girls' playful chatter on the monitor.

Andy walked in soon after. It had been about forty-five minutes and I went to the bottom of the stairs, cleared my throat and singsonged, just like my own mother circa 1981, "*Giiirrrrls!* Dinner's ready!" I didn't have a dinner bell, but I might as well have. Phoebe and Abby marched down the stairs, took a seat at the kitchen table, and we all ate meatballs with tomato sauce together. It probably only lasted about two minutes and forty-six seconds, but it felt, to me, like the most beautiful two minutes and forty-six seconds in human history.

I don't want to in any way suggest that we cracked the dinner code on that particular night and from then on out it was smooth sailing. It turned out, dinner milestones were just like every other milestone—we tended to do a lot of one-step-forward-two-step-backing. There would still be many many nights following this one when it was impossible to occupy Abby as I attempted to make a marinara. And dozens more when Andy and I wouldn't eat until after the kids went to bed or where Andy and I ate one thing while the girls ate a Trader Joe's frozen pizza next to us. It took many more milestones—psychological, physiological, gastronomical—to get to a place where it felt like I figured out how to do family dinner with the kids efficiently, enjoyably, and regularly. But this Meatball Milestone was remarkable in that it was the first time I started to believe what Tom and everyone else had promised me: that sanity might one day return to our asylum, that very soon family dinner was going to turn into something we'd *enjoy*, rather than just *endure*. It was the first time I saw a glimpse of our future—and sometimes a glimpse is all you need.

Where *family dinner was* once the time of day for Andy and me to try out a new recipe from *The Silver Palate* (prekids), or the time of day to plunk down one bottle of bourbon and one bottle of gin on the kitchen counter beside two ice-filled cocktail glasses (postkids), during this next phase of our dinner narrative (the part I'm calling "Family Dinner"), meals became something so much bigger than just the food on our plates. Once Abby turned three and was capable of sitting still for a few minutes, and of not spilling her water twice in two minutes, and one out of every hundred times actually answering the question "How was your day?," dinner finally started resembling the ritual I had grown up with. Slowly, very slowly, it was becoming the emotional anchor to our days, the only time we all set aside our iPhones and Polly Pocket fashion cruise ships to hash out whatever was on the collective family mind. I found that even when the meal was over in a flash, it was sometimes the only time we actually looked at each other, talked to each other, listened to each other. Even today, five years after the Meatball Milestone, it's very possible for me to spend an entire day with my children and somehow not do any of these things in any kind of meaningful way.

It probably won't come as much of a surprise to hear that this phase of family dinner has been my favorite one so far. By 2006, we had settled into a rhythm with the kids and with our own schedules. My friend Pilar from *Real Simple* was starting a parenting magazine—*Cookie*—and she offered me a job there that I couldn't refuse: food, features, and a four-day work week. As luck would have it, I was going to work in the same building as Andy, who was an editor at *GQ*, one floor above my office. (We used to joke that if he jack-hammered through the floor he'd miss me by about ten feet.) Besides being incredibly convenient for dropping off and picking up forgotten house keys, this setup allowed us to occasionally eat lunch together and frequently commute to and from work together. Five times a week, I was now guaranteed at least thirty-three minutes to have an uninterrupted conversation with my husband. And sometimes a weep session—like that one morning on the 8:43, after receiving an email from Phoebe's dance teacher saying that she was "so sorry" I missed the recital and that "I did give the information to your nanny, but I guess that's what happens when you work."

The commute home was a different story. Whatever redeeming qualities we had as respected spouses, professionals, and human beings seemed to disappear between the afternoon hours of three and five o'clock, when time was tight, decisions were made with brutal efficiency, and emails were rapid-fire and clipped. (JR: Train? AW: 6:23. JR: Dinner thoughts? AW: Chili? JR: Done.)

The highlight of the day was pulling into my driveway and walking up the stone steps to our front door. Our living room faced the front yard and both girls would be perched on the couch, staring out the window, waiting for me to come into view. During the winter months, when it was dark *outside* and light *inside*, I would always see them before they'd see me, and even though I'd look forward to this moment all day, I'd make a point to pause, and sear their expectant little faces into my memory. I didn't know a lot, but I knew that when the era of greeting Mom like a long-lost rock star every weeknight at 6:16 p.m. was over, I'd miss it as much as I missed breast-feeding. Every time I walked up those stone steps, I wondered: *Is this the last night I'll see them in the window searching for me?*

I wish I could say that the cheerleading routine they'd perform upon my arrival would last throughout the evening. But the "Mommy's home!" and the "I missed you!" cries would quickly devolve into "I'm hungry," "What's for dinner?" and "I want chips and salsa!" And then I'd think: *Am I imagining things or did Phoebe's Madeline alarm clock, the one in her bedroom, one flight up the stairs on the other side of the house, suddenly just start ticking really loudly?*

And then it was off to the races: The chips and salsa would be doled out slowly since I wanted them to save room for dinner, so we'd play "Chips for Details." (I'll trade you one chip for every good juicy detail about your day.) I'd try, and often fail, to run upstairs and change into sweats just like I saw my mother do before every dinner of my childhood, then run back downstairs to pour myself a drink, just like I never once saw my mother do before any dinner of my childhood. By six thirty, I'd be cooking. In the early days, it was usually something basic (those oven-fried drumsticks (page 165) that, on my best days, had been marinating since the morning and only needed to be shoved into the oven) or something quick (Spicy Shrimp with Yogurt, page 130) or something that could transition right from the chips and salsa (Taco Soup, page 159). At seven-fifteen,

Andy would walk in the front door and make himself a Manhattan. Because I am a good person, I would try to give him at least three minutes to savor his drink.

And then we'd sit.

Over the course of the next few years, the dinners we ate would get more adventurous. This wasn't a conscious decision—it simply had to do with the fact that we were sitting down together. Once the girls were exposed to the foods we ate on a regular basis, there was a significant increase in the number of times a little hand would reach across the table accompanied by the words "Can I try that?" There was still pleading and begging and no-dessert threatening. There were still auxiliary hot dogs and cheese and crackers and peanut butter sandwiches on deck just in case they didn't eat what we were eating, but they were hitting a milestone I liked very much: They were up for adventure. And they took us right along with them.

Great-Grandma Turano's Meatballs

The official Meatball Milestone is from Andy's Great-Grandma Turano and was not only one of the index-card recipes his mom mailed to us when we first got married (page 16), but also so beloved that we painted the recipe inside a kichen cabinet (page 21). It's safe to say that in the fourteen years since we've received that recipe, we've probably made them as many times as Great-Grandma Turano herself did in her ninety-six years. **Total time:** 1 hour

For the Sauce

1 large onion, chopped

2 garlic cloves, chopped

Shake of red pepper flakes

3 tablespoons olive oil

I wanted to do scratch-and-sniff
but my publisher wouldn't let me.

1 6-ounce can tomato paste

1 tablespoon sugar

2 15-ounce cans tomato puree or diced tomatoes

2 tablespoons dried oregano

Few pinches of fennel seeds

Small handful fresh thyme or basil, chopped

In a Dutch oven, sauté the onion, garlic, and pepper flakes in the oil over medium-low heat until onion is soft and just starting to turn golden, about 5 minutes. Add the tomato paste and sugar and stir, mashing the paste and onion mixture together, 1 to 2 minutes. Fill the empty tomato paste can with water and add to pot, stirring until mixed, another 1 to 2 minutes. Add the tomato puree, oregano, fennel, and thyme or basil, and stir. Simmer lazily over low heat, uncovered, for as long as you want: the longer the better. If the sauce gets too thick, add a little water.

For the Meatballs

2 pounds ground beef (or, I hate to even own up to this, but we have been known, in an effort to be healthy, to use ground turkey)

1 cup Italian bread crumbs

1 cup freshly grated Parmesan cheese, plus extra for garnishing

2 eggs, lightly beaten

1 cup chopped parsley

Few pinches of fennel seeds

Salt and pepper

Olive oil, for frying

In a large bowl, combine the beef, bread crumbs, Parmesan cheese, eggs, parsley, fennel, and salt and pepper. Mash together with your hands until thoroughly combined. Roll into balls (the size of golf balls) and set aside on a plate. In a large skillet over medium-high heat, add a big glug of oil. Begin browning the meatballs in batches, turning every 2 to 3 minutes. Remove when browned on all sides (about 5 minutes) and place right into the simmering sauce. Once all the meatballs have been browned and transferred to the sauce, simmer over low heat for at least 30 minutes. Serve over pasta, piled high with more cheese, or, sliced, inside dinner rolls for meatball sliders.

Swedish Meatballs

When Phoebe turned seven, she decided she wanted to celebrate at a restaurant that served Swedish food. And so it was February 2009, at Smörgås Chef in New York City where she had her first Swedish meatball with jammy lingonberry sauce and creamy whipped potatoes. (Needless to say, she was sold on not just the dish but the entire country.) This recipe was adapted from Smörgås Chef and originally appeared in *Bon Appétit* alongside our story of her discovery. It's the real deal. Total time: 1 hour 30 minutes (includes 1 hour chill time)

   1 cup bread crumbs

   1½ teaspoons sugar

   Salt and pepper

   1 teaspoon ground allspice

   ½ teaspoon ground nutmeg

   3⅓ cups beef broth

   4 tablespoons butter

1 cup minced onion

2 thick slices bacon, finely chopped

1 pound ground beef

¾ pound ground pork

3 eggs, lightly beaten

2 tablespoons all-purpose flour

2 tablespoons sour cream

In a medium bowl, whisk together the bread crumbs, sugar, salt, pepper, allspice, and nutmeg. Stir in ⅓ cup of the broth to moisten and set the mixture aside.

Melt 1 tablespoon of the butter in a medium sauté pan over medium heat. Add the onions and sauté until softened and browned, about 3 minutes. Place the onions in a large bowl and set aside to cool. Wipe out the pan and return to medium heat. Add the bacon and cook until the fat is rendered and the bacon is crisp. Remove the bacon from the pan with a slotted spoon and crumble it into the bowl with the onions. Reserve the bacon fat. Using your hands or a wooden spoon, mix the beef, pork, and eggs into the onions and bacon. Once well combined, gently fold in the bread crumb mixture. Refrigerate for 1 hour.

Roll the meat mixture into small balls (about 1 heaping tablespoon of meat per ball). Heat the remaining 3 tablespoons of butter in a large Dutch oven over medium-low heat. Add enough meatballs to form a single layer and brown on all sides. Remove the meatballs from the Dutch oven with a slotted spoon and reserve on a plate. Repeat with remaining meatballs. Once all the meatballs have been browned, whisk together in the Dutch oven 2 tablespoons of reserved bacon fat and the flour until a smooth paste forms. Stir in the remaining 3 cups broth and bring to a simmer, stirring frequently. Add in the meatballs and reduce the heat to low. Simmer gently until the meatballs are fully cooked, about 5 minutes. Remove from heat, stir in the sour cream, and serve with lingonberry preserves (Hello, IKEA!) and mashed potatoes.

October 2006

Mealtime Mind Games

round this time, with a three- and almost-five-year-old at the table, I started to notice something about the way a lot of parents fed their kids who were the same ages as mine. It seemed there were two strict paths to take for a relatively easy go at family dinner:

Path 1: You cook two meals, one for the parents and a separate one, usually of lesser quality or from the freezer, for the kids.

Path 2: You could all eat the same meal, which means that mom and dad will usually be eating food that is "cooked to the weakest link" (i.e., foods that are stripped of sauce, texture, and flavor).

Both paths seemed to lead in the same direction: a nagging feeling that you were doing everything all wrong.

It didn't make sense to me—why did everything have to be so cut-and-dried? Why, for instance, should there be shame in your son eating, say, two of the three things you serve him if it means you only have to cook once and what you cook will be something truly enjoyable? And in my experience, getting stuck in the cooking-to-the-weakest-link rut (which usually means pizza, pasta, and burgers) is going to be the quickest route to sucking all the joy out of a sit-down family dinner. So over the years I developed the following key psychological strategies to ensure that my cooking efforts always felt like a success (even though the casual observer might have a totally different take on things).

Strategy 1:
Picture Your Dinner Plates as Venn Diagrams

As *we were entering* this era of legitimate sit-down family dinner, there were very few meals in our repertoire that every person at the table was eating in the same way, but that never stopped me from making them. Take something as basic as spaghetti with meatballs, with a side of sautéed garlicky spinach. Abby would eat the spaghetti and the meatballs but not the spinach. Phoebe would eat the meatballs and spinach but not the spaghetti. (Don't get me started on having a pasta handicap at the table.) Andy and I, of course, would eat the whole thing like normal people. But, as annoying as all this customizing is, I never consider it *deal-breaker* annoying. (Plus, both of our Italian grandmothers would posthumously disown us if we pulled spaghetti and meatballs from the rotation.) Everybody likes at least two out of three things on the plate—and that's a solid dinner that does not need to be served with a side of peanut butter sandwich. Here is the kind of Venn diagram I've drawn (mostly in my head, until now) that shows you how I try to convince myself we are all eating the same thing.

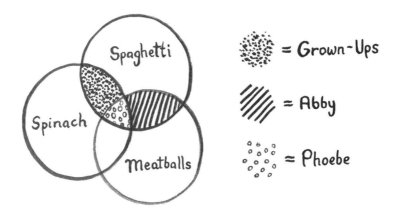

Strategy 2: Denial

If you find the Venn diagram strategy too complicated to wrap your head around, there's another, less mentally arduous route to take. Remember, you are in the hands of a family dinner expert here, so pay close attention to this hard-earned, time-honored piece of advice. I've decided that one of the most effective ways to convince yourself that you are making one thing for everyone (even though you are doing nothing of the sort) is to lock yourself into a state of extreme denial and then proceed with artful self-delusion through every step of the cooking process.

Behold my favorite dinner on earth: Whole Wheat Spaghetti with Caramelized Onions, Spinach, and Parmesan (page 204). I love everything about this dish: I love its pantry-friendliness (it can almost always be whipped together at the last minute), its hands-on cooking time (takes about 15 minutes), its supercool pot-saving trick (you throw the spinach into the pasta pot and drain everything together), and its *deliciousness* (oh boy, oh boy, oh boy). So you think I am going to let Phoebe's pasta hating or Abby's insistence on having it with a little tomato sauce mixed in ("I want it *pink*!") ruin this for me? No way. I refuse. And here's a step-by-step guide to show you how it's done.

✅ **Self-Delusion Moment 1:** I set four identical plates in a grid. This immediately creates the promise (illusion?) of uniformity and order.

. . . .

✅ **Self-Delusion Moment 2:** I earmark the lower right bowl as Abby's and spoon in just the right amount of spaghetti sauce—and a couple hunks of butter. This can barely be called "customizing" since it takes under 10 seconds.

. . . .

✅ **Self-delusion Moment 3:** I earmark the lower left bowl as Phoebe's. And while, yes, the baked potato is not exactly the same thing as whole wheat spaghetti, it's in the "starch" family and hardly takes any extra effort for me to toss the thing in the microwave for 10 minutes.

. . . .

✅ **Self-delusion Moment 4:** Time to apply your Venn diagram psychology: Pasta is done and plated in three out of four bowls. Onions and spinach are done and plated in three out of four bowls. Three out of four! Even though the two kids' bowls are barely related to each other, each can lay claim to having one major component in common with the grown-up version.

See? So easy!

Whole Wheat Spaghetti with Caramelized Onions, Spinach, and Parmesan

(The No-Mind-Game Version)

Total time: 15 minutes

Few glugs of olive oil

3 large onions, sliced

1 pound whole wheat spaghetti

Small handful of thawed frozen spinach or
   big handful of fresh spinach

1 tablespoon balsamic vinegar

Lots of freshly grated Parmesan cheese

Pour the oil into a skillet set over medium-low heat, and cook the onions, stirring every few minutes, for a minimum of 15 minutes and up to 45 minutes. While the onions cook, prepare the spaghetti according to package directions. During the last minute of pasta cooking, add your spinach to the water. Drain the pasta and spinach together. (If integrating spinach into the pasta is going to cause a revolt with certain diners at your table, then just thaw the spinach separately under warm water or cook fresh spinach in a little oil in the pot after you've drained the pasta.) Toss the spaghetti with a little olive oil. Stir the balsamic vinegar into the onions. Serve the pasta in bowls, then heap on the onions, spinach, and Parmesan cheese.

December 2006

The 2.0 Strategy

he first time we gave the girls lamb burgers, they had no idea that what they were eating was any different from the normal turkey or beef burger we usually gave them. This is most likely because we slathered their burgers in ketchup instead of the more traditional mint yogurt sauce that adorned our buns. Did we still mark this down in the Win column? Of course! Because as soon as we were done with the don't-ask-don't-tell portion of the dinner, we showered them with hoorays—as much to redeem ourselves for the trickery as to pump them up with praise. *You tried something new! Congratulations! Hooray!* It was good, right? Right?

Yes, they admitted it was good.

This was a common tactic at the table. We found that once the kids got comfortable with a "kid-friendly" kind of food, it was a logical next step for us to figure out ways to 2.0 that food into grown-up territory. This does not mean I advise leaping immediately from chicken nuggets to chicken cacciatore. It just means you can go from a building-block meal that is as basic as a hamburger and fries to something one small step up. And "one small step" can be defined any way you'd like. For instance, you might think about switching the ingredients (i.e., ground beef to ground lamb) or switching the technique (i.e., roll out the burger California-style instead of just broiling a thick patty), or you can switch the vegetables (French fries to Zucchini Fries); you can add a slice of cheese or a pickle to the plate; you could even just switch the size of the bun. (Sliders!)

On rare, beautiful nights, the girls' eyes would widen and there would be some sort of declaration of eternal love for the new dish followed by a request to have it the next night, too. But this was never our expectation. In our house, debuting something new at the table—no matter how subtly new it may be—is always more about trying the dish than it is about loving it. In fact, just not hating something is considered a victory, a moment worthy of celebration and positive reinforcement. ("Good for you! You didn't spit it out!") We learned to embrace a lukewarm reaction to a new food. A lukewarm reaction was something we could have fun with—it was something we could build on.

Three 2.0 Burgers

There is no shame in serving any of these burgers slathered in ketchup. If it makes you feel better, you can try calling it "tomato coulis." Also, if you want to have the 1.0 version as a backup, that's fine, too—but I find that if you tell your kid there is a backup waiting in the wings for him, then he will only half-heartedly participate in the adventure. Best to hide the old favorite somewhere he won't sniff it out.

Lamb Sliders

Total time: 30 minutes

For the Yogurt Sauce

½ cup plain nonfat yogurt

¼ teaspoon garlic salt

⅛ teaspoon cumin

2 teaspoons fresh lemon juice

Pinch of salt

Freshly ground black pepper to taste

For the Burgers

1¼ pounds ground lamb

¼ cup onion, finely minced

1 tablespoon chopped fresh parsley

1 tablespoon chopped fresh mint

¼ teaspoon dried oregano

Salt and pepper

8 whole wheat dinner rolls

Ketchup (optional)

Cucumber slices (optional)

Preheat the broiler.

To make the yogurt sauce: Whisk together the yogurt, garlic salt, cumin, and lemon juice in a medium bowl. Season with salt and pepper.

To make the burgers: Mix the lamb, onion, parsley, mint, and oregano in a large bowl. Season generously with salt and pepper. Shape the mixture into 8 small ¾-inch-thick patties. Make a small indent with your thumb in the middle of each patty, which will help them retain a flatter shape.

Place the lamb patties on a broiler pan and broil until cooked through, 12 to 14 minutes, flipping once halfway through.

Place the burgers inside the rolls and top with the yogurt sauce (or ketchup, if preferred). Add the cucumber slices (if using).

California-style Turkey Burgers

About the rolling: It really makes no discernible difference in the way the burger tastes, but it prevents the patties from shriveling up into hard little hockey pucks. And psychologically I love that it feels so In-N-Out! Total time: 25 minutes

 1 pound ground turkey meat (preferably dark meat),
    salted and peppered

 1 tablespoon barbecue sauce (any kind)

 2 tablespoons olive oil

 4 whole wheat hamburger buns

 Condiments: mayo, mustard, ketchup,
    Bibb lettuce, pickles (pickles are particularly crucial)

In a large bowl, combine the turkey meat with the barbecue sauce. Shape the mixture into four patties and place two of them a few inches apart from each other on a large plastic cutting board. Cover the patties with plastic wrap, and using a rolling pin, roll the meat so the patties resemble the kinds you see in fast-food restaurants (only much healthier). Repeat with the remaining patties. Fry in the oil in a large skillet over medium heat for about 4 minutes on each side, until cooked through. Place on buns and top with desired condiments. And when it comes to turkey burgers, it's all about the condiments.

Pan-fried Fish Sandwiches

If you are going to make these with Zucchini Fries (page 212), make the fries first so you can reuse the dredging plates. **Total time: 20 minutes**

- 4 whole wheat hamburger buns, toasted
- 4 pieces Fried Flounder (page 143) or mild whitefish such as sole, tilapia, or hake

Tartar sauce or ketchup, for topping

Stuff each bun with flounder and top with tartar sauce.

Three 2.0 French Fries

Of these three recipes, we make the spicy oven fries (aka mega fries) the most often because they are so easy to throw together and also because the kids *inhale* them. If you don't think your kids will go for the spice mixture, just focus on getting them to eat the potatoes with the skins still on, and work your way up to the cayenne and paprika. The chickpea and zucchini fries are not the kind of recipes you'd turn to on a busy weeknight, but on a weekend, if you have some time to spare, I promise you won't regret it. Imagine: French fries with nutritional merit!

Chickpea Fries

Total time: 1 hour (includes 30 minutes for chilling batter)

2 tablespoons olive oil, plus about ¼ cup more for frying

3 cups water

2 teaspoons salt

1½ cups chickpea flour (aka besan, available at Asian specialty stores)

1 teaspoon ground cumin

1 teaspoon garlic powder

½ teaspoon sweet smoked paprika

Oil a small rimmed baking sheet with 1 tablespoon of the oil and set aside.

In a heavy saucepan, bring the water to a boil. Add 1 teaspoon of the salt and 1 tablespoon of the oil and reduce the heat to medium-low.

Add the flour in a steady stream, whisking constantly for about 5 minutes. The batter will become thick and begin to detach from the sides of the pan (like polenta).

Turn off the heat and pour the batter onto the cookie sheet, using a rubber spatula to spread the batter evenly and quickly so it forms a thick pancake-like shape with the thickness of steak fries.

The batter will begin to firm up right away.

Cover the cookie sheet with plastic wrap and chill in the refrigerator for 30 minutes.

While batter is chilling, combine the remaining 1 teaspoon salt, the cumin, garlic powder, and paprika in a small bowl and set aside.

In a large skillet, add ¼ cup olive oil over medium-high heat.

Remove the batter from the fridge and cut into French-fry-type strips on the cookie sheet.

Add the fries to the olive oil and fry for 1 to 2 minutes a side, flipping with a spatula. (Don't crowd the pan.) Remove the fries from the oil and season with the desired amount of spice mixture. If you think the spice mixture might scare off potential converts, then just add salt.

Spicy Oven Fries

Total time: 30 minutes

¼ teaspoon cayenne

½ teaspoon paprika

1 teaspoon garlic salt

3 baking potatoes, cut into wedges (I get 12 wedges per potato)

¼ cup olive oil

Salt and pepper to taste

2 teaspoons water

Preheat the oven to 425°F.

In a small bowl, mix together the cayenne, paprika, and garlic salt. In another medium bowl, toss the potatoes, oil, spice mixture, salt, and pepper with the water. (For whatever reason, I find the steam this water generates in the oven makes them crisp and fluffy.) Line a baking sheet with foil and coat it with cooking spray (crucial—fries will be hard to remove otherwise). Line up your fries in rows and bake for 25 minutes, or until they are crispy and golden.

⭐ *Tip:* Sometimes I fashion a piece of parchment paper into a cone and let the girls carry their stash around.

Zucchini Fries (aka "Green French Fries")

Total time: 35 minutes

1 cup all-purpose flour

2 eggs, whisked

1 cup bread crumbs, salted and peppered

⅛ teaspoon cayenne

½ teaspoon garlic salt

¼ teaspoon paprika

2 medium zucchinis, cut into French fry wedges

Ketchup, for serving

Preheat the oven to 400°F.

Set up the dredging stations: one rimmed plate for the flour, one for the eggs, one for the bread crumbs. Add the cayenne, garlic salt, and paprika to the bread crumbs and mix around with your fingers.

Dip the zucchini sticks first in the flour until lightly coated, then in the eggs. Roll them in the bread crumb mixture until well covered. Transfer the zucchini to a baking sheet lined with foil and bake until they are crispy and golden, 20 to 25 minutes. Serve with ketchup.

February 2007

The Royal Family
(or How We Got Our Kids to Eat Salmon)

e have never been calorie counters in our house. The food pyramid is not something my children would recognize beyond a structure they might like to replicate with LEGOs. There have been a few instances where we talk about our plates resembling rainbows (hence our Rainbow Salad, page 166), but for the most part our philosophy on passing along healthy eating habits to the girls has always been hands-off: If they are eating roughly what we are eating, they are probably doing okay.

During this period of palate expansion, though, we came up with our own version of the food pyramid. Cinderella, Jasmine, Sleeping Beauty, and Ariel had already proven to be excellent bribery booty for toilet training, so we decided to assign royal titles to a few random superfoods we wanted the kids to eat and drink more of:

 * Milk was the prince.

 * Broccoli, with its almighty supply of vitamins and calcium, was the king.

 * Eggs were the queen, since, if we were to believe the headlines, they contained enough omega-3s to triple our children's chances of getting into Stanford.

 * And salmon, pink and delicate, was the princess.

I can't call this strategy foolproof—as both Lady Phoebe and Lady Abby still recoil at the sight of an egg five years later—but I do know that Princess Salmon has enjoyed a long reign. (It certainly didn't hurt that Abby was in her "pink" phase when we introduced the fish.) No matter how it's prepared, somehow we can always count on the girls to wolf it down.

Royal Salmon with Yogurt-Mustard-Dill Sauce

This is such a good weeknight dinner. It comes together so fast and the dipping sauce is just interesting enough to elevate it to something special. Total time: 20 minutes

1 salmon fillet (about 1½ pounds, cut into 6 4-ounce pieces)

Salt and pepper

½ cup plain yogurt

1 heaping teaspoon Dijon mustard

1 tablespoon chopped fresh dill

Squeeze of fresh lemon

Preheat the oven to 450°F.

Sprinkle the salmon with salt and pepper. Line a baking dish with foil, place the salmon in it, and roast for 15 minutes. Meanwhile, in a small bowl, whisk together the yogurt, mustard, dill, lemon, and salt and pepper to taste. Serve salmon pieces with a dollop of sauce.

Sweet Barbecue Salmon

Hoisin sauce is ridiculously sweet, which helps makes this dish an easy sell. Total time: 45 minutes (includes 30 minutes hands-off marinating time)

    1 salmon fillet (about 1¼ pounds)

    1 to 2 tablespoons olive oil

    1 to 2 tablespoons soy sauce

    2 tablespoons hoisin sauce

    Juice from 1 lime (about 2 tablespoons)

Preheat oven to 400°F.

In a small baking dish, marinate the salmon in the oil and soy sauce for about 30 minutes. In a small bowl, whisk together the hoisin sauce and lime juice. Set aside. Roast the salmon for 12 minutes, flesh-side up, then brush on the sauce, turn heat to broil, and broil another 3 minutes.

⭐ *Note:* You can also grill this salmon over medium-hot coals: Grill salmon for 3 to 4 minutes on each side, then brush the flesh side with the hoisin-lime sauce and grill, flesh-side down, for another 3 minutes.

Thai-ish Salmon

Browning the salmon in a skillet and then allowing it to finish cooking in a pool of aromatic coconut milk gives the fish the most delicate texture. A few years later we referred to it on the website as "Salmon for People Who Are Sick of Salmon," and it has been one of the most popular recipes to date. Total time: 30 minutes

2 tablespoons canola oil

1 salmon fillet (about 1½ pounds), salted and peppered

1 tablespoon finely minced fresh lemongrass (white part of the stalk),
available at Asian markets and quality supermarkets

1 tablespoon chopped scallions (white and light green parts)

⅔ cup light coconut milk

Juice from 1 lime (about 2 tablespoons)

1½ teaspoons Thai red curry paste
(available in the Asian section of most grocery stores)

Handful of cilantro, chopped

Handful of basil, chopped

Handful of any vegetables you and the kids like: chopped green beans,
peas, chopped shiitake mushrooms

Heat a large skillet to medium-high heat and add the oil.

Place the salmon in the skillet flesh side down and cook for 3 or 4 minutes, until
nicely browned. Remove from the skillet and set aside.

Reduce the heat to medium-low. Add the lemongrass and scallions and stir
around for 1 minute. Add the coconut milk, lime juice, and curry paste. Whisk
together and let simmer for about 3 minutes.

Add the salmon back in, skin side down, nestling into the sauce. Simmer uncovered for 10 minutes. Add the cilantro, basil, and desired vegetables.

Simmer for another 7 to 8 minutes. Serve with jasmine rice, more cilantro, scallions, and a squeeze of lime.

LAZY PARENT'S DARK SECRET: THE RITUAL

Having a hands-off approach to healthy eating is pretty consistent with our parenting philosophy in general. Have you ever read the instructions on a cast-iron skillet? It goes something like this: *Do not clean this product too well. The fat and flavor left in the pan after cooking helps your skillet build a naturally nonstick surface.* Can I tell you how much I love instructions that reward laziness? Braising is like that, too—the longer you ignore the hunk of beef or pork simmering away in a pot, the more the meat will melt off the bone. So is playtime: No one was happier about that study encouraging parents to give their kids unstructured time with limited parental intervention (not to be confused with limited parental *supervision!*). Apparently this was the secret to getting kids to build imaginations and rich inner lives. (No one would ever accuse me of being a Tiger Mother.)

But my all-time favorite example of laziness, which also happens to qualify as good parenting, is the Ritual. To be more specific, the ritual of a family walk after

dinner on warm summer nights or to the farmers' market every Saturday morning between April and November; the ritual of the kids selecting where they'd like to celebrate their birthday dinner (they choose a country, like Sweden, and then we find a restaurant to match that country); the ritual of dancing to Music Together or Jack White or Taylor Swift or the Nutcracker after dinner and before bed; the ritual of bath-book-bedtime every night and of a bowl of fresh fruit first thing in the morning; the ritual of eating pancakes or bagels in front of *Dora* or the *Back-yardigans* or (later) *iCarly* on Saturday morning; the ritual of me giving Andy a good bottle of bourbon for our anniversary every October. (And don't try to tell me that bourbon has nothing to do with parenting.)

Kids crave routines and rituals—your pediatrician probably told you that at your first baby's first weigh-in. But I think parents—okay, maybe just *this* parent—craves routines and rituals even more. Because, yes, yes, yes, as outlined above, I know it's comforting to my children on some level to know that they'll be able to sit down with their parents every night for dinner, but it's also comforting to me because *there are just so many other things to keep track of.* (I always remember that scene in *I Don't Know How She Does It* when Kate Reddy's boss, who has just lost his wife to cancer, comes to the office completely overwhelmed by all the things his wife did without his noticing. "You wouldn't believe how much there is to remember, Kate," he told her. And to herself Kate says, "Yes, I would.") In other words, when there are twenty-five things on the to-do list already, I don't want to waste energy figuring out how to ensure we have quality time with our kids for the three hours we are with them on a weekday (hence: Family Dinner plus After-Dinner Dancing). I don't want to tap my small supply of creative juices trying to outdo last year's special birthday celebration (hence: Our Pick-a-Country ritual). In other words, when there are so many little things to think about, it's comforting to know that I have a few of the big things running on autopilot.

May 2008

Pork Chops Tonight?

JR: I'm home. We have pork chops. Any ideas?

AW: *Awwww yeeeaaah*. Get mustard apples onions ready.

JR: Onion diced or sliced? Mustard Dijon or grainy?

AW: Sliced. Either. I'll take it from there.

Mustardy Pork Chops with Apples and Onions

Total time: 30 minutes

Olive oil

4 boneless pork chops (about 1¼ pounds), salted and peppered

1 large onion, sliced

1 apple, peeled and slivered to the same width as onion slices

2 tablespoons mustard (Dijon or grainy)

2 tablespoons cider vinegar

¼ cup apple cider, water, or apple juice

Add the oil to a large skillet (that has a lid) over medium-high heat. Brown the pork chops, about 4 minutes on each side. (They do not have to cook through.)

Remove them from the pan and turn the heat to medium-low. Add a little more oil, if necessary, and then add the onions and apples and cook 5 to 7 minutes, until they have wilted.

Add the mustard, vinegar, and cider to the pan, scraping up any brown pork bits from the bottom and bring to a boil for about 1 minute. Add the pork chops back to the pan, nestling them with the onions and apples; reduce to simmer. Cover and cook another 5 minutes, until chops have cooked through. If pan-sauce is liquidy, remove chops and boil sauce for another minute.

September 2008
Entertaining, Part 3

I know what you're thinking: enough already about Andy's Pork Ragù! And didn't I already write about how to cook for dinner guests without humiliating (or hurting) yourself way back in Part 1? I did, yes, but that was 1998. When Steve Madden slides were in style! I need to make sure something is very clear: Entertaining when you are in your twenties, in your first small apartment, with no money and no kids, is a completely different beast from entertaining in your thirties or forties when both you and your guests have a real kitchen, real kids, and real expectations. To begin with, you are probably no longer cooking for people who are mostly subsisting on ramen noodles, Hot Pockets, and that dirt-cheap Thai spot around the corner. At least that was the case for me. Because during the ten years that elapsed between first attempting to cook for people and this point, a lot had happened. Chefs became celebrities. Michael Pollan became a superhero. And a lot of my friends became food snobs.

I mean that in the nicest possible way.

These were the friends I was learning from and working with, the ones who could appreciate not just the deliciousness but the sustainability of our whole grilled mackerel and the in seasonness of our peppery arugula salad. The only problem is, I would stress about cooking for food snobs in a way that I wouldn't for normal types. Quite often during this period, on the day before food-snob guests arrived, I would find myself reexamining everything in my repertoire, everything in my pantry, and every shred of self-worth I had worked so hard to cultivate in my career as a grown-up. (Nope, not proud of this.) The plastic bottle of raspberry-lime seltzer water that I picked up by the case at Trader Joe's suddenly looked crass when one of these guests requested a glass of Pellegrino before

Pork Shoulder Ragù with Papparadelle (page 179).

starting on the wine. (He looked at the bottle, looked at the glass, then said, "I'll try anything once!") When discerning guests came over, I'd rearrange the contents of my refrigerator—hiding Andy's "lite" (aka heart-healthy aka processed) butter behind my organic real butter or making sure the produce from the farmers' market and jars of homemade pickles were front-row center.

Needless to say, this behavior was completely confounding to Andy. "What is wrong with you?" he once asked when I told him I was going to drive to a decidedly out-of-the-way Italian specialty market to pick up my favorite fresh ricotta for a pizza I was thinking of making. "You're acting like you've never cooked anything before. Why are you making this so hard on yourself?"

Needless to say, this drove me nuts. How could he not recognize an up-the-ante situation when it presented itself?

Because he is an emotionally stable person. Who always ended up bringing me back down to earth. And so did the kids, of course. By necessity, having them around forced me to cool it on the impress-my-friends instinct because I'd have to ask myself things like: Does it really make sense for me to spend an entire Saturday morning in pursuit of truffled pecorino on one of the only days of the week I get to spend with my daughters? Why am I making seven different salads instead of just one beautifully simple salad that both the kids and grown-ups will like? What exactly am I trying to prove?

That's actually the punch line to all this: No matter how much I fretted about menu planning for food-snob friends and their kids, no matter how many miles I'd drive for the freshest, bestest ingredient that would crown me Most Valuable Cook in the exclusive inner circle of my own warped mind, the menu invariably would end up looking exactly the same as it did when we'd cook for people who wouldn't be able to pick a butternut squash out of a lineup. After five years cooking with/for/around kids, we realized that we were pretty much only capable of cooking in one gear: simply. And it turned out that was the only gear we needed, no matter who was sitting at the table.

Go-To No-Fret Impress-Your-Friends Entertaining Menus for Each Season

We've had really good luck making these menus for families—snobby food families and otherwise. It was easy to find them because in my diary, I usually add a note underneath the lineup that says something like *Perfect!*

FALL: Braised Beef Short Ribs (page 40), Kale with Avocado and Pickled Onions (page 249)

WINTER: Pork Shoulder Ragù with Pappardelle (page 179), Sautéed Chard with Horseradish (page 244)

SPRING: Salad Pizza (page 276)

SUMMER: Bourbon-Marinated Grilled Pork Tenderloin (page 71) with Grilled Peaches (page 72), Old-Fashioned Coleslaw (page 242)

COOK A SIGNATURE

Another strategy I fall back on when I'm menu-planning for dinner guests is the cook-a-signature strategy. By signature, I don't mean the tuna and white bean casserole your grandma Sadie was famous for—I mean a much-heralded recipe that has been developed by one of the Greats (Julia, Jacques, Marcella), a time-tested, guaranteed showstopper that has already been ingested and enjoyed in millions of homes before yours, sometimes even on holidays and special occasions. They're sophisticated. They're special. They're classic. They say, "I know something about food." You still have to cook it, and generally these kinds of dishes are more time-consuming than, say, Andy's pork ragù—but there's a lot less stress involved when you know you're going with a sure thing.

Here are some of my favorites. You probably have at least one or two of these cookbooks on your shelf already.

✳ Giuliano Bugialli's minestrone, from *The Fine Art of Italian Cooking*

✳ Julia Child's beef bourgignon or coq au vin, from *Mastering the Art of French Cooking*

✳ Nobu Matsuhisa's miso-glazed black cod, from *Nobu: The Cookbook*

✳ Marcella Hazan's bolognese, from *The Classic Italian Cookbook*

✳ David Chang's roasted brussels sprouts (the one that calls for Rice Krispies), from *Momofuku*

✳ Mario Batali's beef cheek ravioli, from *The Babbo Cookbook*

November 2008

• ▪ ▪ • • • • ▪ ▪ ▪ • • • ▪ ▪ • • • ▪ ▪ • • • • ▪ • •

Todd and Anne: Pasta Night

You know the penultimate line in *Charlotte's Web*? It goes like this: "It is not often that someone comes along who is a true friend and a good writer." I would revise it to "It is not often that someone comes along who is a true friend and also a good cook." And this was the quote that came to mind when we first went to dinner at Todd and Anne's house.

Todd and Anne were food snobs in the best possible way. They loved to cook and eat good food without standing on a platform. They loved the farmers' market and Trader Joe's, and, like Michelle and Bill from our Brooklyn days, got really *into* cooking a meal for us. But the best part of all—unlike our food-loving friends from work who all seemed to live in the same square mile in Brooklyn, Todd and Anne lived five minutes away from us and had two kids just about the same ages as Abby and Phoebe who were always underfoot in the kitchen. Before we knew them well, I remember a local friend referring to Todd as "the guy who drives to *Piermont* on Fridays just to go to their farmers' market." Piermont was across the Hudson River, about a thirty-minute drive away from our town. She delivered the description as one might have delivered the line "He's the guy who talks to the pigeons and wears shoes that don't match."

Eating dinner with Todd and Anne was like eating dinner in our own house with our own family but more fun because they were always trying new recipes (Todd's Minty Pea Dip was a huge hit when I wrote about it on the blog) or introducing us to new ingredients (I had seen beluga lentils but had never tried them before they served us a four-star-restaurant-worthy bowl of beluga lentil soup with anchovies and chestnuts.) We'd go camping with them in the summer, where Anne, a professional musician who plays French horn for the Metropolitan Opera, would play guitar and sing like an angel around the campfire. In the spring, we'd all drag our kids out of bed early and caravan an hour north to have breakfast al fresco at a diamond-in-the-rough organic farm that served real sourdough pancakes and breakfast burritos with watercress. And at least once a winter we'd all get together to make pasta from scratch.

Organizing this activity for two families is probably complicated, but I wouldn't know because Todd and Anne are also the kinds of people who decide on something and then do all the legwork behind the scenes to make it happen (another reason why we keep them around). The first time we all made pasta from scratch—a cold, snowy night—this legwork included consulting three or four cookbooks for a composite homemade pasta dough recipe that looked good, figuring out a dish (Todd decided on fettuccine with leeks and bacon), digging up the manual pasta machine from the basement, and last, making sure the house was stocked with bourbon, which we sipped as we cranked.

Their house—a Victorian three times as tall as it was wide—was seemingly

built to host parents cranking out pasta and cradling bourbons on winter nights. In the exposed-brick kitchen, there is always something hearty and bacon-y frying in a cast-iron pan or being chopped on a cutting board that looks so well-worn it ought to be a hundred years old. Year-round, twinkly white Christmas lights frame large windows that overlook the Hudson River. And year-round, some old band that Todd and Andy have just rediscovered on the live music archive Wolfgang's Vault, is playing in the background—often with the kids air-guitaring right along with them.

Making pasta from scratch was the kind of endeavor that I would've once called a "someday" project. As in, "Someday, when the kids are older and I have more time I'll attempt to do that." That was the best part about having friends like Todd and Anne. When you feel like you're all in it together, someday suddenly seems a lot less intimidating. Someday suddenly feels . . . here.

Homemade Fettuccine with Leeks and Bacon

The problem with homemade pasta is that once you make it, your pasta standards go way up and you find yourself driving a few extra miles to the specialty store to pick up a pack of good stuff instead of the perfectly fine box of Barilla. Fresh pasta is so good you don't need to do more than add butter and cheese to make it a world-class dinner—but I can't really imagine you're going to complain about this preparation either. Also: If you make this with store-bought pasta, the sun will still rise in the morning.
Total time: 2 hours (includes 1 hour rising time)

> 2 cups all-purpose flour, plus additional for kneading
>
> 3 large eggs
>
> 1 teaspoon water
>
> 1 teaspoon olive oil
>
> 1 teaspoon salt
>
> 4 slices good-quality thick-cut smoked bacon,
>   chopped into small pieces

4 leeks, well rinsed, trimmed, and chopped

1 cup grated Parmesan cheese, for serving

Pepper, for serving

In a food processor, blend the first four ingredients (except for the additional flour for kneading) and pulse until mixture just begins to form a ball.

On a lightly floured surface, knead the dough, incorporating additional flour when necessary, until the dough is smooth and somewhat elastic.

Flatten the dough into a rectangle shape, and cover with an overturned bowl. Let sit for one hour. Using a pasta machine, roll the dough on the widest setting eight or nine times, folding the dough in half after each time and dusting with flour to prevent sticking.

Turn the dial to the next narrower setting and feed the dough through the machine, once at each setting (without folding) until you reach the narrowest setting. The dough gets smooth and long at this point and you will need a few extra sets of hands to help out. Cut your long sheet in half to make it easier to handle.

Using the fettuccine attachment for your pasta machine, crank out some noodles, snipping them with kitchen scissors as they emerge from the machine.

As you make fettuccine, set it aside in bird's-nest piles and let it dry for about 10 minutes.

In a large skillet over medium heat, add the bacon and cook until crispy. Remove the bacon from the pan and reserve for later.

Remove half of the bacon fat remaining in the pan. (I usually use a paper towel to absorb it, but please do this carefully, because the bacon fat is hot.) Add the leeks to the pan and cook until soft, about 5 minutes.

While the leeks are cooking, bring a large pot of salted water to a boil and begin cooking pasta. Fresh pasta only takes 2 to 3 minutes to cook. Drain, reserving about ½ cup pasta water.

Add the bacon back into the pan along with the leeks and a little pasta water and stir until the sauce looks thicker and slightly emulsified. Add the pasta to the skillet and toss with tongs.

Serve with the grated Parmesan cheese and pepper.

Todd's Minty Pea Dip

Todd whipped up this dip for us during peak produce months, and I was shocked to discover that it was made from frozen peas. Served with some crusty bread slices, this humble little dip can easily hold its own alongside summer produce behemoths like corn and tomatoes. It also happens to be versatile (we've had it as a dip, spread on a sandwich for dinner, mixed with ricotta and sealed inside ravioli) and, unlike corn and tomatoes, can be enjoyed year-round. Total time: 10 minutes

> 1 cup frozen peas, thawed
>
> ⅔ cup loosely packed fresh mint leaves, washed
>
> 2 tablespoons freshly grated Parmesan cheese, plus more for garnishing
>
> Juice from ½ lemon (about 1 tablespoon)
>
> ¼ cup olive oil
>
> Salt to taste

In a food processor, whirl all the ingredients until it is the consistency of chunky guacamole. (You can play around with the consistency. If you like it creamier, add more oil. Chunkier? Add more peas.)

Garnish with some more shredded Parmesan cheese and serve with baguette slices or spread across a piece of crusty bread.

Note: Don't make this dip ahead of time if you are serving to guests. The mint will turn black if it sits around too long.

Beluga Lentil Soup with Anchovies

Don't be turned off by the anchovies. You won't notice any fishy flavor in this soup. The anchovies just add a beautiful salty dimension that I promise you will miss if you omit. And no one's going to arrest you if you add cooked crumbled sausages here, either. Total time: 45 minutes

½ large onion, chopped

1 large carrot, peeled and chopped

1 stalk celery, chopped

2 to 3 flat-fillet anchovies, such as Cento, minced

2 tablespoons olive oil

Salt and pepper to taste

1 garlic clove, minced

1 cup beluga lentils

4 cups chicken or vegetable broth

Grated Parmesan cheese, for serving

In a large saucepan over medium heat, sauté the onion, carrot, celery, and anchovies in 1 tablespoon of the oil until slightly softened. Add the salt and pepper. (Remember, anchovies are salty, so don't go crazy.) Add the garlic and stir for about 30 seconds.

Add the lentils and stir them until they look like shiny beautiful caviar and are coated in oil. Add the broth, bring to a boil, and then lower the heat to a simmer. Keep an eye on the lentils, making sure you always have enough liquid in the pot. You want them to be covered by about 1 inch of liquid. Add more stock or water as necessary.

Test for doneness starting at 20 minutes. Lentils should be able to hold their shape but still be tender. Cook them for another 5 to 10 minutes if necessary. Spoon the soup into bowls and top each bowl with Parmesan cheese and a generous drizzle of oil.

July 2009

Vacation Cooking: My Drill Sergeant of Leisure

When I was growing up, we never took typical family vacations. We never booked a house on the Cape for a week or went to Fort Myers in February; we never sat at the kitchen table with a map of the country circling national parks we wanted to visit like I imagined most families doing. The exception was Bermuda. For a few years in a row, when we were little, we'd stay at the Princess Hotel, a dreamy resort overlooking the ocean where the waiters held silver domed trays and wore white tuxes and where I'd return from dinner to a chocolate mint on my pillow. But even for these trips, we never stayed longer than a few days, a Thursday to a Sunday. Part of the reason for this was that my mother, once she found her calling as an attorney, turned into a workaholic—today, at seventy-five, as partner in her own law firm, she still works harder than all of her children combined—and, like all workaholics, she derives pleasure from work, thereby rendering the need to get pleasure elsewhere useless. (I've always gotten the feeling that she finds vacation from reading ninety-five-page contracts a whole lot more stressful than reading those ninety-five-page contracts.)

Another reason we never went on typical vacations was that my sister, Lynn, was a nationally ranked tennis player who competed in tournaments all over the country. Naturally, the whole family would tag along with her on these trips no matter where they were—Charlestown, West Virginia, Raleigh, North Carolina, Indianapolis. They were always during July and August, and the organizers seemed to find some sick pleasure in selecting venues where the average temperature was a hundred degrees in the shade and never ever near a water park with one of those long, twisty mountain slides. But the truth was, I didn't mind. I was ten, eleven, twelve years old. All I needed was a hotel pool to be happy.

But now that I am not a kid—now that I am a grown-up and I have kids of my *own*—vacation is a different story altogether. I need the pool, yes, but I also need a whole lot more. Most of the time I need a kitchen. I need a grill. I need to go to a place with lots to do. In fact, from the moment we arrive at wherever we happen to be vacationing, Andy and I are crafting ways to make sure we are squeezing the maximum amount of pleasure out of every moment of our waking hours. We take our vacations seriously. Before we have finished our morning coffee we have a plan for the day, one that usually includes exercise for the grown-ups (we usually tag-team our workouts while the kids watch their morning TV), a large chunk of time in or near a pool or beach, some sort of afternoon adventure that involves exploring the local terrain (like a road trip or a hike or a bike ride), and of course, shopping for dinner that we will make in our own kitchen while drinking gin and tonics.

One morning when we were on vacation in South Carolina (where Andy's parents have a house near the beach), the girls were finishing up watching an episode of *The Backyardigans*, and Andy looked at the clock.

"It's ten o'clock in the morning and we still don't have a plan," he said.

"It's only ten in the morning," I said, taking a sip of my iced coffee that Andy had prepared the night before so it would be ready for us when we woke up.

My Drill Sergeant of Leisure
(aka Andy) takes on a salmon.

"Yes, but we have a lot to do today."

"We do?" I asked. The way he said it made it sound as if we were on deadline for something serious. "Like what?"

He started ticking things off on his fingers. "We have to go to the *pool*, we have to go to the *beach*, we have to try out that new *kite* that my dad bought for the kids. I want to go for a *run* and I assume you do, too. We have to decide whether we want to go to that *dock* you just read about to pick up some shrimp, and if we don't, we have to figure out what to make for *dinner* sooner rather than later because at six o'clock I need to be right there on that *deck* drinking my gin and tonic."

Now there was a deadline I could get excited about! Because of behavior like this, I nicknamed Andy "My Drill Sergeant of Leisure." My Drill Sergeant of Leisure shows up the second the plane's wheels touch down. My Drill Sergeant of Leisure shows up first thing in the morning, turns to me in bed, and says with a straight face, "You have some serious decisions to make" (usually something like: Pool or beach? Grouper or mahimahi?) He can't help himself. It's not that he can't relax—it's the opposite of that actually. For both of us, taking a few minutes in the morning to think about the day's structure ensures that we'll get to do all the things that help relax us the *most*. (Stay with me, here.) That means we know what we're having for dinner before we've finished the morning paper. And if we haven't already shopped for all the ingredients we need to make that dinner happen (almost always the freshest piece of fish we can find, grilled, plus a medley of colorful, easy, barely cooked or no-cook salads) we will refer to our Drill Sergeant's schedule to figure out the best time to hit the market without interrupting the natural flow of the day.

While most people can't think of anything more stressful than coming up with an hour-by-hour plan to chill out on vacation, I can't think of anything more stressful than being unprepared for our favorite time of day. Because to deprive ourselves of even one spectacular vacation dinner is, for us, no vacation at all.

Vacation Meal Planning Made Easy!

In case you aren't "lucky" enough to have a Drill Sergeant of Leisure in your own home, I've made vacation meal planning simple. Pick one meal from the Mains section and two or three from the Salads and Starch sections and then you can go about your day doing whatever you please. Recipes are on the following pages, unless otherwise indicated.

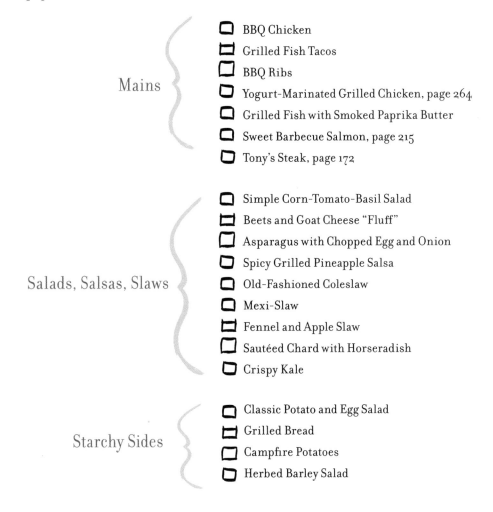

Mains
- ☐ BBQ Chicken
- ☐ Grilled Fish Tacos
- ☐ BBQ Ribs
- ☐ Yogurt-Marinated Grilled Chicken, page 264
- ☐ Grilled Fish with Smoked Paprika Butter
- ☐ Sweet Barbecue Salmon, page 215
- ☐ Tony's Steak, page 172

Salads, Salsas, Slaws
- ☐ Simple Corn-Tomato-Basil Salad
- ☐ Beets and Goat Cheese "Fluff"
- ☐ Asparagus with Chopped Egg and Onion
- ☐ Spicy Grilled Pineapple Salsa
- ☐ Old-Fashioned Coleslaw
- ☐ Mexi-Slaw
- ☐ Fennel and Apple Slaw
- ☐ Sautéed Chard with Horseradish
- ☐ Crispy Kale

Starchy Sides
- ☐ Classic Potato and Egg Salad
- ☐ Grilled Bread
- ☐ Campfire Potatoes
- ☐ Herbed Barley Salad

Grilled Fish Tacos + Spicy Grilled Pineapple Salsa + Mexi-Slaw = Perfect Vacation Dinner

BBQ Chicken

Drizzle chicken pieces (**drumsticks and thighs**) with **canola oil, salt**, and **pepper**. When the grill is hot, grill the chicken (no sauce yet) for a total of 8 to 10 minutes, turning all the while. Brush the chicken with the **barbecue sauce** (see below) and cook for another 4 minutes, basting with the sauce the entire time and turning pieces frequently so they don't burn.

Barbecue Sauce

If you make extra sauce, it keeps in the fridge for up to 2 weeks and works well with ribs and pork tenderloin, too. Total time: 15 minutes

2 teaspoons Worcestershire sauce

1 shot bourbon

1 teaspoon hot sauce

$1/3$ cup cider vinegar

3 tablespoons Dijon mustard

1 garlic clove, minced

$1/2$ cup ketchup

1 tablespoon fresh lemon juice

$1/2$ cup brown sugar

$1/4$ cup molasses

Salt and pepper

1 dried chile pepper

Combine all ingredients in a small saucepan over medium heat. Cook for 7 to 8 minutes, until thickened. Remove from the heat and let cool.

Grilled Fish Tacos

Prepare your grill. Marinate a **1-pound piece of firm whitefish** (such as swordfish or mahimahi) in a little **olive oil, salt,** and **pepper**. About 5 minutes before you grill, add a squeeze of **lime.** Once grill is hot, grill the fish 4 to 5 minutes on each side, depending on thickness. The fish is done when it's firm to the touch without being rock hard. Remove the fish from the grill and break it apart into chunks. Meanwhile, place as many **tortillas** (corn or flour, whatever you prefer) as can fit on the grill. Flip over after 30 seconds, grill a little longer, and then transfer to a platter. Assemble the tacos with tortillas, fish, and one of the sides listed on page 236.

BBQ Ribs

Smear **rib rub** (see below) on the meaty side of **2 rib racks** until coated. (You'll have some rub left over; store and save it for next time.) Place the ribs on a cookie sheet, cover with foil, and bake at 300°F for 3 hours. Remove and set aside. When your fire's ready (you don't want to put the ribs over a raging fire, so let it die down a little until it's about medium heat), grill the ribs for 2 minutes on each side to get a little char going. Then brush the meaty side generously with **Barbecue Sauce** (opposite page; or you can use your favorite store-bought brand). Keep flipping, a minute or so on each side, being careful not to burn but getting the sauce nice and caramelized. Cover and cook for 5 minutes. Remove from the heat, and slice the ribs along the bones on a cutting board.

Rub for Ribs

Makes enough for 4 rib racks

1 tablespoon smoked paprika

1 tablespoon paprika

2 teaspoons celery seed

2 tablespoons brown sugar

2 teaspoons kosher salt

$1/2$ teaspoon cayenne

1 teaspoon garlic salt

$1/2$ teaspoon freshly ground black pepper

With a spice grinder or mortar and pestle, grind all the ingredients together until everything is crushed. If you don't have a mortar and pestle or spice grinder, add the spices to a zipper-lock plastic bag and crush them with a rolling pin. If you don't have a rolling pin, I think it's time to hit the kitchen store.

Grilled Fish with Smoked Paprika Butter

This is the kind of recipe you want in your arsenal for those times when the fish is so fresh you feel guilty messing with it. Prepare your grill. Marinate a 1-pound piece of firm **whitefish** (such as tilefish, swordfish, striped bass, mahimahi) in a little **olive oil, salt,** and **pepper**. (Add a squeeze of **lemon** to the fish 5 minutes before you grill.) While grill is heating up, make some smoked paprika butter: Beat together **½ stick unsalted butter** (at room temperature) with **1 tablespoon smoked paprika** and a large pinch of kosher or sea salt until it's blended together. Melt the butter in a small saucepan over low heat and then pour into a small bowl. Once the grill is hot, grill the fish 4 to 5 minutes on each side, depending on thickness, brushing the melted smoked paprika butter as you go. The fish is done when it's firm to the touch without being rock hard. Remove the fish from grill, brush one more time with butter, and serve.

Simple Corn-Tomato-Basil Salad

If it's corn-and-tomato-basil season, you should be arrested for not having some version of this salad on the table. There is no official recipe for this—as with all fresh, peak produce, you don't need to add anything to the **chopped vegetables** beyond **olive oil, scallions, salt**, and **pepper**; proportions of vegetables should be to taste. You don't even have to cook the corn if you don't feel like it. But if you do feel like it: Boil the **corn** for 3 minutes, or cut raw kernels off the cob and fry in olive oil for 3 minutes. (If you want to turn this into a quick fresh salsa for tacos, stir in a few spoonfuls of your favorite salsa.)

Beets and Goat Cheese "Fluff"

Lucky for us, this one falls in the Pink Food category. Phoebe likes these beets without the cheese. Abby likes these beets for painting bright pink lines across her plate. To make: Remove the stems of **5 to 6 beets**. Wrap the beets in foil and roast at 425°F for 40 minutes. While they are cooking, add a drizzle of **heavy cream** or **half-and-half** to a small log of plain **goat cheese** (about 5 ounces) and mash together until cheese is slightly fluffy instead of crumbly. Once the beets are cool, peel and chop them into a fine dice. Top them with goat cheese "fluff," **fresh thyme** (or **tarragon), salt, pepper,** and a drizzle of **olive oil** before serving.

Asparagus with Chopped Egg and Onion

Add **1 pound asparagus** (trimmed) to boiling water and cook for 2½ to 3 minutes depending on thickness. Drain and immediately plunge the spears in ice water to stop cooking and preserve their bright green color. Remove from the ice bath and pat dry with paper towels. Chop **1 hard-boiled egg** into small pieces and sprinkle them over the chilled asparagus (or over half the asparagus if you, like me, have egg haters in the house) along with **1 tablespoon finely minced red onion** and drizzle with a **mustardy vinaigrette** (such as the Basic Vinaigrette on page 163).

Spicy Grilled Pineapple Salsa

This is a must if you picked the fish tacos (and also works with the Bourbon-Marinated Grilled Pork Tenderloin on page 71). You're basically just replacing the tomatoes in a traditional salsa with pineapple. Brush **9 large fresh pineapple rings** (remove the tough core if you are using the cross-sections of a fresh pineapple) with a little **vegetable oil** and place on the grill over medium heat for about 3 minutes on each side until the flesh looks golden and caramelized. Remove from the grill to a cutting board, chop up, and add to a medium bowl. Toss with **1 small jalapeño** pepper (minced, pith and seeds removed), the juice from **1 lime** (about 2 tablespoons), **⅓ cup chopped fresh cilantro**, **2 tablespoons red onion** (minced), **salt**, and **pepper**.

Old-Fashioned Coleslaw

In a large bowl, whisk together **⅓ cup cider vinegar**, **1 teaspoon prepared horseradish**, **4 heaping tablespoons mayonnaise**, **½ teaspoon celery seed**, **1 tablespoon sugar**, and **salt** and **pepper** to taste. Set aside. Shred **½ head green cabbage** (about 5 cups) as thinly as possible (with a mandoline or the shredding disk of a food processor). Add to the dressing and toss to combine. Serve right away.

Mexi-Slaw

In a large bowl, whisk together **½ cup sour cream**, the juice from **1 small lime** (about 2 tablespoons), **2 teaspoons sugar, ¼ teaspoon ground cumin, 3 chopped scallions** (white and light green parts), and **¼ cup chopped fresh cilantro**. Add **1 small head red cabbage** that has been shredded as finely as possible (with a mandoline or the shredding disk of a food processor, about 5 cups of cabbage total) and toss. Add **salt** and **pepper**. This is best served with fish tacos.

Fennel and Apple Slaw

In a medium bowl, whisk together the following: **⅓ cup apple cider vinegar, 2 tablespoons mayonnaise, 1 tablespoon Dijon mustard, 2 teaspoons celery seed, 1 teaspoon sugar,** and **salt** and **pepper** to taste. Then add to the bowl and toss: **2 thinly sliced bulbs fresh fennel** (use a mandoline or the slicing disk of food processor), **2 peeled and thinly sliced Granny Smith apples** (or whatever you can find—the more tart the apple the better; cut apples into matchsticks) **1 tablespoon chopped fresh cilantro,** and **1 tablespoon sunflower seeds**.

Sautéed Chard with Horseradish

Add **2 tablespoons olive oil** to a skillet over medium-low heat. Add **½ small chopped onion, salt,** and **pepper,** and cook until softened, about 2 minutes. Add **1 bunch washed and destemmed chard,** and sauté until it wilts, chopping with kitchen scissors in the pan once it has shrunken and become more manageable. Stir in **1 teaspoon grated prepared horseradish** (such as Gold's) and **1 teaspoon of white balsamic vinegar** (or white wine vinegar or tarragon vinegar) and serve.

Crispy Kale

The easiest way to prepare **kale**—and the way we prepare it the most—is to simply sauté a big pile of it in **olive oil** with **salt** and a few drops of **balsamic vinegar** over medium-high heat. Like most greens, a huge mound of kale will shrivel down significantly, but unlike most greens, kale tends to get crunchy if it sits on medium-high heat long enough. (And, for me, that's a good thing.) The trick is to trim the stems and chop it roughly into chip-size pieces.

Classic Potato and Egg Salad

This was my favorite potato salad growing up. So much so that I'd make my mother prepare twice the amount so I could always have some for breakfast. (My argument: How is it so different from eggs with hash browns?) Add **4 eggs** to a pot of water, turn the heat to high, and as soon as the water boils, remove from the heat and cover. They will be perfectly hard-boiled after 14 minutes. Meanwhile, peel about **7 or 8 (2¾ pounds) medium potatoes** (Yukon Golds, red, or fingerlings) and boil for 15 minutes (until a sharp knife easily slides through the flesh) and let cool. Finely dice the potatoes and add to a bowl. Once the eggs are cool, remove shells and dice finely. In a small bowl, whisk together **4 heaping tablespoons mayo** and **1 heaping tablespoon Dijon mustard.** Toss everything together along with a little more than **2 tablespoons chopped red onion** (I don't like too much of it), a few chopped **sweet pickles** if you'd like, a handful of chopped fresh **parsley,** and **salt** and **pepper** to taste. If the salad seems dry or gloppy, drizzle in a little sweet pickle juice and toss to loosen.

Grilled Bread

This is the "psychological latch" food for the girls: No matter what new recipe is gracing the dinner plate on any given night, they will see their favorite "toast" and feel comfortable with whatever is surrounding it. To prepare: In a small bowl, add **salt** to some **olive oil**. (Phoebe sometimes asks me to add chopped fresh **parsley** or **chives** or finely minced **garlic** to the oil.) Brush the sliced **baguette** with oil, sprinkle with salt, and grill facedown for about 2 minutes, checking to make sure it doesn't burn.

Campfire Potatoes with Crème Fraîche

Place **1 cup small unpeeled, unchopped potatoes** on 2 separate pieces of foil (2 cups potatoes total). To each mound of potatoes, add a little **olive oil, salt, and pepper,** then wrap in foil and put them on the grill grate for 30 minutes. (Listen to them—if they sound really sizzly, check to make sure they're not burning. Move the foil packets around to make sure they cook evenly.) When they're cooked, dump the potatoes into a bowl and smash with a fork, just enough so that the flesh bursts out of their skin. Pour a little more **olive oil** on top, a squeeze of **lemon**, whatever chopped **fresh herbs** you've got (mint, thyme, parsley, seriously whatever!), and **4 generous dollops sour cream** or crème fraîche.

Herbed Barley Salad

Bring **1 cup pearl barley** that has been rinsed and picked over, **1 teaspoon salt,** and 3 cups water to a boil in a medium pot. Cover and simmer for 50 minutes, until the barley is firm but cooked through. Toss with a handful of **chopped herbs** (parsley, chives, thyme), **3 tablespoons olive oil, salt, pepper, 3 chopped scallions** (white and light green parts), **¼ cup freshly grated Parmesan cheese,** and a generous squeeze of **lemon.** Sometimes, instead of the herbs, I'll toss in about 2 tablespoons of store-bought pesto.

DEAR GRILL-O-PHOBE

Dear Andy,

You know how much I care about making sure a nice dinner is on the table every night. You know how I love to cook, how proud I am of the fact that I can perfectly pan-fry Brussels sprouts, which Abby inhales like gumdrops; that Phoebe's most requested summer meal is whole mackerel, and that the four of us sit down together and eat the same dinner at least five times a week.

I was thinking about all that the other night as I watched you out the kitchen window, grilling the girls' favorite chicken on the patio. I was inside, aproned and alone, chopping tomatoes, but I might as well have been cradling a cobbler with oven-mitted hands. There you were—outside in the twilight, refereeing some insane tetherball game between Abby and the dog, chucking a football with Phoebe while simultaneously flipping and rearranging the scene-stealing meat on the Weber, Dark & Stormy in hand.

This whole tableau: It should have warmed my maternal heart. But I have to be honest here—it did the exact opposite. It sent me spiraling. How, after all these years, do I not know how to grill? How have I become that woman, the one who turns over the tongs—her self-worth—to the man of the house as soon as the weather turns?

My college feminist theory professor would kick me with her Doc Maartens, but I'm ready to ask for help. Your help. I don't want to be inside anymore, rinsing greens. I want to be the griller. I want a taste of the glory! I'm not terribly ambitious. I have zero interest in experimenting with applewood chips, cedar planks, or mesquite. I just want to be able to stand outside, partake in some ball throwing, and grill our favorite yogurt-marinated chicken for the family without humiliating (or hurting) myself. I'm asking for your help.

Jenny

Dear Jenny,

Please don't tell me that this is what you were up, tossing and turning about, the other night at 3:00 a.m., when—or was I dreaming this?—I asked you what was wrong and you said "Nothing" but you might as well have said "Everything." It wasn't, right? Right? What we need is a plan of action. I hate to shatter the self-serving illusion that grilling is anything short of manly, highly specialized work—definitely not for the womenfolk—but . . . it's not hard. Or intimidating. Or even complicated. It is, as you are about to see, embarrassingly easy. To do it right, you will need five things: a Weber grill, a charcoal chimney, a newspaper, charcoal, and some olive oil.

Let's start with a simple, clarifying thought experiment: Think of the grill as a stovetop. Makes it easier, right? And so, the first thing you will need to do is turn your burner on. You do this with your charcoal chimney. You know that thing out on the patio that you keep trying to throw away? See how it's divided inside by some wire mesh? Stuff two sheets of crumpled newspaper into the smaller compartment, and set it paper side down on the lower grate of the grill; then, fill the upper compartment with charcoal, all the way up, until it crests the top of the chimney. Light the newspaper, making sure it catches, and go make yourself a Dark & Stormy. Much smoke will ensue, but don't be alarmed. After 15 or 20 minutes, when the flames have died down and the coals on top are going gray around the edges, empty the chimney into the grill, spreading the coals evenly as you do. (The goal is to avoid a big pile of hot coals in the middle of the grill.) Replace top grate (i.e, the cooking surface, i.e. your pan) to get it nice and hot, and go play some tetherball.

In 10 minutes, your coals will be mostly white, glowing pink at the center. You should be burning at medium-high heat. Brush the grate with olive oil, and using your tongs, lay the chicken down, leaving some space between each piece. The chicken, which has been pounded thin to allow for tenderness and even cooking (read: minimal stressing over its doneness), shouldn't take more than 7 to 8 minutes total. I turn them every couple of minutes, so they don't burn, and move them out to the edges if the fire feels too hot. When they're firm to the touch but not rock hard, you're ready to go. See how manly and dangerous and . . . manly that was? No? Humor me at least.

Love,

Andy

September 2009

Kale: Why the Hell Not?

When Phoebe was in her "Threes" program at nursery school one of the first things she learned about was the weather. The kids would all take turns affixing smiley-face suns or frowny-face storm clouds onto a big poster titled "What's the Weather Today?" She started asking us to describe the sky outside whenever we'd leave the house. "Sunny, Mommy?" "Cloudy, Mommy?" Once, when she asked me this question, the sky happened to be so dark and foreboding that I found myself struggling to use the word *cloudy*. (This is probably the only time being an editor by trade conflicted with the day to day of motherhood.) It wasn't the right word to describe it, but it was the only word in her weather vocabulary. I hesitated. I briefly contemplated saying "really cloudy," but that wasn't right either.

"Ominous," I finally said. "The sky looks *ominous*."

"What does that mean Mommy?"

"It means the sky looks kind of dark and scary."

"Oh. You're right. The sky *is* dark and scary. It *is* ominous."

From then on, whenever the sky looked this way she would correctly identify it as "ominous," much to the shock and delight of any grown-up who was around to hear it.

I had an epiphany about parenting around this moment, an epiphany that most moms and dads probably have way before their child turns three: Kids are game for anything. It's the grown-ups who have the harder time switching things up, letting go of a routine, trying something bigger and better.

Just because the world of institutionalized learning tells kids they need to know the words *sunny*, *cloudy*, and *windy* doesn't mean they are not capable of also learning the words *ominous*, *blustery*, and *scorching*. In fact, to them, there really isn't any difference between the words *cloudy* and *ominous*. Words are just a combination of sounds. It's the grown-ups who inject the shroud of grown-up-ness around "big words" by not using those words. It's not the *kids* who think they can't handle them.

So, to come back to Planet Dinner, if *pizza*, *pasta*, and *nuggets* are the expected words at the dinner table, the "sunny" kind of meals, then why are we not presenting them with some more, uh, "ominous"-sounding meals, like curry, like quinoa, like *kale*. When I posted a kale salad recipe on the blog one of my most loyal readers wrote "Okay even *I'm* going to have a hard time with this one. Kale for kids? You might have just lost me." The thing is, I had the exact same reaction when my friend Naria told me she served kale to her five-year-old. But then I asked myself the same question parents around the world ask their kids every single night at the table: "How will you know if you don't try?" It's up to me and Andy—it's our job—to try things at the table. Constantly. It's up to us to figure out how to come up with a marketing plan for kale at our table. This doesn't mean that they like everything we put in front of them. (They've seen quinoa on the table at least fifty times and, other than a few happy five minutes in 2009, still refuse to go near it.) But I will say that both girls have not only become avid kale fans, they have tried to convince their unsuspecting classmates to try it, too.

Kale with Avocado and Pickled Onions

This was literally the recipe that convinced my kids to like kale. **Total time: 20 minutes**

1 cup water

2 tablespoons red wine vinegar

1 tablespoon sugar

½ teaspoon salt

½ medium red onion, sliced

1 large bunch kale, washed, stems removed, and chopped (8 to 10 cups)

¼ cup olive oil

1 tablespoon balsamic vinegar

Salt and pepper to taste

1 avocado, cut into chunks

In a small saucepan, add the water, red wine vinegar, sugar, and salt and bring to a boil. Add the onion and simmer for 15 minutes. Remove the onion from the pickling liquid with tongs and set aside in a bowl to cool.

Meanwhile, boil the kale (in water, not in pickling liquid!) for 2 minutes. Remove the kale with tongs, pat it dry with paper towels, and add to the bowl with the pickled onions. (If you feel up to it, you can give the kale an ice bath before you add to the bowl, to stop the cooking and preserve the deep rich color.) Toss the onion and kale with the oil, balsamic vinegar, salt, pepper, and avocado.

Kale, Sausage, and White Bean Stew

This recipe won a quick-meal contest on my website. It has all the hallmarks of a weeknight keeper: a quick cook time, a forgiving technique, and . . . sausage! **Total time: 30 minutes**

1 onion, chopped

3 tablespoons olive oil

2 garlic cloves, minced

Salt and pepper to taste

½ teaspoon red pepper flakes

4 to 6 links (about 1¼ pounds) Italian chicken or pork sausage,
   casings removed

1 32-ounce container chicken broth

1 14-ounce can diced tomatoes

2 14-ounce cans cannellini beans, rinsed and drained

1 large bunch kale, washed, stems removed,
   and chopped into small pieces

Drizzle of red wine vinegar (about 2 tablespoons)

Freshly grated Parmesan cheese

Sauté the onion in the oil in a Dutch oven over medium-high heat until softened, about 3 minutes. Add the garlic, salt and pepper, and pepper flakes and cook, stirring 1 minute.

Add in the sausage, breaking it up with a fork, and brown until cooked through, 4 to 5 minutes. Add the broth (add less if you like your stews more chunky, less brothy), tomatoes, and cannellini beans (rinsed and drained). Bring to a boil. Add the kale, simmer until wilted, about 3 minutes. Stir in a drizzle of red wine vinegar and serve stew with a lot of freshly grated Parmesan and crusty bread.

THE FAMILY PART OF FAMILY DINNER

Does this exchange sound familiar to you?

"What'd you do today?"

"What?"

"What'd you do today?"

"Huh?"

"What'd you do today?"

"Mmm, I don't remember."

"How was your day?"

"Good. I need ketchup. Do we have ketchup?"

Over the past few years, we've devised a few techniques to deal with this situation, ways to prod and cajole Phoebe and Abby into sharing and interacting—or, at the barest minimum, stopping for a moment to look up and acknowledge something beyond the food on their plates. These are our most effective.

✳ Mad-Sad-Glad

The most consistently successful of all our methods. Each family member has to share one thing from their day that made them mad, one thing that made them sad, and one thing that made them glad. In addition to initiating some real conversation (we rarely make it all the way around the table, once the kids get going) this has the welcome benefit of clueing you into some things in your kids' lives—anxieties, accomplishments, mean girls at camp, math difficulties, and the always-telling lunch-table politics—that they might otherwise have locked away in a drawer and let fester.

✳ The Negative Assertion

This doesn't deliver the kind of sustained, substantive conversation you get with Mad-Sad-Glad, but it often helps break the ice and get some dinnertime energy flowing. Kids love to prove their parents wrong—or at least our kids love to prove us wrong—so I'll offer up an observation that I know is untrue and wait for the kids to set the record straight. Like this one:

Me: I can't believe you had to stay inside all day at camp today because of the weather.

Abby: No we didn't!

Me: Man, that must have been so boring.

Phoebe: We were outside all day! We hiked down to the river, and had lunch under the poison ivy tree, and . . .

Other options: "Why do you think Ms. Metrano decided to skip math lessons today?" "I can't believe nobody said a word on the bus on the way home this afternoon." "Do you guys ever wonder how an ostrich flies?"

✳ The Misdirection Play

We hardly ever get an answer when we ask our kids something directly ("What did you do at school today?"). I find it helps to take the pressure off a little by asking them to tell a story about someone else. But maybe don't phrase it quite so overtly. Phrase it like this: "So, [your kid's name here], tell me about this new friend of yours, [new friend name here]. Does she have long hair? Does she like watching Boomerang? At recess, is she a cop or a robber?" Bet you anything your kid responds, and when he/she does, you've got them right where you want them.

✳ The Awkward Silence

Join forces with your spouse and resolve to say nothing, not a word. Kids can't hack it. They fill the silence. (Only downside: One of them might feel the urge to fill the silence with something like "Poop on a poop on a poop poop poop.")

✳ The Nuclear Option

To be deployed only in truly desperate situations: "Okay, if you guys don't start telling me about your days, we're not having s'mores tonight." This one has never failed—and believe me, we've wielded it way more than we should ever admit.

October 2009

⋅ ● ⋅ ● ● ⋅ ● ● ⋅ ● ● ⋅ ● ⋅ ● ⋅ ● ⋅ ● ⋅ ● ⋅ ● ⋅ ● ⋅ ● ⋅ ● ⋅ ● ⋅ ● ⋅ ● ⋅ ● ⋅

Control Freak

At *least once a* month I'd be sitting in my office when an email from the class mom would ping in my inbox. The subject head would read: "Help!"

"Can someone bring juice and paper cups to the First Grade Writer's Workshop Celebration this afternoon?"

And then I'd sit there waiting for the "reply-alls" to start pinging.

"No problem!"

"I can bring some lemonade!"

"I'll bring the cups!"

"Looks like I'm too late, but if you still need me, I can do either or both!"

Before I knew it, my inbox was jammed with displays of selfless party supply heroism. When the offers were all stacked up that way, one on top of the other with the same subject line—*Help! Help! Help! Help! Help! Help! Help!*—it was easy to imagine that they were, collectively, saying, *Why are you just sitting there in your office, Jenny? Do something, would you?*

I loved my office. On one wall there was an enormous bulletin board (I called it "my brain") that was covered with inspiring photographs and story layouts, plus about a hundred index cards, each one representing a story idea that was in the works (white card) or that I wanted to be in the works soon (pink card). On another wall were three framed original sketches by a Swedish illustrator named Lisbeth Svarling, whose regular contributions to the magazine made me inexplicably happy. In another corner by the door was a pile of new cookbooks and novels that were delivered daily for my consideration. Next to that were two large jars—one with lightly salted almonds and another with dried cherries—that ensured I'd have visitors all day long. (We called it "friend bait.") Then there was my computer. I think if someone came into my office and offered me a vintage Mercedes in exchange for my iMac, I would've laughed in dismissal. I can't remember the exact model, but let me just say that this thing was big, fast, and—the best part—came with a free tech team only a few floors away. When I'd arrive in the office on Monday morning, after spending the weekend cramming in errands and food shopping and back-to-back birthday parties, nothing made me happier than turning on my lightning-fast Mac with its LED backlit monitor and seeing all my color-coded files lined up one on top of the other. To this day, I associate Apple's signature organ chord—the one that sounds like a meditative *Ommmm* when you press the on button—with feeling *in control.*

But on days when I'd receive all these cry-for-help emails, I didn't want to be in that office. I wanted to be home. I wanted to be five minutes away from school so I could be the paper cup hero. While I was there, maybe I could volunteer to chaperone a class trip and help out with the mosaic art project in the spring? I was still working full-time, and even with my one day off—now moved to Fridays—I still had the most awful habit of romanticizing whatever was happening on the domestic front in my absence. Beyond the classroom stuff were the playdates and after-school activities. I felt especially guilt-stricken by the fact that I couldn't pick up the girls at ballet or pottery and hear the teachers proclaim how gifted my daughters were at pirouetting and glazing.

One year I scheduled a tennis class for the girls on Monday night at a facility consistently referred to as "second best" next to the nicer program across town. The reason I chose it was because they offered a class that ended at six thirty, and it was a walkable distance from a station on my train line. If I timed things right, I could catch the last fifteen minutes of the class. In my mind, those fifteen minutes were different from regular fifteen minutes. They were quality-time minutes. Minutes that I imagined would register in my daughters' impressionable psyches as: "Even though Mom is never ever the paper cup hero, she *did* just take an early train to a different train station and walk here—all so she could watch me practice my *serving* toss. That's how much she loves me."

After those quality fifteen minutes, though, the girls would usually dump their short-throated Prince rackets into my arms and one of them would ask, "Mom, how come you can never come in time for the *whole* lesson?"

I didn't give up, though. To be a working parent was to sign up for a lifelong game of fuzzy math. It always seemed like I was crunching numbers or counting minutes as though the answer to raising happy children lay somewhere in a magical, logical, predictable formula. When Phoebe and Abby were little, I wrote an essay for the *New York Times* about the imaginary Quality Time spreadsheet I kept in my head. On this spreadsheet, I detailed how many hours a week I spent with my kids, with the goal being to have as many or more hours than Devika. (I always "won" this little exercise because I reasoned that hours spent driving the kids places—a big part of Devika's job—were not worth as much as hours at the dinner table or on the floor acting out *Three Billy Goat's Gruff*.) I don't necessarily think this obsessiveness is limited to delusional, emotionally insecure mothers. I've noticed that when Andy has to work late closing a story and misses dinner and bedtime, he's almost always on an earlier train the next night, as though those few extra minutes of eating chips and salsa with the girls before dinner will cancel out his absence from the night before. Though I've never asked him, I'm pretty sure he's trying to make his numbers come out even, too.

As the girls got older, though, the quality-time equation got more complicated. Being around more was no longer just about doing drop-off and pickup or showing up at the classroom party with a stack of paper plates. I found that the problems of a second-grader—even the most garden-variety kinds like "Fill-in-the-blank doesn't want to play with me anymore"—were exponentially more stressful to deal with when I realized that, for the first time in my tenure as a parent, I could do nothing to solve the problem. The only thing I could think of doing in order to feel more in control (or to delude myself into feeling more in control) was be around more to *talk* about the problem.

This was about the time I found myself doing a different kind of math. If I was around more . . . if I left my job, could we make it work financially? If I could figure out a way to work only three days a week (a prize that usually comes with a round-trip ticket to Disneyworld) could I make the hours at work and the hours at home come out even? If I left my job to go totally freelance, how many hours would I have between 8:09 a.m. (when the girls got on the bus) until 2:57 p.m. (when they got off)? And most important: How much would my very own iMac set me back?

But then I'd go to work and get wrapped up in developing one of those ideas on the pink index cards. Or the friend bait would reel in another working mom with the same issues as me and we'd end up saying how happy we were to have each other's support and friendship. Or I'd look around my organized office, where I always felt in control, and think, *How could I ever leave this?* There was always an excuse. After this issue closes, I'll decide. After I write this story, I'll decide. After the book project wraps, I'll decide. And on and on.

The decision I never had the guts to make was made for me. In October 2009, I showed up at my desk, coffee in hand, only to be ushered into a filled-to-capacity conference room and told by two sweating Ralph Lauren–clad execs that *Cookie* was folding (apparently, their numbers weren't adding up) and my services were no longer needed. We weren't the only ones to lose our jobs. The company also folded *Gourmet* and two other magazines that day, and across the country the recession was driving the unemployment rate up to record numbers. In the scheme of things, I was lucky. Andy was employed. We had insurance through his job. Life would go on.

After the announcement, I went back to my office—the one where I always felt in control—and began the dreaded task of boxing up my four-year career at *Cookie.* One by one I removed each index card that held an idea now belonging to someone else. In another corner was a pile of proofs for the cookbook we had been working on for two years. Nothing in that pile—not a recipe, not a word, not a photograph—belonged to me either. I started responding to the outpouring of emails from friends and colleagues who had heard the bad news and said they would keep their ears open for jobs. I thanked them for the support and said I'd be in touch when I figured out what I wanted my next step to be. I don't remember my exact words, but the subtext of each reply was something like: *Help! Help! Help! Help! Help!*

I thought a lot about what my next step could be. I could get another full-time magazine job. Or maybe a cookbook editing job? I could write. I could edit. I could fill in for people on maternity leave until I figured something out. I could also . . . go for a jog in the middle of the day. I could go to Fairway in the middle of

the week. I could make a weeknight dinner that took longer than thirty minutes. I could be at the bus stop every day after school. I could start thinking about family dinner around lunchtime. I could . . . I could . . . start doing what 14 percent of American mothers were already doing: I could start one of those blog things. I could *blog* about something I really believed in. Something that made me happy. I could blog about family dinner.

It wasn't just that I needed a way to fill my days. I knew other parents were struggling to find more time to connect with their kids, too. I heard about the connection problem at school board meetings, at the bus stop, and on the soccer sidelines from working mothers sitting in my friend-bait chair, from Lori (my Dinner Doula guinea pig), from an esteemed guest with multiple degrees and academic chairs on NPR. There was always a trendy culprit to blame for the problem—the omnipresence of cell phones and kids' pathological addiction to social media, the overscheduled child (tennis on Monday, pottery on Tuesday, ice skating Wednesday—you get the idea), the standardized test-driven curriculum in our schools (which results in homework overload but intellectual starvation), our expected 24/7 connectivity with the office—but all of them felt similarly overwhelming, unfixable, seemingly out of our control.

Family dinner was something I could control.

I spent an embarrassing amount of time on GoDaddy.com, the website that tells you if the name you want for your website has already been taken. My first choice was TheProvider.com, which a "squatter" (someone who buys domain names for nothing knowing someone else will buy them from him for much more later) said I could buy it from him for the low price of ten thousand dollars. (I offered him eighty dollars, but he wouldn't budge.) I didn't have a second choice. In spite of the eight thousand options Andy and I came up with over the next month, I couldn't commit to any of them. It had to be perfect. If I learned anything in my magazine career, it was that the title and subtitle can sometimes be the most important part of the story—the part that *convinces* you to read the story. It had to be strong. It had to communicate exactly what the site was about. It had to be broad enough so I could write about things that happened at the table, not just what we ate at the table. It had to be unintimidating. For search reasons, it had to have the words *dinner* and *family* in it, but it couldn't sound like a holier-than-thou family values website. It had to instantly telegraph the idea that dinner was something that had the potential to make you and your family really happy, that dinner had the potential to change your life.

Was that too much to ask for?

It was Andy who finally came up with Dinner: A Love Story (and the tagline: It all begins at the family table). We were driving south on I-95 on our way to his parents' house for Thanksgiving. As soon as he said it, I knew it was the right one. From the backseat, Abby told me to stop screaming because she couldn't hear *Ratatouille* on the DVD player. GoDaddy.com told me the name was mine if I wanted it. I wanted it!

Dinner: A Love Story, the blog, was born six months after I lost my job and quickly became the emotional bread-and-butter (as opposed to the financial bread-and-butter) of my new life as a freelancer. And so now, instead of obsessing about the number of hours I was away from my children, or the number of minutes I managed to catch of the tennis lesson, or how many lost opportunities there were to be the paper cup hero, I began obsessing over different numbers.

I began obsessing over my Google Analytics numbers. Google Analytics is the application that tells you everything you could ever want to know about your website readers except their names: how many there are, which posts they read, which website sent them, what country they live in, how many minutes and seconds they stay, how many pages they visited, what keywords and phrases they Googled to find me (my favorite: "jenny rosenstrach gin and tonic") and a lot more stuff that I haven't figured out yet. Needless to say, my GA page with its charts and graphs and beautifully precise measurements on things like "bounce rate percentages" was bookmarked as a favorite. Andy would come in the kitchen, catch me poring over my numbers and ask, "Looking in the mirror again?"

It's research, I'd plead. *So I know what my readers are responding to!*

But it was more than that. For the first time since I had kids—maybe even since I started working—I felt what it was like to be in control of my life. I could reply, "I'll bring the juice!" to the class mom's email. I could be at the bus stop whenever I wanted to. I could be at drop-off *and* pickup for every activity. (It should be noted, however, that the activity schlepping turned out to be the absolute *bane of my existence*.) And I was in control of something that was exclusively mine. This was a powerful drug, and before I knew it, I had turned into my mother. I considered working every bit as fun as vacation. I didn't know what all my work on the site was going to lead to or how long it was going to last, but I don't think I ever stopped working to ask myself either question. All I knew was that the numbers were adding up to something good.

Five Recipes on Dinner:
A Love Story with the Best Numbers
(i.e., Most Popular!)

Best Vegetarian: Peanut Butter Noodles

This peanut butter noodle recipe (known to most of the world as sesame noodles) is from my friend, mother of two, and onetime *Gourmet* magazine staffer Melissa Roberts, whose kids lived and breathed peanut butter. In the original recipe, she called for peanut butter that is not all natural because it apparently affects the texture. But I find that the dinner still works with the all-natural kind, too. If you have any leftover sauce after tossing with the noodles, try it drizzled over steamed spinach goma-ae-style. **Total time: 25 minutes**

1 pound udon noodles or spaghetti

1 small garlic clove

1-inch piece peeled fresh ginger

½ cup smooth peanut butter

⅔ cup warm water

2 tablespoons soy sauce

1 tablespoon Asian sesame oil

1 tablespoon red wine or cider vinegar

1 teaspoon sugar

½ to 1 teaspoon red pepper flakes

Any combination of the following toppings: sliced cucumbers, chopped peanuts, sugar snap peas, and shredded chicken if you need to please a meat-eater

Prepare the noodles according to package instructions. Set aside.

With the motor running, drop the garlic and ginger into the bowl of a food processor and process until finely chopped. Add the peanut butter, water, soy sauce, sesame oil, vinegar, sugar, and pepper flakes and process until smooth.

Toss with the noodles and add the desired toppings.

Best Dessert: Apple "Gazette"

Most people of course know this as an apple "galette," but Abby once called it a gazette by accident, so that's its official title in our house. My favorite thing about this recipe is that unlike most baked goods, it can be thrown together casually with room for error. (I am not a baker, so I need a *lot* of room.) You can slice the apples right into the middle of the crust to save on bowl cleanup, too. Cortland, Granny Smith, Jonathan, Northern Spy, and McIntosh are all excellent pie-baking apples. **Total time: 1 hour**

1 9-inch frozen pie crust, such as Pillsbury or Trader Joe's
   (or if you have Martha Stewart's pâte brisée in the freezer, lucky you!)

3 to 4 apples, peeled and sliced (about 1½ pounds or 4 cups)

¼ cup sugar

½ teaspoon cinnamon

Dash of nutmeg

Juice from ½ lemon

6 to 8 dots of butter

1 egg, beaten

Preheat the oven to 400°F.

Lay the pie crust on top of a cookie sheet. Peel and thinly slice the apples directly into the center of the crust, leaving about a 1-inch border around the perimeter of the dough. Sprinkle the apples with the sugar, cinnamon, nutmeg, and lemon juice. Using your hands, toss everything together gently, then pleat the crust around the perimeter of the apples. (Most of the center of the pie will be exposed, like a tart.) Dot the apples with butter and brush the crust with egg wash. (This is an excellent task for kids.)

Bake for 20 minutes. Turn down the heat to 350°F and bake another 20 minutes, until crust is golden and the apples are a little bubbly. If the apples look dry on top, stir them around a bit to coat with juice. If the crust is looking too brown before the apples are bubbly, cover the galette with foil. Once the galette is cool, Abby likes to sprinkle it with powdered sugar, but this step is not required.

Best Grilling: Yogurt-Marinated Grilled Chicken

We never liked grilled chicken—it was always too rubbery or dry—until we discovered the yogurt technique. Now it's our number one choice for summer dinner. On the blog we called it "Grilled Chicken for People Who Hate Grilled Chicken." **Total time: 3 hours 20 minutes (includes 3 hours marinating time)**

½ cup plain yogurt

1 garlic clove, chopped

2 teaspoons salt

Juice from 1½ lemons (about ⅓ cup)

Good squeeze of honey

1 tablespoon olive oil

Very healthy dose of freshly ground black pepper

4 to 5 boneless chicken breasts (about 1½ pounds),
   pounded (see sidebar, page 12)

In a medium bowl, whisk together the yogurt, garlic, salt, lemon juice, honey, oil, and pepper until emulsified. Pour the yogurt marinade into zipper-lock plastic bag. Add the chicken to the bag and mush around until coated. Seal and refrigerate for a minimum of 3 hours. When the grill is ready (and oiled), shake off the excess yogurt from chicken breasts and grill 3 to 4 minutes on each side, until flesh is firm but not rock hard.

Best Beef: Belgian Beef Stew

I grew up eating the traditional tomato-based beef stew—the kind that goes well with a mound of egg noodles. This one is the Belgian brothy version and is topped off with a dollop of mustard. Just the detail to elevate a classic kid dinner into a grown-up one.
Total time: 1 hour

1 tablespoon olive oil

2 garlic cloves

1 sirloin steak (about 1½ pounds), patted dry, salted, and cut into 1-inch
   chunks

1 large onion, chopped

1 12-ounce bottle of good-quality dark beer

1 bay leaf

Leaves from 2 sprigs fresh thyme

1 cup peeled and sliced carrots

Salt and pepper to taste

2 pounds red potatoes, peeled and quartered

Dijon mustard, for serving

In a Dutch oven, heat the oil and 1 garlic clove (halved horizontally) over medium-high heat until the garlic turns golden, 1 to 2 minutes. Remove the garlic and discard. Add the steak to the oil, in batches, and brown on all sides, salting and peppering as you go. Set the steak aside.

Add the onion to the pan, reduce the heat to medium-low, and cook until the onion is soft and sweating, about 8 minutes. Then add the steak and its juices back into pan, with the beer, bay leaf, and thyme. Bring to a boil, scraping the bottom of the pan as you go. Reduce the heat to low and cover. Simmer for 20 minutes. Chop the remaining garlic clove and add to the pan along with the carrots. Meanwhile, boil the potatoes in salted water for about 15 minutes, until a knife meets no resistance slicing through them.

Cook stew for another 25 minutes, until the carrots are tender. Serve over boiled potatoes and top with the dollops of Dijon mustard.

You'll need a spoon to drink up the broth.

Best Chicken: Baked Chicken in Creamy Tomato Sauce

I couldn't believe how popular this recipe was with my readers. I had eaten it at my friend Vanessa's house—she found some version of it first in *Olive* magazine—and when I shared it on the blog, people went crazy. I think it has something to do with the mascarpone. Everyone has their worn-out baked chicken dish, but the mascarpone manages to make it a little special without turning off the kids. Total time: 50 minutes

3 to 4 large boneless chicken breasts, rinsed and patted dry

3 tablespoons olive oil

1 small onion, finely chopped

2 garlic cloves, minced

1 15-ounce can chopped tomatoes

3 tablespoons mascarpone

Handful of fresh basil, roughly chopped

Preheat the oven to 350°F.

In an ovenproof skillet or Dutch oven, brown the chicken breasts over high heat in the oil, about 2 minutes on each side. Remove the breasts from the pan. (They do not have to be cooked through.) Turn down the heat to medium-low and add the onion and garlic. After about 2 minutes, stir in the tomatoes and simmer for 10 to 15 minutes. Stir in mascarpone and basil. Add chicken breasts back to pan, immersing them in sauce, and bake uncovered for 20 minutes, flipping halfway through.

May 2010

. . . .

Rising to the Occasion

It's true that losing my job was both traumatic and clarifying, and that I might describe the time around this event as "before I got canned" and "after I got canned." But that wasn't exactly the case. A more accurate summation might be "before yeast" and "after yeast." Because right after I lost my job, I discovered the book *My Bread* by Jim Lahey. Lahey is the man behind Sullivan Street Bakery (among other popular New York spots) and his popularity probably peaked the day Mark Bittman ran his no-knead bread recipe in the *New York Times* Dining section. The recipe was something of a sensation—a whole generation of amateur bakers intimidated by the conventional punching and rolling step (aka kneading) became instant converts. It was one of Bittman's most-read columns in ten years and spawned an entire cookbook featuring other no-knead recipes that were just as exciting as the now world-famous bread.

Of course, had I not lost my job, I would have never picked up Lahey's book in the first place. That's because every single recipe in the book called for an ingredient that was a virtual deal breaker for anyone who had kids and also a job.

Every recipe contained yeast.

There are other instructions and ingredients that intimidate me—phyllo dough, egg poaching, grilling a Porterhouse—but none of these tasks seemed to speak to the condition of my life as profoundly as yeast did. In my mind, there was no overlap on the Venn diagram between people who worked with yeast and people like me, who seemed to spend way too much time in a state of semi-urgency—even when the task at hand was just folding laundry. To me, if you were comfortable working with yeast, it usually meant you were regularly making recipes that required yeast. Which usually meant that you had a reserve of patience as well as the kind of life that regularly allowed for *rising time*. The only rising that happened regularly in my house was Abby at inhuman hours in the morning.

But when I flipped through Lahey's book and came across the recipe for his crispy thin pizza crust—the same crispy thin crust that lined the pizzas I had devoured at his restaurants several dozen euphoric times—I had a clarifying moment: I don't have a job. I no longer walk around exhausted all the time craving sleep. I now have a life—at least for the time being—in which two hours of rising time (which is what the pizza recipe called for) would not upend my day or my sanity.

If the rest of the world was caught up in a no-knead bread revolution, I was caught up in a no-knead pizza crust revolution. At Trader Joe's I found a sick pleasure in bypassing the perfectly fine store-bought balls of pizza dough, reaching instead for the triple-pack of Fleischmann's active dry yeast that once taunted me from the baking ingredient shelf. And we would absolutely tear through those yeast packs—making homemade pizza about once a week for the first year of my new life. I'm not talking about the kind of pizza you make by sprinkling shredded cheese over jarred sauce. I'm talking pizza that always made good use of our fresh farmers' market loot or pizza that may or may not include cheese. We experimented with different toppings all the time—arugula and ricotta, green tomatoes and aged provolone. The kids would occasionally take a bite of these—and in the case of our salad pizza devour them—but for the most part, they stuck with their favorite: marinara and mozzarella, maybe sausage. Which was fine with me because it didn't involve a whole lot of extra work on our ends. We'd just draw an imaginary line down the center of the pizzas and make one half for them and the other half for us. We call these "split-personality" pizzas, and in our minds it's the ultimate family dinner—you can have three separate meals on one crust and still feel like you're all eating the same thing.

Six Pizzas

If *you have just* read this little ode to yeast and wondered why on earth you picked up this hateful book with stories about people who have time to make homemade pizza crust, please take a big Lamaze breath. Remember, those kids hanging on your apron won't always be hanging on your apron. And until they grow out of that phase, you are encouraged to replace the homemade dough in the following pizza recipes with the store-bought variety now available just about anywhere.

Pizza Crust

I love Jim Lahey's crust because it's thin, crispy, and so very reliable. I can't ever remember a night where it didn't work. When we're feeling healthy, we replace the white flour with whole wheat flour—if you want to be sneaky about it with the kids, you can start by just replacing half with whole wheat flour. We usually use one ball of dough for one dinner and then freeze the extra for another dinner later. To thaw, remove from freezer about two to three hours before using and work it with your hands if it's still stiff. Makes two 16-ounce balls of dough; each ball of dough makes 1 cookie-sheet-size pizza Total time: 2 hours 5 minutes (includes 2-hour hands-off rise time)

> 3¾ cups all-purpose flour
>
> 2½ teaspoons instant or other active dry yeast
>
> ¾ teaspoon salt
>
> ¾ teaspoon sugar
>
> 1⅓ cups water, room temperature
>
> Olive oil, for greasing

In a medium bowl, stir together the flour, yeast, salt, and sugar. Add the water, and using a wooden spoon or your hand, mix until blended, at least 30 seconds.

The dough will be stiff, not wet and sticky. Cover the bowl and let it sit at room temperature until the dough has more than doubled in volume, about 2 hours. Divide the dough in two and shape each section into flattened balls. If you are only making one pizza, freeze the other ball in a freezer storage bag. If you rub a little olive oil on your fingers and on the ball of dough before bagging, it will be less sticky to negotiate.

Pick your desired pizza from the following pages and proceed as directed.

Pizza Sauce

Makes 3 cups of sauce, enough for two 11 x 17-inch pizzas Total time: 30 to 40 minutes

2 garlic cloves, minced

4 to 5 glugs of olive oil

1 small onion, chopped

Salt and pepper to taste

Few shakes of red pepper flakes

1 28-ounce can diced tomatoes (or tomato puree)

6 shakes oregano

4 to 5 basil leaves, chopped (optional)

In a medium saucepan over low heat, sauté the garlic in the oil for 1 to 2 minutes, until fragrant. Add the onion, salt and pepper, and pepper flakes, and turn up the heat slightly. Stir until the onions have softened, about 4 minutes. Add the tomatoes and oregano. Stir, bring to a boil, and then simmer uncovered for 30 minutes. (But 20 minutes is fine, too, if the kids are losing it.) If you have basil, definitely add a few shreds during the last 5 minutes that it simmers.

Pizza 1: Sausage and Ricotta Pizza

You will always see this combo on one side of our split-personality pizzas. (If you are doing the split pizza, remember to halve the ingredients below.) Total time: 35 to 40 minutes

Olive oil, for greasing

1 16-ounce ball homemade pizza dough (see page 270)
or your favorite store-bought variety

1½ cups Pizza Sauce (see page 271)
or your favorite store-bought variety

1 link sweet or hot Italian sausage, casing removed,
crumbled and cooked

1 8-ounce ball fresh mozzarella, thinly sliced

6 to 10 spoonfuls fresh ricotta

¼ cup freshly grated Parmesan cheese

Preheat the oven to 500°F.

Using your fingers or a pastry brush, grease a 17 x 12-inch rimmed baking sheet with the oil. Drop your pizza dough into the center of the baking sheet, and using your fingers, press out and flatten the dough so it spreads as close as possible to all four corners. This might seem difficult, but persist—the thin crust will be worth it.

Add the sauce to dough, spreading with a spoon. Sprinkle with sausage and top with the mozzarella. Add the ricotta and Parmesan cheese on top. Bake for 15 to 20 minutes, until the cheese is bubbly.

If the crust is browning faster than the toppings are cooking, cover with foil and continue to bake.

Pizza 2: Mushroom and Onion Pizza on Whole Wheat Crust

For this one, try replacing 2 cups of the flour in the pizza crust recipe for whole wheat flour. It adds a nice nutty flavor. Total time: 35 minutes

4 tablespoons olive oil, plus more for brushing

1 16-ounce ball homemade pizza dough (see page 270)
    or your favorite store-bought variety

1 medium onion, sliced

1½ cups mushrooms (any kind—if you can find maittake, try them;
    they are my favorite) sliced or chopped

Leaves from 2 sprigs fresh thyme

¼ teaspoon red pepper flakes

Tiniest pinch of nutmeg (barely ⅛ teaspoon)

Salt and pepper to taste

1 8-ounce ball fresh mozzarella, thinly sliced

Freshly grated Parmesan cheese

Chopped fresh parsley (optional)

Preheat the oven to 500°F.

Using your fingers or a pastry brush, grease a 17 x 12-inch rimmed baking sheet with 1 tablespoon of the oil. Drop your pizza dough into the center of the baking sheet, and using your fingers, press out and flatten the dough so it spreads as close as possible to all four corners. This might seem difficult, but persist—the thin crust will be worth it.

In a medium bowl, toss together the onion, mushrooms, thyme, pepper flakes, nutmeg, and salt and pepper with the remaining oil.

With our split-personality pizza (sausage and ricotta for the girls; arugula, ricotta, and lemon for Mom and Dad), everyone goes home happy.

Top the dough with mozzarella slices so it covers as much of the crust as possible. Top with the onion-mushroom mixture, brushing any exposed dough (specifically the edges) with extra oil. Bake for 12 to 15 minutes, until the cheese is bubbly and golden. If the crust is browning faster than the toppings are cooking, cover with foil and continue to bake.

Add the Parmesan cheese and a little fresh parsley (if using) when serving.

Pizza 3: Salad Pizza

This was inspired by the salad pizza I grew up gorging on at Sal's Pizzeria in Mamaroneck, New York. The girls love it, too—good thing or I'd have to start wondering if they were related to me. **Total time: 30 minutes**

Olive oil, for greasing

1 16-ounce ball homemade pizza dough (see page 270)
    or your favorite store-bought variety

1½ cups Pizza Sauce (see page 271)
    or your favorite store-bought variety

½ cup olive oil

¼ cup red wine vinegar

3 shakes dried oregano

Salt and pepper to taste

1 small head Boston or Bibb lettuce,
    shredded or chopped

1 cup cherry or grape tomatoes, halved

2 tablespoons finely minced red onion

½ cup freshly grated Parmesan cheese

Preheat the oven to 500°F.

Using your fingers or a pastry brush, grease a 17 x 12-inch rimmed baking sheet with the oil. Drop your pizza dough into the center of the baking sheet, and using your fingers, press out and flatten the dough so it spreads as close as possible to all four corners. This might seem difficult, but persist—the thin crust will be worth it.

Bake the crust for 8 minutes. Remove from the oven, add the sauce, and brush the exposed perimeter with olive oil. Bake for another 5 minutes, until the crust is golden and sauce is warm.

While the crust is baking, make your salad. In a large bowl, whisk together the oil, vinegar, oregano, salt, and pepper. Add the lettuce, tomatoes, onion, and Parmesan cheese, and toss.

When the pizza crust is finished baking, let cool slightly and top with the salad. (To prevent a soggy crust and oily fingers, make sure excess salad dressing does not spill onto pizza.) Serve with a lot of napkins. It gets messy.

Pizza 4: Zucchini and Feta Pizza

If you don't have feta, ricotta will work, too. Just don't mix it into the zucchini. Add it in small dollops on top before baking. Total time: 40 minutes

> Olive oil, for greasing
>
> 1 16-ounce ball homemade pizza dough (see page 270)
>   or your favorite store-bought variety
>
> 2 medium zucchini, shredded (about 2 cups)
>
> ½ cup olive oil

1 cup crumbled feta

Zest from ½ lemon

Freshly ground black pepper

1 8-ounce ball fresh mozzarella, thinly sliced

Handful chopped fresh mint

Preheat the oven to 500°F.

Using your fingers or a pastry brush, grease a 17 x 12-inch rimmed baking sheet with the oil. Drop your pizza dough into the center of the baking sheet, and using your fingers, press out and flatten the dough so it spreads as close as possible to all four corners. This might seem difficult, but persist—the thin crust will be worth it.

In a large bowl, toss the zucchini with the oil, feta, lemon zest, and pepper. Distribute the mozzarella on the crust evenly and then top with the zucchini and feta mixture. Bake for 15 minutes, until the crust looks crispy and golden and the cheese is bubbly.

If the crust is browning faster than the toppings are cooking, cover with foil and continue to bake.

Remove from the oven, sprinkle on the mint, and serve.

Pizza 5: White Pizza with Arugula, Parmesan, Lemon, and Ricotta

This is best when you can find market-fresh, peppery arugula. **Total time: 35 minutes**

Olive oil, for greasing and brushing

1 16-ounce ball homemade pizza dough (see page 270)
  or your favorite store-bought variety

1 8-ounce ball fresh mozzarella, thinly sliced

Few handfuls of arugula

½ cup freshly grated Parmesan cheese

⅓ cup olive oil

Juice from ½ lemon (about 2 tablespoons)

Salt and pepper to taste

12 dollops of fresh ricotta

Fresh oregano (optional)

Preheat the oven to 500°F. Using your fingers or a pastry brush, grease a 17 x 12-inch rimmed baking sheet with the oil. Drop your pizza dough into the center of the baking sheet, and using your fingers, press out and flatten the dough so it spreads as close as possible to all four corners. This might seem difficult, but persist—the thin crust will be worth it.

Cover the dough with mozzarella and brush exposed edge of the crust with a little oil. Bake for 15 minutes, until the crust is crispy and the cheese is bubbly. (If the cheese starts to bubble before the crust looks done, cover the center of pizza with foil.)

While the pizza bakes, toss together the arugula, Parmesan cheese, olive oil, lemon juice, and salt and pepper. When the pizza crust is ready, let it cool for about 2 minutes and then top with the salad. Add the ricotta and finish with a few grinds of pepper and oregano (if using).

Pizza 6: Pan-fried Hawaiian Pizza

The pan-fried pizza move comes in handy during the summer when you don't want to turn the oven to 500°F. Total time: 20 minutes Makes 2 pizzas

Olive oil, for frying and brushing

4 ounces ham or prosciutto, chopped

1 16-ounce ball homemade pizza dough (see page 270)
or your favorite store-bought variety, split into 2 8-ounce balls

1 cup Pizza Sauce (see page 271)
or your favorite store-bought variety

1 8-ounce ball fresh mozzarella, thinly sliced

1½ cups pineapple cubes

4 or 5 fresh basil leaves, shredded

Preheat the broiler.

Add a little oil to a medium cast-iron pan and fry the ham over medium-low heat until it's a little brown and crispy, about 3 minutes. Set aside.

Roll each pizza dough half into circles the size of your cast-iron pan. The dough will probably be slightly thicker than what you're used to.

Heat the pan to medium and add about 1 tablespoon of olive oil. Add 1 piece of the rolled-out dough. Cook for 2 to 3 minutes, until the dough is bubbly on top and browned underneath. Flip, add half of the sauce, half of the mozzarella, half of the ham, and half of the pineapple. Cook another 2 minutes, until the bottom is cooked, then slip under the broiler for 2 to 3 minutes, until the cheese looks bubbly and the pineapple is slightly caramelized. Top with basil. Remove the pizza from the pan, and repeat with the other piece of dough.

June 2011

Running Late

JR: Got stuck on phone with M. Can you start dinner?

AW: Yup. What do we have?

JR: Chicken thighs should be in fridge thawing . . .

AW: With braised leeks?

JR: Inspired! Start in skillet, add broth, finish in oven?

AW: With a touch of cream.

JR: Wow! We're cooking with cream now?

AW: Good cholesterol check this morning.

JR: Got it. Can we whisk with a little Dijon?

AW: Can't go wrong with that, my brother.

Pan-roasted Chicken Thighs with Braised Leeks

As with all browning, to get a nice sear on the chicken, it's helpful to start with room-temperature meat. Total time: 30 minutes

3 tablespoons olive oil

1 garlic clove, halved

1 pound boneless or bone-in chicken thighs, salted and peppered

Seven-Ingredient Dinner:
Magic words to working parents.

3 large leeks, well rinsed, trimmed, and cut into 2-inch-long pieces

¾ cup chicken broth

¼ cup cream

1 heaping tablespoon Dijon mustard

Preheat the oven to 375°F.

Heat a large ovenproof skillet over medium heat and add 2 tablespoons of the oil. Swirl the garlic in the oil for about 1 minute (do not let it burn) and discard.

Turn up the heat to medium-high. Add the chicken thighs and brown on both sides, about 4 minutes total. Remove the chicken with a slotted spoon. Add the remaining oil and leeks. Cook until the leeks have slightly softened, 2 minutes. Mix the chicken back with the leeks and add the broth. Bring to a boil, then transfer to the oven.

Bake for 10 minutes. While the chicken is baking, whisk together the cream and mustard. During the last 2 minutes of cooking, add the creamy mustard to the leeks and stir until combined. Serve with rice.

Fall 2011

. . . .

Love Is Homemade Stock

hen Andy and I were first dating we'd do this thing when we'd say good-bye. We'd start walking in opposite directions and turn back to look at each other as we got farther and farther away. We'd keep craning our necks for as long as we could—until the other person was too blurry in the distance or until a pack of drunk thick-necked frat boys interrupted our line of vision. (Do I need to remind you that we met in college?) Every time we would do this—and for several years after, when we would part from a corner on Second Avenue and West Fifty-seventh Street to our separate offices in New York City—I'd get a young-and-in-love endorphin rush.

Is it a sad state of affairs or a happy one when two kids, one Boston terrier, and nearly twenty years later, I still get this same exact brand of rush today but for totally different reasons? Like the time when Andy came home from a solo shopping trip and unpacked the ketchup—even though I was the one to squeeze the bottle dry and hadn't even reminded him that we needed to replenish. Or the time he gave me a Wüsthof paring knife (my first quality piece of cooking equipment) as a congratulatory gift for taking the GMAT. (Perhaps this was his tactful way of telling me that my short-lived plan to go to business school was *so not me*.) Or the many times I'd overhear him playing the part of Swiper at six in the morning, locked into an intense game of Dora Dollhouse with Abby, as I'd sleep in down the hall. (If it were *me* on morning duty, we'd play Dora the old-fashioned way: by turning on Nick Jr.) But mostly I'm thinking about the half-dozen instances when I've come downstairs after kissing the girls good night only to discover the carcass of the roast chicken we just ate for dinner submerged and simmering away in our 5½-quart Le Creuset Dutch oven. This meant that Andy was making me homemade stock. It meant that while I went about my after-kids-go-to-bed routine (which usually included any combination of Jon Stewart, Tina Fey, or my *Friday Night Lights* heroes Coach and Tami Taylor) that a big batch of stock was just getting tastier and richer and more delicious and, with a stash of it in the freezer, that all kinds of dinner possibilities (Bugialli's signature minestone!) would be presenting themselves in the next few weeks. I think the first time Andy surprised me with this, my heart actually fluttered.

Because for a working mother of two, having a stash of makes-anything-special homemade stock in the freezer was and is just about the most romantic thing I could imagine. Yes, of course I could use the Tetra Pack organic broths that are readily available in every supermarket and more than decent in flavor

Homemade Chicken Stock: whatever's in the vegetable bin . . . throw it in the pot!

and quality. But that's the point. So could everyone else in the world with $3.89 to spare. No one really *needs* homemade stock. Homemade stock is a luxury most people cannot afford. Not in the material sense but in terms of time. Who has the time and energy to add one more task to the to-do list after the cooking, the feeding, the math-homework "helping," the eat-your-broccoli-ing, the cleaning, the dishwashing, the backpack unpacking, the lunch packing, the bathing, the bedtime storying, the back tickling, the please-just-one-more-kiss-goodnighting?

Somehow the guy I married did. (How on earth did that happen?) More important than the fact that using homemade stock instead of the store-bought kind made soups and stews taste a zillion times better, he knew that it made me happy. It's not like I've been married for as long as our parents have been married, and it's not like I'm an expert just because I've written a bunch of words inside two covers, but for the life of me, I'm not sure I can think of a better definition of love.

Roast Chicken

Before you have your chicken stock, you have to have your chicken. My Dinner Doula client Lori says you can't call yourself an official mother until you know how to roast a chicken, which, of course, is ridiculous. I find a whole roast chicken satisfying in my house for a different reason: It has two drumsticks and I have two kids. No fighting! Total time: 1 hour 40 minutes

6 potatoes (Yukon Gold or red), cut into chunks

1 small onion, chopped into chunks

3 medium carrots, peeled and cut into chunks

1 tablespoon olive oil

Salt and pepper

1 whole roasting chicken, about 4 pounds

1 lemon, pricked several times with a knife

1 small bunch fresh thyme

2 tablespoons butter, melted

Preheat the oven to 425°F.

Arrange the potatoes, onion, and carrots in a baking dish. Toss with the oil and sprinkle with salt and pepper. Place in oven and roast for 15 minutes.

Meanwhile, rinse the inside and outside of chicken under cold water and pat dry. Stuff the cavity with lemon and thyme and tie the legs together with butcher's twine.

After the carrots and potatoes have roasted for 15 minutes, place the chicken, breast side up (see tip), on top of the vegetables. Brush the chicken skin with butter and season with salt and pepper. Continue roasting until the chicken is a golden brown and the juices run clear when the thigh is pierced with a fork, about 1 hour and 15 minutes, or 18 to 20 minutes per pound. Remove the chicken from the oven, carve, and serve with the vegetables.

⭐ *Tip:* I finally heard an easy way to figure out which way is breast side up. You want your chicken to look like "a desperate woman." Since this is, in theory, a family cookbook, I'll leave it to you to figure out what that means.

Andy's Homemade Chicken Stock

Eventually, you're going to strain this whole thing, so don't worry about the size of whatever you are throwing into the pot. Total time: 2 to 5 hours

To a large stockpot, add the following ingredients in no particular order or quantities: everything salvaged from your **whole roast chicken** (bones, skin, meat, everything); **1 large onion** (you don't even have to peel it, but make sure you at least halve it); a little **Parmesan rind** (I always freeze the heels of my wedges for this purpose); a handful of **celery stalks** and **carrots** (the baby variety or the real sticks); **herbs** (parsley, sage, rosemary, thyme); and any other **vegetable** you might otherwise chuck into the garbage within a few hours anyway: Peppers? Zucchini? Scallions? Parsnips? Green beans? In they go.

Cover with water and bring to a boil. Then reduce the heat to a simmer and keep on the stovetop for at least 2 hours and up to 4 or 5. Add more water if it reduces too much. Remove from the heat and allow to cool a little.

Pour the broth through a strainer into a large bowl. (The pot is probably heavy, so be very careful when you do this.) Let cool some more, then freeze 2- to 3-cup portions in freezer storage bags, unless you know you will be using the stock within a few days. Remember to flatten bags before freezing to make for easy thawing.

To thaw, run the bags of frozen broth under warm water in the sink for 2 to 3 minutes.

Chicken Soup with Orzo

My favorite chicken noodle soups are the ones that aren't overly brothy. The shredded chicken and orzo in this one makes it taste almost like chicken and dumplings. I freeze in single-serving batches and have for weekend lunches or quick-thaw dinners. Total time: 1 hour 30 minutes

1 large onion, chopped

3 carrots, peeled and chopped

3 stalks celery, chopped

Salt and pepper to taste

2 tablespoons olive oil, plus more for serving

$\frac{1}{2}$ cup white wine

6 cups homemade chicken stock (page 289) or store-bought chicken broth,
   plus up to 2 cups more as needed

$1\frac{1}{2}$ pounds boneless or bone-in chicken breasts,
   rinsed, patted dry, and cut into 4-inch chunks

Parmesan cheese rind (optional)

$1\frac{1}{2}$ cups orzo

$\frac{1}{4}$ cup loosely packed chopped fresh parsley, for serving

Parmesan cheese, for serving

In a large stockpot over medium-low heat, sauté the onion, carrots, celery, salt, and pepper in the oil for 10 to 12 minutes.

Add the wine and turn up the heat to high; until the liquid has completely reduced. Add the stock and bring to a boil.

Add the chicken and Parmesan rind (if using) and bring the soup to a boil. Add more stock, if necessary, to make sure the chicken is fully immersed. Reduce the heat to low and simmer for 30 minutes.

After the chicken has thoroughly cooked through, using two forks, shred the cubes of chicken while it's in the pot. Just before serving, bring the soup back up to a boil and season with salt. Add the orzo and cook for another 7 minutes, until it is al dente. If the soup gets too thick from the pasta starch, add up to 2 more cups of stock until it reaches the desired consistency. Remove the rind and serve with parsley, pepper, oil, Parmesan cheese, and big hunks of crusty bread or Ritz crackers.

Tomato and White Bean Soup

I came up with this recipe on a snow day when school was canceled and the roads were impassable, and I had no choice but to put away my work to concoct some hearty, warm-your-bones meals. That day I had no excuse not to soak dry beans for six hours, but when I use canned cannellinis, it seamlessly transforms into a quick weeknight go-to. It's also delicious with chopped shrimp mixed in. **Total time: 30 minutes**

1 tablespoon olive oil, plus more for garnish

1 slice thick-cut smoky bacon

½ large onion, chopped

1 medium piece celery, chopped

1 large carrot, peeled and chopped

Salt and pepper to taste

1 teaspoon chopped fresh rosemary (optional)

1 14-ounce can diced tomatoes, a few tablespoons set aside

3 15-ounce cans cannellini beans, 2 cans with their liquid
   and 1 can drained and set aside

1 cup homemade chicken stock (page 289) or
   unsalted store-bought chicken broth,
   plus a little extra for thinning out

Freshly grated Parmesan cheese

In a large stockpot or Dutch oven, heat the oil over low heat and add the bacon. Cook 8 to 10 minutes, until the fat is rendered and the bacon is crisp. Remove the bacon with a slotted spoon and set aside. Add the onion, celery, carrot, salt and pepper, and rosemary (if using) and cook until the vegetables are soft, about 8 minutes.

Add the diced tomatoes, 2 cans of beans plus their liquid, and the stock into the pot. The liquid level should be just barely above beans and vegetables. Bring to a simmer and cook until warmed through, about 10 minutes.

Turn off the heat. Puree with a handheld immersion blender or in batches in the blender (see warning). Add more stock if necessary and season with more salt and pepper to taste. Mix in the reserved can of beans, reserved tomatoes, and the bacon (crumbled into bits) and bring soup back up to a simmer. Garnish with Parmesan cheese and a drizzle of oil. Serve with crusty bread.

Warning: If you don't have an immersion blender, you can use your regular blender. Blend in batches, keeping in mind you shouldn't shut the lid tightly or the trapped steam may cause a bean soup explosion. Hold the lid with your hand and keep it slightly ajar so some steam can escape as you blend. Place batches of pureed soup into a large bowl as you go, and when you are finished, add the whole thing back to the pot.

2012– ?

In Summation

erhaps you have just read this book from cover to cover and you are now inspired to start a family dinner ritual in your own home. Congratulations! Sometimes the hardest part is making the choice and committing to it. Well, it's also hard trying to figure out how you're going to get home in time, who's going to cook, what you're going to do about your kids' aversion to pasta and salt and water and eating. Okay, fine. There's no part that is exactly perfectly *easy* when you are just starting out, but as I hope you've gathered over the course of reading the previous 293 pages, the more you do it, the easier it will get and the more you put into it, the more you'll get out of it.

About those 293 pages. That was a lot to process, right? I think it might help all of us to do a quick review of the material we have covered so you feel like you have a better handle on how to begin and what to expect.

Let's review.

☑ *Rule 1: If you have a kid under three, you might not want to include him or her in the family dinner festivities just yet.* Tending to a toddler at the table—his milk spilling, his green hating, his inability to articulate how multidimensional your marinara is—takes its toll on the rest of the diners' satisfaction, especially the cook's. You won't be able to concentrate on any kind of conversation or enjoy what you just spent some time preparing, let alone be able to savor your family's only unplugged moment of the day. You will, in fact, only be setting yourself up for failure. That can be hard to recover from and could have potentially fatal results for the ritual itself. Eating in shifts made so much more sense for our family. Even if the girls were eating microscopic bits of turkey with six pieces of steamed broccoli and, two hours later, Andy and I would sit down to lamb chops and quinoa, we had convinced ourselves it was family dinner. This was because a) we always prepared our childrens' meal; b) we always sat with them while they ate; and c) we were training ourselves to get out of the office in time to do all this.

☑ *Rule 2: Don't force yourself to cook every night.* We are no longer living in the same world we grew up in—no one expects you to produce a hot made-from-scratch meal every night. But if you are one of those moms who finds it extremely satisfying to produce a hot made-from-scratch meal for your kids, then do it when you can and let it go when you can't. (By this point in my parenting career, shouldn't I know that telling mothers not to feel guilty is like telling Paula Deen not to use butter?)

☑ *Rule 3: Restaurants are your friends.* After you've cooked a few nights in a row, reward yourself with dinner out—whether it's a hot dog from a vendor at the park or takeout from everyone's favorite falafel house or a sit-down affair at the fancy Italian place. Besides giving you a break, this will give you ideas for dinner when you are back in your kitchen wishing you were at the fancy Italian place.

☑ *Rule 4: If you can, think about pushing bedtime later.* **My kids have always gone to bed on the later end (since we usually get home from work between six thirty and seven), and logistically I find this makes life a little easier around dinnertime. There are enough things going against you already with this whole endeavor—might as well control the clock. If your kids are starving and you can't imagine how they will last that long, ply them with a healthy snack at five thirty. If you can swing it, you can most likely give yourself a comfortable half hour to drink a glass of wine, talk to the kids, and get a simple meal on the table.**

☑ *Rule 5: Employ the two-out-of-three philosophy.* **Everyone has his or her own criteria for what defines a successful family dinner, but these are mine:**

1. Every member of the family is accounted for and seated, facing one another.

2. There is a wholesome meal on the table.

3. Everyone is eating (more or less) the same thing.

You may have other variables, like if the TV is off and no punches or peas are thrown between siblings, but the three above are the biggies for me. If I can honestly say that I've hit two of these three truths, then you better believe I'm marking it down in the Successful Family Dinner column. That means it counts if everyone is at the table eating a Domino's pizza. If mom and dad are eating grilled mackerel while their kids are seated next to them chowing down on turkey burgers, that counts, too. If only dad is there, but you're all eating grilled double-cut lamb chops and kale salad, you can also feel pretty good about your dinner situation.

☑ *Rule 6: In other words, stop looking at what you're doing wrong and focus on what you're doing right.*

Dinner: A Love Story

☑ *Rule 7: Cook within your culinary comfort zone.* **When you're starting out, cook what you're comfortable with. Remember, the name of the game is eliminating as many obstacles as you can—so really, why would you start with a quinoa pilaf that requires you to hunt down some sort of special smoked paprika? Start with something you can make without a recipe. Start with scrambled eggs. Or a hamburger made with really good beef. Or pasta with a no-cook tomato sauce. Or with your grandmother's seventy-five-ingredient curry if you are capable of making it on autopilot. I find bobbing back and forth between a cookbook and a skillet while also trying to catch up with my children who I haven't seen all day requires concentration powers I do not have—especially when a glass of wine is involved.**

☑ *Rule 8: I'm not going to lie. It helps to eat good food as you do all this.* **The ultimate goal (at least in my house) is to make dinner a ritual, and putting together something that you want to eat—that you are excited to eat—is going to help a lot with establishing that ritual. If you cook good food, it will build on itself. Your family will look forward to it. You will look forward to it. You will get addicted to eating well and watching your family eat well. Is it essential that you braise an osso buco on a Tuesday night? Of course not. But is a market-fresh frittata going to be more satisfying than a frozen pizza? My hunch is yes. (And by the way, that frittata—page 117—takes the same amount of time as the frozen pizza. If only my children liked eggs.) But my point is, even though the most important part of family dinner is the family part, I do not want to dismiss the role of caring about what you cook in the equation. The more you care, the more you'll cook, and the more you cook, the better you'll get, and the better you get, the more firmly the family dinner ritual will take hold. It's probably going to be a long time before my kids recognize in a conscious way that eating a meal with someone who loves them satisfies some deep psychological need. But for now I'm pretty sure they're psyched to show up just for the pork chops. And I have no problem with that.**

☑ *Rule 9: Last, keep it in perspective.* **A few summers ago, I was having dinner at a friend's house. She is about ten years ahead of me in the parenting game and I've always looked to her for advice on everything from day camps to birthday cake bakeries to how to best survive third-grade clique drama without ending up in the headlines. She has three daughters, each one more accomplished than the** next. At the time of this dinner, the oldest was about to start her junior year in college, the middle one, a homebody, was getting ready to leave for her freshman year at a big school in the Midwest, and the youngest, a high school sophomore, had just returned from doing volunteer work in South America. None of them were at the dinner table with us. In fact, none of them were in the house—until about halfway through our delicious grilled salmon, at which point the middle daughter wandered into the kitchen and opened the fridge.

"Hi, honey," my friend said. "There's some salmon here if you want it."

"Nah," the almost-college-freshman said. "I'm going to Jack's tonight." Jack was her boyfriend. She wandered out of the kitchen and we heard the back screen door creak open then slam shut.

My friend rolled her eyes. "You know, when they were little, dinner was such a pain in the ass. All the kids did was complain about what I cooked. It was such a thankless job." She went on, "Now that they're older I'll cook anything they ask for. I'll cook five different meals if it means they'll all sit down with me for dinner."

I call up this scene all the time. Whenever I catch myself in a dinner table standoff with one of the girls. Whenever I've spent an hour making something that ends up getting scraped into the dog's dish. I call it up and then force myself to think: Lucky. Feel lucky. They are sitting at the table. They are seven and nine years old. They still get excited about a jungle gym with monkey bars and sprint into my arms if I haven't seen them all day. If my daughter doesn't eat those beautiful, just-caught sweet scallops that I cooked to absolute perfection, I need to just take a few deep breaths . . . and let it go.

It's just a scallop.

Acknowledgments

I *found that writing a* book was a lot like being a parent—I spent a lot of my time looking around at everyone else who has done it before me, wondering how on earth they seem to manage it so effortlessly. The book you have just read was an absolute labor of love, with an emphasis on the labor part. I don't know how it would have happened without the support of the following people:

My Dinner: A Love Story readers: I knew what I was writing was interesting to me, and the three people around my dinner table, but I had no idea that tales of pork chops mixed with reviews of childrens' books mixed with family living would mean something to you guys, too. I love that for every "Yum! This was delicious!" you write comments like "Thank you for bringing peace to an otherwise no-good day." It's hard to overstate how much that real-world feedback (and such *well-written* real-world feedback) means to a lonely blogger sitting in her pajamas at the kitchen table banging out 300 words on mashed potatoes. A thousand thank-yous.

My editor and friend, Lee Boudreaux: I'm married to a book editor so I know how many authors and launches and pitches and bidding wars and writer complaints you are juggling on an hourly basis. And yet, not once since I landed on your doorstep, have I ever felt like I was anything but the only person in your orbit. Thank you for your tireless enthusiasm, your thoughtful reads, quick turnarounds, and your diplomatic reassurance whenever I was ready to lose it.

My agent, Elyse Cheney: For pushing me in directions I would never think to take. And for taking one look at my dinner diary back in 2009 and saying "I will represent this project," even though the blog was months away from launching and neither of us had any real sense of what "this project" even was.

The team at Ecco: Dan Halpern, Abigail Holstein, Rachel Bressler, Allison Saltzman, Leah Carlson-Stanisic, Mark Ferguson, Michael McKenzie, Leslie Cohen, Samantha Choy, and Ben Tomek. Thank you all for believing in the blog, the book, and the bumper stickers!

Yolanda Edwards: I'm waiting to discover the boundaries of your generosity —whether it's as small as hand-me-downs and flea-market finds or as huge as photography counsel, design feedback, and personal cheerleading. I feel lucky to have you on my speed-dial.

Rory Evans: Thank you for making everything I've written cleaner and better— not just this book (which I could've never published without your stamp of approval), but all those stories about garlic and coffee and how to get ahead for the holiday *right now*. And a huge thank-you for reading my blog so religiously and for commenting on posts with such heart.

Pilar Guzman: For letting me piggyback on your shooting star; for telling me my jeans were too big and my ambitions too small; for encouraging me to be a writer as much as an editor; for teaching me everything I know about design; for always coming through for me when I need you.

Adam Rapoport: For letting Andy and me be *Bon Appetit*'s Bro-Viders! For guest-posting on DALS before DALS was really even DALS, and for teaching me (among other things) that tonic should be superfizzy, a burger should be loosely packed, Bud should be in a can, and music should come on loud immediately following a toast—and should preferably be the Rolling Stones.

Fred Woodward, Jennifer Livingston, Mike Paterniti, Sara Corbett, Naomi Nista, Lori Leibovich, Melissa Vaughan, Chelsea Cardinal, Laurie Sandell, Lia Ronnen, Ava Savitsky, Devin Friedman, Kendra Harpster, Kristina DiMatteo, Kate Porterfield, Joel Lovell, Alanna Stang, Melissa Roberts, Sally Schultheiss: Each of you let me use your personal stories, your photos, your illustrations, your ideas, your massive social media networks, or your wise counsel for one reason: You believed in what I was doing and you wanted to help. Coming from magazines, I'm somewhat used to the idea (only somewhat) of being surrounded by so many talented people, but what really amazes me day after day is being surrounded by talented people who are also capable of such big acts of kindness.

Ed Nammour: For spending an entire day shooting (and many more days thinking about and putting together) the official *Dinner: A Love Story* video, which, I might add, rocks because of you. You went way beyond the job description of "neighbor" and for that I will be eternally grateful.

Joanna Goddard, Deb Perelman, Brooke Reynolds, Caroline Fennessy Campion, Gabrielle Blair, Phyllis Grant, Carina Schott: For being instrumental in building my audience when my daily readership was in the double digits, and for being so inspiring with your regular roll-out of high-quality content. With you guys around, the relentlessness of blogging seems not just more manageable, but way more fun.

Jennifer Causey: For the beautiful photographs and for your calm, cool, collectedness on our shoot. Thank you especially for making my day-to-day life look like its best self—the world you shot here in these pages is definitely a place I'd like to live every day.

My friends at the Dobbs Ferry Public Library and the Hastings Station Café: You all somehow convinced me that I had a place to report to every workday—regardless of whether I showed up or not. And Avi—the only reason any of these sentences make sense is because you brew a badass cup of Barrington. Those caffeine hits fueled at least 75 percent of the words in this book.

James White: For your patience teaching this old dog all your cool new tricks; Griffin Waldau and Ava Savitsky (again) for the website's signature logo and design; Heather Jones for your thorough recipe testing; and Lauren Palmieri for your testing, your cooking, and your Babbo-level pasta twirling!

My loyal locals: Anne Scharer, Todd Lawlor, Bonnie Stelzer, Jonathan Abady, Susan Dominus, Jennifer Aaronson, Carolyn Bloom, Robin Helman, Jenny Goldstock, Liz Gould Vales, Tom Vales, Shannon Johnson, Mary Salke-Roth, Marcie Cuff, Cindy DeRose, Catherine Kelly, Jeff Gordinier, Julie Schrader, Claudia Heitler, Lori Slater, Helene and Seth Godin: Don't ever stop grabbing me at the farmers' market or Old Navy or the school hallway to tell me how much you loved the ragù or the Avgolemeno or the dumb joke I made in last week's post. Your encouragement and friendship has been nicer than I could have imagined and keeps me going!

The Original *Original* DALS team: My parents, Jody and Ivan Rosenstrach; Andy's parents, Emily and Steve Ward; my sister, Lynn Zerbib; my brother, Phil Rosenstrach; my siblings-in-law Nick Zerbib, Trish, and Tony "Tony's Steak" Ward. Plus, a big humungous thank-you to the next generation of supercool DALS eaters: Sophia, Aidan, Luca, Alison, Amanda, Owen, and Nathan—each of you in your own special way has given me grist for the mill.

Phoebe and Abby: Everything—not just dinner—seems more fun when I see it through your eyes. This book would literally not exist without you. Thank you for waiting at the table while your mother takes forty-five pictures of the cheeseburgers that you are starving for. Thank you for being so game for anything and everything. I love you very much, and I forgive you for not liking eggs.

Andy: Your daughter said it best when she noted that the moment you enter the house after work is like the part in every song when the beat finally kicks in. I couldn't have said it any better, except I might extend that metaphor to my life in general. I won the lottery that day in 1992 when I met you in your Yankee hat, and not a day goes by that I don't thank my lucky stars for finding someone whose favorite form of procrastination is to braise a pork shoulder, to nail the perfect tagline, to pour his heart into writing 1,000-word blog posts, and to build me up while asking for nothing in return. This book is as much yours as it is mine.

Index

*J*enny Rosenstrach *is the* creator of Dinner: A Love Story, the website devoted to family dinner, and the coauthor of *Time for Dinner: Strategies, Recipes, Inspiration for Family Meals Every Night of the Week*. She was the features director at *Cookie* magazine for four years, and before that, the special projects editor at *Real Simple* for five years. Her essays and articles have appeared in numerous national publications and anthologies, including *Real Simple, Cookie, Martha Stewart Living, Whole Living*, and the *New York Times*. She and her husband, Andy Ward, cowrite "The Providers," a column in *Bon Appétit*. They live in Westchester County, New York, with their two daughters.